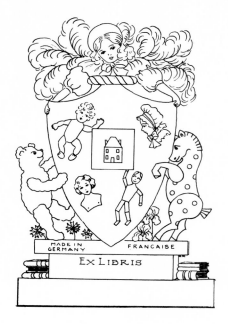

MADE IN
GERMANY   FRANCAISE

Ex Libris

Women molding doll heads in Sonneburg, Germany. Swivel heads, two to a mold, can be seen in foreground, with stacked molds beside first window. Second woman is pouring slip from ordinary pitcher. Fourth woman is working on shoulder heads and their molds, stacked by her window, show large pour-hole opening for this type.

All-Bisque & Half-Bisque Dolls

Genevieve Angione

PHOTOGRAPHY
Color plates by Louis Ouzer
Black and white by Charles F. Angione
Rochester, N.Y.

Thomas Nelson & Sons

Design by Harold Leach

Library of Congress Catalog Card Number: 76-77265

Printed in the United States of America

Acknowledgment

Grateful thanks are due to many people but especially to:

Marianne DeNunez not only for her help but also for allowing me to try my hand at porcelain doll making in her studio in Arleta, California.

Astry Campbell for allowing me the same privilege in her Short Hills, New Jersey, studio and for sharing her knowledge.

Spinning Wheel for the use of material which has previously appeared in its pages.

Dorothy Coleman for dropping her own research work to dash off a note or answer a telephone cheerfully and always interestedly.

Collector friends who, without turning a hair, gave us their precious prizes to be photographed.

And to dealer friends and acquaintances who have kept their sharp eyes open for many of these little charmers.

To my family,
who have so patiently lived
with me and the dolls
for so many years

Contributing Collectors

Mrs. Helen Brewer, Cambridge, N.Y.
Mrs. Astry Campbell, Short Hills, N.J.
Mrs. Bess Goldfinger, New York City
Miss Jessie Hardy, Avon, N.Y.
Mrs. Gladyse H. Hilsdorf, Fayetteville, N.Y.
Mrs. Peggy Millar, Brookfield Center, Conn.
Mrs. Margaret W. Strong, Rochester, N.Y.
Mrs. Margaret Whitton, Wilton, Conn.
And, of course, the author.

Author's Note

This is a book about all-bisque and half-bisque dolls from various periods, the 1850s to Occupied Japan. That is not what it started out to be at all, but that is what it became. There are just too many of these neglected small ones and they will help collectors to know more about all dolls, one fondly hopes.

All-bisque fanciers, however, should not be surprised if they have specimens in their collections which are not included in this work. It is virtually impossible for one book to contain, or one author to own or to borrow, a sample of every doll made in this field because they were apparently numberless. Almost without exception, though, collectible dolls will fit into one of the categories detailed here.

The word "detailed" is used deliberately because at times this seems more like a catalogue than a book. There is very little documentation of these dolls and we have to start somewhere. It may be possible at some future time to do a revision or perhaps a supplement as identified dolls are shared by their owners.

And it proved to be impossible to place these dolls in consecutive order because some German firms continued in operation generation after generation, always following the trends of the times. After trying many methods of classification it was finally decided that *type* was the common denominator rather than attempting to arrange them by age. So, at times the chronicle will appear to be retrograding but it is the fault, if any, of the dolls and not the author's wandering mind.

The nomenclature for this special section of dolldom is explained as specialized words and terms crop up in the text. This should be useful to the general collector because these little dolls are made of the same materials and by the same processes as parts of the larger ones.

The only exception to this is the first three short chapters in which a working knowledge of production methods and materials and terminologies is given in some detail for the benefit of those who have no personal contact with the manufacture of these items.

Anyone who is working in the ceramic field today is asked to bear in mind that the information and methods detailed here pertain to old German production and not to advanced modern materials and operations.

GENEVIEVE ANGIONE

Rochester, N.Y.
May 1968

Contents

The Ceramic Field

Doll language is largely made up of terms borrowed from other fields and differs not only between areas in this country but also when compared to the terminology in Europe. Work has been going on for years in the United States to standardize the proper terms because it is vital for a collector to know exactly what is meant in a lecture, on a list, or in a book or a magazine.

These chapters are in no way intended to be a crash course in the ceramic arts, nor are they intended to flaunt or to imply any deep reservoir of knowledge on the subject. They were written by a layman for laymen, by a collector for other collectors, and with a great deal of generous help from outside sources.

Through the years, bit by bit, sometimes quite by accident, a collector picks up some of the basic information which *should* make terms understandable but sometimes serves only to compound the confusion. It is essential to have a rudimentary knowledge of the sources of these terms, of the processes from which they arise, and the materials involved if one is to be a knowledgeable collector.

The word "ceramic" is used to indicate the entire field of fired clay articles, whether high-fired or low-fired. It is a word like "lace," which also indicates an entire field of patterns, materials, methods, and workmanship covering a great area of time. For descriptive purposes there are divisions of terms among professional ceramists which the public should understand to some degree at least.

Innumerable deposits of all kinds of clay dot the earth and provide mankind with everything from bricks and sewer pipes to the finest luxuries and the commonest everyday necessities. Early in history man learned to form items from clay and to sun bake, and later to fire, them into every state from passable usefulness to superb quality.

All clay items are classified according to their chemical makeup, the use to which they are put, the type of firing they require, and so on. So, we have brick clay, pottery and ball clays, stoneware and porcelain clays. These clays are used either by themselves or as part of a carefully compounded mixture.

We are concerned as doll collectors with objects made from porcelain clays and, like lace, they can vary greatly, have entirely different names, and come from various periods. Just as lace can be classified as to country of origin, by pattern and width, by type of material such as silk, linen, cotton or even modern synthetics, handmade or machine-made, natural or dyed color, so can ceramics be identified by their own peculiarities.

Because of the ceramic classification according to the clays used, the factories have names which generally reflect their types of operation— brickyards, pottery works, and the like. The factories in which we are interested were, and still are, called "porcelain works," although their production could be varied to meet changing times, public demands, or profitable contract orders.

In the doll field we are dealing primarily with the products of European factories which were built generations ago and operated under what we would term "impossible working conditions." To those workers of long ago, however, it must have presented a much different picture because starvation was an ever-present factor in their lives.

We are also dealing with mass production, so the establishment of any kind of porcelain plant must have been a very expensive undertaking. It might be well to start right there, with special reference to dolls.

Even if a factory building could be found to convert to this purpose, that was only the beginning. Walk-in kilns (this is pronounced "kill" and "kills" by professionals) had to be built. From existing illustrations these factory kilns varied greatly in shape, in size, and in their location with relation to the rest of the plant. While they did not necessarily feel that they had to protect the workers, the owners certainly wanted to protect their products through the various firing operations, and some factory kilns appear to have opened onto covered passages somewhat similar to modern breezeways which run between a house and a garage.

Every type of kiln and every type of fuel known to man was used at one time or another—wood, coal, charcoal, and coke, then on into oil, gas, and finally electricity. Aside from the excellent controllability of electricity, the most outstanding change in kiln operation was the development of the continuous kiln, tunnel or circular track, used in modern plants.

In the early days of mass production a factory also had to have convenient land for the tons of fuel necessary to run the kiln fires because they were stoked like furnaces to produce the intense heat required. Coal was a problem all by itself. Because it contained slag and other impurities, European coal burned very irregularly and made control of all areas of a loaded kiln very difficult. Not infrequently, poor temperature control in some sections during the firing process produced loads which fell below the firm's standards. Coke and charcoal were used by some operators in an attempt to overcome this handicap.

A German worker who migrated to the United States after World War I reported that Armand Marseille solved the firing problem by importing the very superior and slow burning English coal for his plant. The cost of such an operation must have been tremendous but Armand Marseille seems to have been a very rich man.

In mass production it took hours to load a kiln with all the trays which held the doll heads and/or parts. Many more hours were required to bring the firing up to temperature and as much as an additional 48 hours for the kilns to cool off before they could be unloaded. Since these small articles were made by the thousands every day, there had to be at least several kilns to keep even a moderately large production flowing smoothly.

The buildings presented more problems. Tons of plaster had to be kept in dry storage, both plaster of Paris for mold making and casting plaster for making models. Hundreds of molds of each size item had to be made and stored between working periods because they had to dry out thoroughly after being used several times in order to produce good ware when used again. Generally a set of molds can be used about fifty times satisfactorily. Hundreds of mesh-bottomed kiln trays had to be available at all times because they were used in several operations.

There had to be rooms in which the molds could be made, more rooms where the molds could be filled, and released heads and/or parts had to have room in which to dry. Other rooms with benches were needed for the finishers and there had to be relatively dustfree rooms with more benches and drying racks where the decorators could work.

All of these rooms had to have many windows because the sun provided most of the light. No such operation could have been handled without office space, bookkeeping quarters, and sales rooms. It was in these sales rooms, we are told, that some manufacturers displayed with great pride the various prizes for which they vied so vigorously at expositions, exhibitions, and trade fairs all over the world. Europe's climate being what it is, there at least had to be coatrooms for the employees, as well as some sort of toilet facilities.

Added to all this, there had to be storage rooms for the inventory of finished products, as well as shipping areas with the attendant storage for boxes and other shipping materials. Tremendous proportions of their products had to be prepared for the ocean voyage to America.

It is well for us to remember also that workers did not commute by bus, train, plane or automobile to follow an industry which needed their manpower. With only a basic crew of highly skilled artisans—sculptors, mold masters, kiln operators, and painters—the local people had to be taught the processing and handling. The establishment of such a plant in an area was truly important to the common people.

However, there is a tendency for us, a hundred years later, to assume that stories from one area of production are also true of others. The most frequently quoted references apply to the making of cheap, hand carved, wooden dolls.

It is common knowledge that whole families and even whole villages in southern Germany made these crude wooden dolls by the millions. We know that is true. Some stories also tell us that the men who financed these operations never permitted any group or any village to have the complete patterns for any object because they did not want "spares" bootlegged to competitors. That is understandable.

These wooden items could have been gathered up in any kind of containers, lurched over bad roads in horsedrawn carts or carried in baskets on men's backs to an assembly depot where they could have been finished and shipped. No harm could have come to them except possibly a sticklike arm or leg occasionally broken.

There doubtless is some basis in fact for all the tales we are told about dolls being made in the homes before they were made in factories—but where are the dolls and how do we identify them? Old trade directories list countless individuals and firms as "toymakers" but that in no way indicates that they produced or assembled dolls with porcelain parts made at home. "Cottage industries" appear to have dealt with objects of wood, or the dressing of dolls, or the manufacture of such items as doll shoes and hats. For us to presume that porcelain products were handled in this fashion is at least questionable.

Farming out valuable molds and expensive clay products for heads to be poured by individuals in their homes, which sometimes housed three generations, is not a too reasonable supposition, old tales notwithstanding. To believe that tender, frail, dry, unfired clay could be fired in small kilns, manned by different people, is not too reasonable either. Unfired ware certainly could not have been safely transported except by hand, in very small quantities, and only for a very short distance. And this is without taking into consideration any rigors of the weather.

The only stage at which porcelain items could have been safely sent into homes was after they were biscuit-fired—that is, hard, unglazed, and undecorated. At this stage the sanding could have been done in homes, with most of the family helping, because it was, and still is, just monotonous rubbing with an abrasive until the pieces are smooth.

Some people suggest that the complexion coating of bisque, or the painting of china heads, was done in homes for small firms or for those just getting started. This also poses a great many problems, however. Fired and sanded pieces can be transported in any kind of packing—cloth, paper, sawdust or excelsior. But the painted pieces must be handled carefully before they are refired to prevent scratches, smearing, smudges, and clinging bits of foreign matter.

Under these circumstances, home decorating would have been a time-consuming, inefficient system fraught with great danger of damage and of loss from unavoidable accidents. The consensus among modern workers in the field is that any such operations were the exceptions rather than the rule and that this work was done under strict supervision in factories, no matter how inadequate the "factories" may have been by our standards.

Then, too, Germans were not, and are not, of such easy-going temperaments that such slipshod arrangements as these would have been satisfactory for very long, if at all. The consistent quality of their products also argues against such disorganized methods.

Further, it is sometimes said that individual potters made fancy articles in their spare time to add to family finances. Maybe they did, but doll heads were not ordinarily made of potter's clay, so that also would not apply. With only a very few notable exceptions, doll heads were not made of ceramic clay, either, we must bear in mind.

Because we have stringent child-labor laws, we are inclined to forget or to misunderstand general working conditions in other times. Children frequently outnumbered the adults in small villages all over the world generations ago and everywhere they were pressed into service to earn the barest living for a family. German law then, as now, was adamant with respect to a basic education for every citizen. But, after twelve or fourteen years of age (it is now fourteen), it was mandatory that citizens learn a trade if they could not attend a college or a university, or enter an established family business.

This national control of the poor could account for the stories of early morning and late evening chores for children of all ages. Nowadays in Germany trades are learned at special trade schools but in the period we are considering there were no such things as trade schools in scattered villages. One learned a trade by being an apprentice and it is quite possible that one's entire childhood was considered an apprenticeship in whatever trade was available in his given area. The children we have reference to just happened to learn the porcelain trade by geographic accident of birth in porcelain-manufacturing areas.

Endlessly repeated stories are told about the work done by German children but this work was no doubt much like that done by children everywhere in those times. American farm children, for instance, helped with chores before and after school and all during vacation. City children sold papers and did all kinds of "leg work" for their elders. English children worked long and hard in the textile industries and Welsh children worked in coal mines. There were no laws anywhere to prevent this exploitation of minors. That German children worked in their village factories and shops should not strike us as so unusual.

In such a situation as this, it takes very little imagination to picture the possibilities for outsiders to make money without much investment. We know that molds were sometimes released after they had been used because papier mâché, which is also a water absorption molding method, can be used in worn porcelain molds, for instance. Sometimes this release was by outright sale of molds that were beginning to wear but it also appears to have been by "gentlemen's agreements" at other times because, highly competitive though they were, German (and French) doll manufacturers were frequently either blood relatives, in-laws, or great personal friends and they all helped each other in emergencies.

It is still impossible to do this kind of work on an enormous scale without accumulating "seconds" and natural overages in production. In a cut-throat business such as dolls, where constant change was the chief selling point, such accumulations would pose still more sales and storage problems.

Some of the fired material which warped badly or cracked or sagged in the firing could be ground into various grades of "grog" and had many industrial uses. Grog was one of the substances used to make the textured clothing on Snow Babies, for example.

So, buyers to cart all this unwanted material away at a price, for whatever purpose, were a blessed necessity rather than a nuisance. Modern collectors should remember this when dolls *appear* to be similar and yet vary widely in quality, decorating, and types of bodies. They could very well have started out in the same kiln and parted after that first firing.

2

Manufacturing Processes

No doll head (or anything else to be molded) can be larger than the original model. In fact, after it is cast it will be smaller than the model because of the natural shrinkage in the firing. There is no way to increase the size except to make a new and larger model. On the other hand, anything can be reduced to the disappearing point.

For the benefit of those who have never tried it, or have never seen it done, a description of this complicated process could be interesting.

We live in an age of show-and-tell but old German manufacturers guarded their methods and materials jealously, so old books tell us very little. By questioning modern artists, a working knowledge of the business can be gained because they are duplicating all these operations and they have had to rediscover many of these secrets for themselves.

To make a head, for instance, a model is needed and it must be considerably bigger than the finished product is to be, no matter how large. This can be sculped from any material which will produce a good mold. Different artists today prefer different materials and they agree that this must also have been the case in Germany long ago. There are people who believe that the Germans used wax but many contemporary working artists argue that wax is a very precarious medium which is not suitable for this work because it would be affected by the heat which generates in the plaster of Paris molds while they are setting.

At any rate, if the model makes a perfect "master mold," the duplicating process can be started. To be technical about it, all casting molds are "negatives" and, of course, castings are "positive" impressions from the molds, or duplicates of the original model.

To put a head into production, a "master mold" is made from the model and from this master mold a "mold block" is created of the hardest material available, because the mold block will be used to make many working molds. It is quite possible to use metal for the mold block, although this would be an expensive method. Nowadays some large manufacturers use a metal pattern from which many master molds can be made and this makes it possible to have unlimited mold blocks and production molds. Individual artists and small studios, however, use some substance similar to a product called "Hydrocal." At any rate, the mold block must be as impervious as possible to water because the molds are made of plaster of Paris mixed with water.

The largest size heads will come from the first and largest mold and, because doll heads are made from porcelain clay compounds, they will shrink 20 to 25 per cent in the firing. In order to provide a very graduated reduction in head sizes, a ceramic head can also be cast from this first set of molds, because ceramic shrinks only about 10 per cent. By using one of the fired porcelain heads and the fired ceramic head, two new, smaller sizes can be created.

Thus it goes, right down the line to provide excellent downward graduation.

This molding process to get smaller heads also explains why heads with a single number get smaller as the numbers get smaller; for example, a size 20 head is enormous and an 8 is medium size. But, in the fractional sizes, as the heads get smaller the size numbers increase.

After a head has been reduced to size 1 or 0, miniaturization can begin. The first casting would be size 1/0, the second reduction 2/0, or, in some of the old German firms, 0/1 and 0/2. In these sizes the figure indicates the number of the reduction.

For instance, there are two heads available for measurement which have the same face, stock number, and manufacturer. The size 0 is almost 10 inches in circumference and the size 11/0 is only slightly over 5 inches. Europeans use centimeters instead of inches and millimeters instead of half or quarter inches, so these heads indicate that the manufacturer rigidly held shrinkage down to 10 millimeters per model, or slightly less than our half inch. This accounts for their 11/0 which would be a size 10/0 by our measurements.

Production Methods

In the old molding method, when clay was rolled out like piecrust on a flat surface which was probably covered with a moist cloth, cut into the proper size pieces, then hand pressed into the molds, the consistency of the clay was undoubtedly more like those of the clays used for dinnerware.

Bru used this method and it is not known exactly when it was abandoned, although it is strongly suspected that when Paul Gerard took over the factory the manufacturing method was changed. The great advantage of the hand-pressed process was that the material did not warp out of shape. The very desirable "applied ears" were made from rolled clay. They were cut out just like cookies and attached to the head after it had been turned out of the mold.

The vast majority of manufacturers, however, used the "poured" method.

Clay generally cannot be used as it comes from the earth. It must be ground, sieved, washed, and then mixed with other necessary ingredients to become a workable paste. A proper clay mixture can be "opened." In other words, this paste will accept fine sand and other materials which are also necessary to its composition if fine products are to result. When the required liquids are added, the resulting soft, thick, creamy white liquid is called "slip."

One of the most important added ingredients is feldspar (also spelled "felspar"), a hard, crystalline mineral, an excellent fluxing agent which causes the other ingredients to bind together. It is essential to good production because it reduces shrinkage even while the objects are drying. Then, at high temperatures in the kiln, the materials fuse, or melt together, and the shrinkage increases again. Ground feldspar in the proper proportions must be added to the slip and thoroughly mixed through it to ensure the evenness of this shrinkage throughout the whole object. Because of this, slip must always be very thoroughly remixed before each pouring to ensure uniform distribution of the feldspar and consequently uniform shrinkage.

The production of the various clay compounds, called "clay bodies" by ceramists, is an independent industry today because individual workers in clay do not have the chemical background or the necessary facilities to make their own. Countless controlled test firings are necessary to ensure the proper proportions of each mixture.

Among modern ceramists feldspar is frequently mentioned and as frequently blamed for the slight yellowness of modern porcelain. Like everyone else, professionals admire the stark whiteness of old porcelain but irremovable traces of iron in our feldspar are the cause of the yellow or creamy tone.

The thick plaster of Paris molds in which poured objects are formed are generally in two pieces which are held together in today's studios with binders cut from automobile tire tubes or live rubber binders made for the trade. This obviously was not the method used in Europe generations ago. Clamps were used which were very similar to those used in the furniture industry; stout cord properly tied or wire with a cloth covering would both have been quite practical.

Molds can be in any number of pieces, incidentally, depending on the elaborate detail of the finished piece. These extra mold pieces are necessary to prevent "undercutting," which makes it impossible to remove an object from the molds after it has set. It is less expensive to provide multi-part molds, especially in mass production, than separately to mold and subsequently to "apply" hats, for instance, on dolls.

The plaster molds absorb the liquid from the clay and this creates the desired thickness of the form. When the proper thickness of the clay has "set up," the core of unset slip is poured off and can be used again as soon as the air bubbles are dispersed. The partially emptied molds are then tilted to drain and to harden further.

When unmolded, the pieces are of a grayish-green putty color, and to the trade this is known as "greenware." The name is not in reference to the color but because of the fact that the objects are unfired and hence unusable, like green fruit. Greenware is extremely tender when it is wet and subject to damage even in the most gentle handling.

At a safe time during this wet period (ceramists call this the "leather" stage), the eye sockets are cut, sew holes opened, mouths cut, the edges of shoulder plates cut straight, and ears pierced. When the pieces are firm enough to be handled easily, separately molded hanging curls can be added, long rolls of clay can be braided and flattened for coronets, hand-made flowers and leaves placed in the hair, and so forth.

To an experienced operator the process is as simple as mending a pieshell or adding a fluted rim to a crust is to a good baker. The greenware is moistened with slip at the proper spot, the part to be added is also moistened on the under side with slip, and then they are firmly pressed together to eliminate air pockets until a bond forms between them as the wet slip starts to dry again. Teacup handles are a notable example of this adding process.

Most of the marks by which we identify porcelain items are "incised" in the material and in mass production the figures and/or trademarks were generally incorporated in the molds. Like the word "intaglio," "incised" means "to cut into, to form, or make an imprint or mark upon."

On the other hand, because modern artists handle each piece personally, many of them "inscribe" their names or identifications with a sharp instrument during the greenware stage. Occasionally a modern ceramist adopts a painted insignia which can be fired onto the pieces, generally using black for the color. This can be sanded off, of course, if the piece is a fine reproduction which is to be sold for what it is not, but in complexion-coated items that spot of pink color is also removed, which helps the buyer to identify a reproduction or a fake item.

Marks can also be "impressed" in this soft material through the use of metal stamps, for instance, like those used in hot wax. It appears to have been done in some porcelain works but the method requires pressure and such pressure involves the danger of warping. Because there is enough accidental warping during the firing process, it is not easy to believe that the old German doll manufacturers would have added to these possibilities when incising was so much easier. Incising also eliminated all possibility of error and required no additional worker time which would have added to the costs. Marks are always sharper from new molds and this may be the answer to the impressed appearance of some doll marks.

Greenware is left to air dry on open shelves and when it is thoroughly dry, without any feeling whatever of dampness or chill, it is pure white again unless the slip was precolored to save one decorating operation. In dolls this is pink to eliminate the complexion coating. At this point it is ready for the painstaking "finishing" process which cleans it up, removes mold marks, sharpens features, and makes it ready for the kiln.

This finishing work is now done with a variety of small artists' tools and material wrapped around a finger—silk chiffon, organdy, and the like. Sponges, both wet and dry, are also used. One tool which intrigues an amateur is a metal rod which holds small pieces of very fine-grained sponge, much as a tweezer would, and thus enabling the operator to smooth such difficult places as the sides of the noses on dolls' heads and the finger depressions in hands.

No matter what tools are used, however, this is a dusty job and the soft clay is so powdery it seems to be held together by nothing more than wishful thinking.

High firing (the Germans are said to have used up to 2,732° F.) makes these fragile pieces so sturdy they can withstand the most vigorous sanding. It is largely this polishing or sanding which produces the texture by which these objects are graded, providing good porcelain slip (or clay body) was used in the beginning and received proper handling throughout the entire operation.

Skill is perhaps the most important factor in porcelain manufacture, with good workmanship a close second. The clay must be fired to the proper maturity. The greenware must be meticulously trimmed and cleaned. The sanding has to be thorough. Then good decorating and the proper firing of the decorating completes a truly artistic endeavor.

The firing process is easier to explain on a smaller scale than to try to reconstruct mass German methods.

Modern electric kilns are remarkable pieces of equipment, although sometimes even the manufacturers do not know what makes one kiln function perfectly while another one defies control. Made up of substantial layers of porous firebrick, even a small "test" kiln only 6 inches by 6 inches square will hold quite a few assorted heads, arms, and legs of moderate size.

The top or front is removed and the pieces to be fired are placed on the floor, standing on the straight edges which are an essential part of the finishing process. These are the rims on swivel heads, the bases of shoulder heads, and the tops of arms and legs which do not have elbow and knee joints. Bent arms and legs, arms cut at an angle instead of straight across, such as those used for kid bodied Brus, or ball tops which fit into pin-jointed elbow and knee joints, lay flat on the floor or shelf in a modern kiln. European production fired such pieces and small all-bisques in the trays previously mentioned.

Very little clearance is necessary between pieces for the heat to circulate, so an assortment is necessary to use up all the available space.

The timing of each firing is governed by a "cone." These are slender, pointed pieces of prefired material which flop over like warm candles when the desired temperature has been reached. These cones are prefired to various temperatures so that they collapse when the heat of the kiln goes above their individual resistance points.

Porcelain handlers talk a jargon all their own, saying such things as, "I fired those to Cone 5 but next time I am going to fire to Cone 6. It may be better with this new slip I'm trying . . . at least I'll know." Even an inexperienced glance at the cone charts shows relatively small increases in firing temperatures between each cone number but these differences are critical. Underfiring causes a disfiguring mottled appearance much like external mildew; overfiring causes bumps like warts and/or sagging, as in the case of the cones themselves.

After the kiln is loaded and the top or front has been carefully replaced, the cone is checked again to be sure it can be seen through the peekhole in the front kiln wall. In walk-in kilns, which are constructed of brick, individual bricks at eye level in several places around the circumference are not cemented in place and serve as peekholes when they are withdrawn from the kiln wall.

The slender cones, incidentally, are always prepared in advance. They stand in little firebrick cups, held upright by clay packed around their bases. If this clay does not have time to dry properly, the heat can cause it to explode and the cone falls out of sight, thoroughly confusing the operator.

The electricity is turned on after the final cone check and a timer is set for the first peek. All during the firing period the bright red-orange glow from inside the kiln can be seen through the slight cracks between the several layers of brick which make up the height of the kiln.

When the little cone has collapsed out of sight, the electricity is turned off and the kiln is left undisturbed to cool. Even with a small test kiln this takes several hours. When it is cool to the touch, the top is removed and then it is left to go down to room temperature. The pieces inside are now "biscuit."

When these pieces leave the kiln they are pure white (unless precolored) and beautiful to see, but they are surprisingly rough to the touch. It is the laborious hand sanding which produces the desired finish. There is an ultrasmoothness which frequently distinguishes new pieces from old ones, no matter how faithful or beautiful the reproduction. Entirely different from old European slip, good modern slip is factory compounded and it sands to an almost slippery finish. There is a slight drag to the satin finish of old bisque when it is handled which is missing from modern products.

The invisible dust which forms from the sanding is removed by a bath to prevent it from fusing to the parts during the next firing and causing roughness which cannot be removed without damage to the coloring.

cro *3*

The Products

Bisque. This word is a corruption of the word "biscuit." When the pure white ware comes out of the kiln after the first firing, before it is decorated or glazed, it is "biscuit."

The term is originally from the French and it is rather interesting to run it down. The definition of the French *biscuit* is *gâteau sec. Gâteau* is "cake, tart"; *sec* is "dry, dried, harsh, unfeeling, gaunt, spare, barren, bald, curt, tart, sharp." The word "bisque," on the other hand, is generally accepted as a type of thick, creamy soup. It is also used as a term in some sports.

Somewhere, somehow, perhaps through mispronunciation or perhaps by deliberate intent, the word "bisque" crept into the porcelain language and it is generally accepted to mean *"decorated or tinted* biscuit." Some people feel that it is the second firing, or the color coat, which brought about the use of the word. There is a type of European plain cake which, after it is baked into loaves, is cut into slices and rebaked until it is hard and crisp—it is *"sec"* to the *n*th degree. To an American, however, it would be a "cracker" and not a "biscuit," so the term apparently did not originate in this country.

All of this adds very little to the derivation of the term "bisque" but the word is so entrenched now that there is not a particle of sense in trying to eliminate it. To set some standards for it would be more pertinent.

In the doll world the word "bisque" is accepted to mean an entire doll, a doll head and/or shoulder plate, or doll limbs which are tinted to some semblance of skin tone. Properly done, this tinting is a wonderfully lasting, rather lifelike, and scrubbable finish. To other antique collectors it is any unglazed, tinted figurine, knickknack, decorative vase, flower basket, or the like, because the tinted items have more general appeal.

There are and always were many kinds of clay bodies which could be fired, there is and always was good and bad workmanship, but the old adages still apply: You cannot make a silk purse out of a sow's ear nor can a boy do a man's work.

Good dolls and/or dolls' parts cannot be made from poor materials or by inadequately trained workers. It is because of these variables that such anomalous expressions as "salt" and "sugar" bisque arise. Generally they mean coarse or poor quality. The use of them should be viewed with caution because such words as excellent, very good, ordinary, poor, or very poor are much more accurate and meaningful.

The all-over complexion tint is the first step in preparing the sanded doll, heads, and/or parts which are to become bisque (in the vernacular). Paint which appears to be a henna color is used for this. A wad of lamb's wool enclosed in a piece of China silk is used to "pad" the color to an even, streakless state of perfection. This takes a bit of doing because as the silk and wool absorb the excess paint, it can be transferred to a previously finished area. Satisfactory pieces are left on the tops of standing dowel sticks to air dry sufficiently to permit handling without harm. They are then fired to fuse the color.

It is interesting to note in old books about doll-factory operations that this complexion tint was not laid on and brought to perfection by one worker. Beginners in the decorating rooms simply swabbed on spots of the basic color, then the pieces were passed to a more skilled worker who spread it evenly. They were finally passed to handlers who were responsible for the finished padding.

After the first color firing and cooling, the pieces are then "featured." This includes eyebrows, sometimes both eyes and eyelashes, and lips. Before or after all this, molded hair must be painted and padded to the proper color. These steps can take more than one firing unless one is a skilled artist because eyebrows and lashes, for instance, take a great deal of handling of the head in order to get the proper angle from which to apply each brush stroke. There is no reason to believe that, judging by the prices charged for their dolls (or wares of any kind), German manufacturers fired oftener than need be. In mass production it is very likely that the pieces had time to dry sufficiently as they passed through the factory processes and were safe to handle by the time they reached the painters who specialized in brows and lashes, for instance. They were made by the thousands every day so there had to be time for them to dry somewhere along the line.

The same is true of the "blushing" which is applied to the backs of hands and the tops of bare feet, as well as the fingernails and toenails which were sometimes indicated in red. Legs which have shoes and socks could have been painted in two firings at most, with sufficient drying time between the applications of paint.

How this kind of tedious, painstaking work could have been done in badly heated and uncooled factories, with wholly inadequate lighting, by ordinary workers without today's prescription eyeglasses, is most difficult to understand. It becomes even more difficult to understand if, having criticized countless old German products, one personally tries to do it even under the most expert and patient supervision!

China. The word "china" comes from the name of the Asiatic country where clay was first fired into useful articles many centuries ago. In the early days of the Oriental trade, ships could not come back empty so, besides decorated chinaware, which was sometimes referred to as "trade china," they are said also to have brought back blank articles. These were then decorated in England and became "English china." Whether or not decorated china was accepted as "trade" for European merchandise, and the blank items were decorated in England, the stories have been repeated so many times that there could be some truth in either or both statements.

Very loosely translated, "china" means any kind of fired ware which has been glazed—specifically *tableware*.

To American doll collectors the term "china" is used to denote whole dolls or dolls with heads and limbs which have been glazed.

Although they have long been in service in the retail tableware establishments, the terms "underglaze" and "overglaze" are not understood. Probably because it sounds so logical and saves hours of explanatory debate, clerks in tableware departments warn purchasers that some china must be carefully washed or the designs will wear off with greater or lesser dispatch. Good china clerks know what is meant by customers' questions about wearing qualities of the designs and give the answers the public has come to understand.

Proper china decorating does not wear off or wash off but it is not controlled by underglazing.

Glazes closely resemble glass and have various characteristics and classifications, such as colored or uncolored, transparent or opaque, soft or hard, and so forth, according to their chemical makeup.

Soft or low-fire glazes are used on pottery and ceramics because these clays cannot withstand high firing temperatures. Soft glazes also have a tendency to craze, as every housewife knows who has kept food warm on a platter or a dish in an oven. Hard or high-fire glazes, such as those used on porcelain, do not do this because the porcelain clays withstand much higher temperatures than the glazes.

Even today the composition of glazes used in the ceramic field are among the most closely guarded secrets of the trade, each studio or factory believing its own to be the best.

The production of china has to be a highly controlled operation. In mass production, most factories prefer to use the *overglaze* method. This system provides for the glazing of all objects *before* the first firing but after they are cleaned and finished, because all faulty or warped pieces can be discarded before the decorating. Because porcelain clays are fired at high temperatures, the decorating colors penetrate the glaze during the second firing and have an attractive *underglaze* appearance.

In the *underglaze* method, the operation is reversed. The decorations are applied after the ware has been cleaned and finished, before the first firing, and then glazed.

Individual artists use either system, depending on their skill, experience, or personal preference. Improperly applied, the glaze not only runs off and puddles during the firing but also blisters and bubbles, ruining the objects. Those who cannot preglaze must fire, then glaze and fire again. It is a longer process but it is surer and prevents the glazing of culls.

Properly glazed china pieces come from the kiln ready to be decorated. Overglaze paints, which have special adhering qualities, are used for this work whether the decorating is to be freehand or decals. The second firing makes the colors permanent.

Old doll heads sometimes are found almost featureless and the remaining paint flakes and washes off readily. Unless we are willing to believe that German factories sometimes released unfired heads, or heads painted with ordinary paint, another explanation must be found.

Close examination of such heads leads one to the supposition, and it is purely supposition, that these could have been overages or even slight "seconds" which were sold to individuals or small firms which were either unable to build a kiln or unable to operate one properly. Because they were glazed and fired before they were sold, such heads could also have been decorated by families or in ordinary shops with overglaze paints. When thoroughly dried they could have been sold to bargain-hunting buyers, of which there was always a bumper crop.

Many such heads have been examined by the author through the years and there is a lackluster quality about them which is puzzling. Where the paint has or does wash off, there is the glaze underneath in perfect condition. Unfortunately, too, they are sometimes very desirable types to modern collectors, and they have prompted much inquiry and guesswork.

Old stories and records in this country use the word "china" in referring to Grandma's favorite dolls and to the family heirloom dinnerware. Grandma got the word from her parents and they heard it at the store where the dishes and the dolls or doll heads were purchased because old catalogues from which the storekeeper bought his supplies listed them both by the same name.

These old catalogues are interesting, especially in view of today's controversies over language. Many American areas had their own "China Works" whose famous-name products were described as: "near china," "semiporcelain," or "white ware." Imported products were listed as: Austrian, Bavarian, French or Japanese "china." Even Haviland was called "Limoges China."

After generations of use in our factories, advertising, stores, and homes, doll collectors quite naturally picked up the term with the dolls and now it is firmly established and has, at least for Americans, its own meaning. So, what the English, for example, may call "a porcelain head" would be simply a china head to us, even though it was made from porcelain clay and, unfortunately, not necessarily a good one by our rather high American standards. This is the danger of contradictory descriptive terms.

Ordinarily a china head is left white with only the hair, lips, cheeks, eyes (unless it is glass eyed), and eyebrows colored. Some very desirable chinas have a complexion coat, however, and they are commonly and quite erroneously referred to as "pink lustre" by people who should know better. They should be called "pink toned" because lustre paint has a metallic content—copper, silver, or gold—and sometimes an added color, as in the case of grape lustre, which has purple added. It is the pink complexion coat which makes these dolls different and desirable and lustre paint has no part in it whatever.

Lustre is sometimes used in chest decorations, molded earrings, snoods, and swags, or in fancy painted shoes, garters, and stocking tops. In these instances the reference to the trim is quite proper and necessary.

Porcelain. Porcelain has always been the cream of the ceramic art. The word itself comes from an earlier term which meant "shell." Fine, translucent, almost shell-like, true porcelain frequently has a clear, sharp sound when tapped even with a fingernail and it is all of these qualities of fineness which the word inadequately conveys to Americans. This is apparently why even the finest domestic American products were referred to as "semiporcelain."

The important ingredient in porcelain is kaolin and this comes from the Chinese "Kaoling," meaning "high hill or ridge," the Chinese area from which the first, white, superfine clay came to Europe.

Various explanations are on record covering the introduction of kaolin to European porcelain makers. We are concerned only with the fact that it *was* brought from the Orient and it *did* make a tremendous change in the industry, starting in the early 1700s.

Valuable French deposits of kaolin were discovered in the Limoges area in the 1760s and, in less than a century, led to the world supremacy of all the porcelain products manufactured there. Through the years, "Limoges, France," which was actually the address of the various makers, became synonymous with "highest quality."

Like other clays, kaolin from one area differs from all others because of the basic and purely local substances which disintegrated to produce it, chiefly feldspar rocks. Even after careful processing it always contains impurities from the parent rock, such as quartz, feldspar, and mica, which must be taken into account when blending a working mixture.

This soft, earthy material is dry to the touch, has good shaping characteristics when mixed with liquids, retains its color after firing, and is fire resistant, which reduces the shrinkage.

We have American deposits of this very necessary clay in Georgia, for example, and it plays an important role in our industrial as well as our personal lives. Kaolin is frequently the fine working ingredient in brass and silver polishes, and it is used in the commercial polishing of such widely diverse articles as glass and plastic eyeglass frames. Various types of kaolin clays are used for ceramics, paper, paint, ink, plastics, and other process industries. It is also used for talcum powder and refined for zinc sterate.

Besides the special clay body from which porcelain is made, the shell-like quality starts in the molds. The gradual "setting up" or thickening of the form next to the mold is watched very carefully by the operator.

As in all molded ware, the slip is poured into an opening at the end of the mold and the mold is poured full. As the slip begins to set from the absorption of the liquids by the plaster molds, more slip is added to keep the mold full. The worker watches the edges of this pouring hole to determine the thickness of the form within the mold. Inasmuch as the weather, for instance, can hasten or delay the thickening of the clay, this is a job for an expert.

At this point the technicalities of the porcelain art get a bit complicated for people outside the field because size and shape also enter the picture.

A very large porcelain doll head, for instance, would have to be poured with thicker walls than a tiny object of any kind. Then, too, an object which is almost complete can be poured much thinner than an object with a large opening. The larger the opening the greater the possibilities that the object will warp in the firing.

The next step is the same as in all poured products—the excess slip is poured out through the hole by which it was poured in. When sufficiently set to be unmolded, the item is called "greenware," and is set aside to dry enough to be handled.

Porcelain is glazed either before or after the first firing, depending on the method preferred by the individual manufacturers, either artists working alone or in factories. And it is decorated like china.

There are doll heads which carry the marks of famous porcelain works such as the crossed swords of Meissen or any of the marks of KPM (Königliche Porcellan Manufactur). Among the far more numerous unmarked heads, however, those which have a very thin shell of high quality and fine decorating are considered by Americans to be porcelain. Such heads, when held over a bright light in a darkened room, are thin enough to glow from the light and they often are frighteningly thin about the nostrils, in the eye corners, and at the ends of the mouth.

This division of *porcelain* and *china* which has been established in the doll world is not the doing of modern collectors. They have simply inherited the situation. Professional ceramists protest this division because both porcelain and china are made of porcelain slip. It all boils down to the fact that there has to be some way by which the buyer can judge the quality of the ware offered for sale and the seller can describe and advertise it.

The so-called "china" heads were only toys for children and they had to be cheap. As the twentieth century approached, there was less and less reason for quality and more and more reason for quantity production because these items were no longer reserved for the rich. Now that the twentieth century is more than half over, we find ourselves with more "china" heads available than the lovely, thin, "porcelain" types. A collector with any degree of advancement differentiates between the two kinds, just as collectors in any other field search for degrees of perfection in the objects they desire. China heads which are incised **Germany** across the back, as well as many which have just figures incised in the shoulder plate, do not command the admiration and the price of the earlier types because the quality is inferior, no matter what you call them or what you say they are made of, and it is rightly so.

It is a simple fact of life among the people who are spending the money and are not professionally trained in the ceramic arts. If they buy "porcelain" they are entitled to high quality and workmanship and if they buy "china" the great difference should be reflected in the price.

Parian. This is another trouble-making word.

The word "Parian" refers to the Island of Paros in the Aegean Sea, noted for its beautiful marble, although other Greek islands also produce excellent marble. As doll collectors we use the word to indicate starkly white, beautiful, almost grainless biscuit ware. Marble experts tell us that in the actual Parian marble, however, the color can vary to creamy white because of the mineral content of the island earth. And the grain of the marble, they say, can vary from fine to coarse.

It is all very interesting but we are talking about marble and doll heads are not made of marble. So, how did the word "Parian" get into doll language?

In his recent book, *Dolls,* John Noble, who is the Curator of the Toy Collection of The Museum of the City of New York, gives some background which should interest all collectors. He says in part, pages 34-35:

"In London, at the Great Exhibition of 1851, a statuette called 'The Captive Slave' attracted a great deal of attention and publicity. A reduced copy of a statue by Hiram Powers, an American artist, it was made of a new biscuit china* called 'Parian Ware.' Pure white, dense, and finely textured, this material did resemble marble to some degree. The original statuette found its way to the Victoria and Albert Museum, and reproductions, somewhat reduced in size, were soon on sale, and must have been very popular, to judge from the numbers still to be found in London antique shops."

He further says, "It is not surprising that this 'Parian look' was adopted before long by dollmakers, and the heads which they produced were unlike any that had yet been made.

"These heads have been loosely classified by collectors as 'Parians,' and the name is very suitable, as long as we realize that the term is a general one, and does not necessarily mean that they were made from actual Parian Ware. They are in fact to be found in various grades of chinaware, some exquisitely fine and brilliant, others quite coarse and dull. (The replicas of 'The Captive Slave,' presumably made of the real Parian Ware, have a curious soapy sheen to them and this writer has not yet seen an old doll's head made of this specific material.)"

Parian Ware, consequently, is accepted to mean art objects which are pure white, unglazed, and of extremely fine, almost textureless, slightly soapy quality.

These specifications for Parian Ware cover all objects made of the material. This is another instance where doll collectors borrowed a term from another field, and, to use it properly, their dolls should live up to the requirements laid down for such objects. So, if you have a *pure white,* fine-grained, undecorated doll head with a slightly soapy sheen, it may very well be a real Parian Ware doll head, since the manufacturers are supposed to have taken up the fad after 1851.

To be quite frank about it, this author has no desire for one and it does

---

*If the book is reissued, the author says the word *china* will be changed to *porcelain.*

not take much serious thinking to come to the opinion that these dolls would not have been very appealing to children. And we do presume that the doll heads we seek were originally made primarily for children.

Among museum directors and curators, dedicated people who are responsible for the classification of objects which must be accurately catalogued and publicly displayed, dolls or doll heads are not loosely labeled Parian. Knowledgeable art dealers, whose living depends on their accurate appraisal of objects to be offered for sale and guaranteed to be genuine, often flatly deny that dolls and doll heads were ever made of Parian.

Many serious researchers and some advanced collectors agree with these experts. After all, the dolls called Parian are not pure white. Indeed, in many instances, they are not the finest quality bisque. Their resemblance to Parian Ware derives from the fact that they are *not complexion coated* and nothing more. They have colored hair, painted eyes, eyebrows, lips, and cheeks. Added to that is the fact that they do not have a soapy sheen.

Another point to be considered is that the so-called Parian heads were made in Germany. We know this and at least up to this time there is no argument about it. Thus far no research has uncovered proof that the Germans ever said they were producing Parian Ware heads. They had every right to be proud of their own stark white bisque or bisque porcelain heads.

In his *Book of Ceramics,* which is completely addressed to professional ceramists, Pravoslav Rada lists Parian as "Bisque Porcelain." The composition of one formula for producing Parian is given as 60 per cent feldspar and 40 per cent kaolin and the firing temperature is from 1,280 to 1,320 degrees C. These temperatures on our Fahrenheit scale are 300 to 400 degrees less than the temperatures the Germans reportedly used in doll production.

Just by way of comparison for the layman, this formula for Parian differs greatly from a recipe given for Bone Porcelain, for instance, which contains kaolin, feldspar, bone-ash, and quartz. These ingredients must be juggled to make the best compound. As has been pointed out before, all of these ingredients vary geographically and require a great deal of experimentation to function at the highest level. This is why European factories guarded their secrets well and little or no record can be found of what they used or how they used it. The same situation prevails today.

We do know that there is a very good reason why dolls of this type are generaly decorated in pastel colors, however. Intense color must be built up of thin painted layers on the unglazed surfaces and each painted layer had to be individually fired. What often appears to be, or is said to be, black or dark brown "glazed" hair on these dolls may be the natural gloss which comes from the volatile oils in the coloring medium because of the density of the application of color. The beautiful satin-black complexion coat known generally as "Nubian" may have taken up to five or six trips to the kiln. Before the advent of the airbrush there was just no other way to achieve that flawless black on the unglazed surfaces. Some fine modern ceramists still prefer the old method.

Dolls of this quality may also have applied decorations, such as swags or flowers in the hair, molded earrings, fancy collars, breastplates, and the like. During the firing of the features some or all of these decorations may be glazed, resulting in a truly magnificent doll head but compounding the description problems by adding another type of ware to the head.

Here again there is an argument with the "pure" ceramists. For identification and classification purposes, doll collectors usually refer to these decorations as "china" trimmings. In most instances it makes a great deal of difference in the price and also, if a collector is seeking such a doll, she recognizes this description in an advertisement or uses the term in her letters to doll dealers so that they can be sure of her requirements.

It does not harm the dolls when we do not call these trimmings "glazed porcelain" and it certainly helps everyone else to have these language distinctions which are understood by the people who are spending and accepting the money.

Long before most doll collectors were the least bit interested in the subject, old-time dealers had a common expression by which Parian objects were judged. They said Parian had to be "white as snow and smooth as a used bar of soap." They also referred to any glazed trim on bisque objects as "china trim," so at least in America it is an expression of long standing.

In recent years the designation of Parian among doll people of all kinds has turned into an "almost anything goes" affair. Almost anything which is not complexion coated is included in the Parian classification and some heads with a very pale complexion coat are referred to as "tinted Parian." The term has been both lightly and loosely used and, unfortunately, European and American views often differ widely on what can and cannot be considered Parian. Most Americans, both collectors and dealers, are attempting to maintain high standards for so-called Parian dolls and insisting that only basically pure white heads which have been featured qualify for this classification.

To protect the investment of the advanced collector, as well as the buying power of the novice, something obviously has to be done about standards and it is up to the collectors themselves to do it or they will see their hobby priced out of existence.

The easiest way to correct this specific problem is to set standards and to insist that really fine-textured, lovely doll heads without all-over complexion tinting be called "Parian-quality," for instance. This will be in complete accord with the movement to call the complexion tinted chinas "pink toned" instead of the completely erroneous "pink lustre," unidentified dolls which meet other standards "French-type" instead of "French," and flat-topped bisque heads with stringing holes "Belton-type" instead of "Belton."

By changing the designation to "Parian-quality" all the coarse, rough, white bisque heads with only feature decoration can be ruled out even by a novice. By insisting on fine-grained, pure white Parian-quality, all complexion tinted and off-color dolls will be eliminated.

The old term, "china trimmed," has served so well for so long it could be retained to avoid a great deal of confusion. Those who wish to say "porcelain trimmed" would be free to do so and eventually everyone would profit from the clarification.

Exaggeration adds nothing to the intrinsic value of anything and that is especially true of dolls. To an experienced or to a studious collector, a true description often pinpoints a valuable connection between periods or changes in production. Like assigning the true age to a doll, the proper standardized descriptions help everyone.

Half Dolls {#ch}

Half Dolls

There is no mistaking a half doll because there are not enough kinds to confuse even a beginning collector, at least in the twenty years of this author's searching.

Some modern ceramists, or perhaps it is the mold makers, have produced at least one new pair. One is the body of the well-known little seated bisque boy in a large straw hat who perched on the edges of numberless fish bowls with a pole and a thread line in his hands. The little girl has a high bonnet but the figurine from which she comes is not as familiar as the boy. But these are classified as "reproduction half dolls" and reproductions are another story entirely.

In 1950 when Janet P. Johl wrote *Still More About Dolls,* she described half dolls (page 162) as: "The head and body, to the waist is of bisque, in one piece." On page 163 she illustrated the elderly couple. Since that time they have been given the name "half dolls" and it is most appropriate in the opinion of most collectors because it pinpoints the type.

Incised: **Germany** along the waist at the edge in back, they all have many things in common. They have bisque hands with very short forearm allowances on which to attach the sawdust stuffed cloth arms and the cloth tops of the arms enter the torsos through narrow shoulder slits in the bisque. The arms apparently were glued in the factory but if the dolls have to be redressed, many collectors fasten strings into the cloth arm ends so they can be tied together because when the glue dries out the arms slip out quite readily.

The half dolls have bisque legs which end in mid-calf and all the stockings are white. The molded shoes have slight heels and front bows; in the women and girls they are painted blue and in the men and boys they are bright yellow. The women and girls have pink cloth bodies; the men and boys have dark brown. None of them can sit because the tightly stuffed legs are attached to the bases of the bodies without any movement allowance.

All the eyes are blue with black pupils and lid linings; the one-stroke brows are in reddish blond. The adults are 6½ inches, the children are usually 4½ inches although the children can be found in larger sizes. The author has never been able to find the adults in larger sizes, however. Both of the young couple have light blond hair and so do all the children; the old gentleman's hair is very light gray; the elderly woman has no hair showing.

All the bisque is good, the modeling is detailed and lifelike, and the finishing and decorating of the torsos is excellent.

No. 1 With a slightly turned head, this lady has center parted hair with a molded top band which was not picked up in color, good waves around the face, and a large braided bun in back. Her neckerchief and molded underblouse are white, the blouse is a pretty shade of green.

No 2 Also with a turned head, this gentleman has excellently molded hair from a side part and an elegant curling moustache. His shirt is white

1 & 2 Author's collection

with molded flowing tie colored brown and suspenders done in pale blue. His pants are worth notice because the selvage of the velvet serves as a cuff without bulk.

No. 3 The little boy's head is quite turned, he has good bangs, a white shirt, and light blue bow tie.

The little girl is more colorful. Her side parted bob has a molded pink bow. The blouse is white with a yellow "bertha" collar which has a pink ruffled edge and there is a small blue breast bow.

Unlike the mother and father, these two children often appear as shoulder heads. The boy is cut below the bow and the girl at the circular collar. They have been seen in sizes up to almost 4 inches.

No. 4 This old gentleman has side-painted eyes and very pleasant wrinkles between his eyebrows, at the outside corners of his eyes and around his mouth. He wears a molded rimless cap with a front tassel which has a string molded to the center crown and it is painted brown. His ascot is white and the double-breasted charcoal gray jacket has a molded closure and buttons. There is a black spot of paint under his left eye which should

3

4

3 Author's collection; 4 Strong collection

have been removed, unless someone thought it would look like a mole. It is not always present.

No. 5 The lady has the same pleasant, slightly wrinkled face as her companion and she has an even wider smile. Her head bandanna is gray-green with a knot in back. The center closing on her brown jacket has molded buttons and her white underblouse can be seen at the neck edge. The selvage of the brown velvet used for her dress was utilized for wide, bulkless cuffs.

No. 6 These turned head children are usually considered to be the youngsters for the older couple, although they surely are grandchildren. Because they are not as "gussied up" as the other pair, the association is quite natural and for some reason they always appear to be more shy than the other boy and girl.

The girl's hair is molded in a braid around the head, a style many Europeans still like and many Americans remember from their childhood. Something had to be done with the long hair in the hot weather and this was

6 *Strong collection*

another of the "somethings" to do with it. Her jacket is blue and the high-necked underblouse is white.

The boy has close cropped hair, a maroon jacket, and a white blouse with the molded front band picked up in pale blue.

It should be noted that all these colors vary in any given number of sets. Without any Madison Avenue training in consumer psychology, these old German manufacturers knew very well the power of color to attract attention. Whether they were aware of it or not, they also knew that buyers lingered over merchandise with a choice of colors and the lingering was almost always fatal.

Researching in Germany during the summer of 1968, the Colemans happened upon some information about half-bisque dolls which they gladly shared.

On page 385 of the 1911 *Deutsche Spielwaren-Zeitung,* there is an illustrated advertisement by Hertwig & Co., Katzhutte, Thuringia. Because the advertisement is in the lower left corner of a right hand page, it could not be copied well but the dolls are unmistakable.

All-Bisques

What is a doll?

Nonsensical arguments notwithstanding, a doll is a humanized toy, a plaything. It makes no difference whether it is a sumptuous creation for the entertainment of a reigning queen or a rag doll for the amusement of a child.

There are no hard and fast rules which can be laid down and relentlessly applied, but a doll does NOT have a molded base attached to it. We cannot say that a doll must have moving parts because some dolls are "frozen" and yet they are not figurines nor are they votive statues. Some dolls have only half bodies and yet they are dolls, not pincushion tops. Thus it goes, but a doll is a toy forever.

Doll collectors have their preferences, often based on what they did or did not have as children and just as often controlled by what they can or cannot afford. Some collectors are omniverous and seek anything pertaining to dolls, including figurines holding dolls, jewelry in the form of dolls, paintings containing dolls, books about dolls, as well as doll banks, lamps, clocks, and the like.

Among the truly collectible dolls, the all-bisques hold more than an alphabetical first place with many hobbyists. Some women collect nothing else, some buy them as "dolls for dolls," and others keep a little world of all-bisques apart from their more spectacular prizes, proud of both kinds.

All-bisques have many attractive qualities.

Anybody who can thread a needle can dress them in bits of lace and ribbon, most of the jointed ones are easy to restring, and it only takes a few tries to turn out an acceptable wig if the hair is not molded. They can be beautifully displayed in groups under glass domes or in shadow boxes with a piece or two of dollhouse furniture and miniature items. Dozens of them will also live quite comfortably and be instantly accessible in the drawers of a spool-thread cabinet from an old store.

There are in existence, but rarely in retail circulation, all-bisques with elbow, knee, or both knee and elbow joints. They also come with shoulder or hip and shoulder joints, with stiff or swivel necks, with molded hair or with wigs, with open or closed mouths, painted or set glass eyes, and with glass eyes that sleep.

Collectors divide these dolls into French, German, and Japanese but it is well to remember that while millions of them are incised with the word **Germany** or with figures which we now recognize as the type the Germans used, it is almost impossible to establish definitely the French origin for the finer old types thought to be French. Japanese dolls are identifiable by their inferior workmanship if they are not marked.

Among the millions that are unmarked, it is quite within the limits of credibility that the German factories made some, if not all, of them. We are positive that the Germans made many or most of the early French doll heads because there are printed records in which the French themselves complain about it. If they could not or did not make heads, there is no real proof as yet that they made many whole all-bisque dolls that can be classified as "early."

The entire area of the origin of unmarked dolls is quite confused and this includes all dolls, not only all-bisques.

Collectors should bear in mind that many of these firms were owned by a sole proprietor or a pair of partners and no production records for stockholders had to be maintained. Many of them seem to have sold their entire production to jobbers or contract bidders and hence did not have to advertise in trade journals. There also was no income tax as modern manufacturers know it, no Social Security, unemployment, or pension plans which required elaborate personnel record-keeping. Records of modern manufacturers will be available for research long after they have gone. This was not true in Germany or anywhere else for that matter in those times.

Added to this dearth of material from one century to the next, two devastating wars first crippled and then decimated the German doll industry. Consequently, we have only surviving Trade Directories, catalogues, individual trade fliers, old magazines and books, plus hearsay, of course, to use for research—along with the dolls themselves.

And it is surprising what the dolls can tell us. Keen observation and detailed records of the dolls which pass through our hands gradually build up funds of pertinent information which are priceless. Inasmuch as we are living in an age which looks perpetually and anxiously into the future, it behooves those of us who are preoccupied with the past to compare our observations and to share our knowledge generously with others.

Because of the great lack of authentic data, in these pages acceptably French dolls are grouped together, both early and late; so-called French dolls are classified as French-type; some German and Japanese dolls are identifiable, and, in other instances, the reader is invited to guess along with the rest of us or to tell us if we are wrong.

Aside from Frozen Charlottes, all-bisques fall into three stringing classifications:

Pegs were used in some of the oldest and nicest types. In this method we now draw rubber through the body and through the holes in the arms, or the arms and legs, and then hold the rubber firmly by forcing glued wooden pegs into the holes. However, many old dolls have pieces of what appears to be linen string caught in the original pegs.

Wire was used for many years, looped and bent over the outer edges of the limbs. This fell out of favor and then returned, as an economy measure, many years later. The old wire is generally brass if the doll is in original condition and the later dolls usually have "hard wire," although many inexpensive specimens have common, poorly galvanized wire which rusts readily.

The third type, which is also rubber strung, has stringing loops molded to the tops of the arms and the insides of the legs, or the arms only. These loops fit into shoulder and thigh holes in the torso, and, in some of the French and French-type, the arms fit into molded shoulder sockets just like those in jointed composition bodies.

It should be noted here that dating all-bisques is not the primary consideration of this book. There is no way of knowing how long certain types remained popular or, which adds to the total confusion, how often some of them were revived, or whether the molds were sold to secondary manufacturers when something new was created.

Some types can be found in old American wholesale catalogues but apparently the most desirable kinds went directly to expensive toy shops and department stores, either through resident European brokers or the stores' own traveling buyers.

Many all-bisques are very old, others are old, some are pre-World War I, and some are postwar. Readers of this book will be firmly convinced that World War I caused many and great changes, not only in the lives of the people of the world, but also in commerce and industry, and especially in the toy field.

French

Not many all-bisques are identifiably French and arbitrarily assigning a French origin to an unmarked doll accomplishes nothing. Late French specimens, which are generally the least desirable, are marked but very few old ones enjoy that distinction.

No. 7 It is most fortunate that this 8½-inch doll is incised on the head and the body with two sizes of the same figure 6 and that all her limbs are marked on the flanges with a smaller size of the same figure. By further happy coincidence, it is a French type of numeral, such as are found on F.G. dolls, for instance.

If it were not for all this, she would surely be subjected to the argument that her original head had been removed and a small French Fashion head substituted.

Her French eyes are very pale, threadless blue, with dark outer rims and large pupils. The upper and lower painted lashes and the dark blond, feathered eyebrows are typically French. She has red eye and nose dots, a very well done mouth, her original cork dome, and the remains of a lovely light blond mohair wig on a good cloth cap.

The modeling is all very good and the hands are exquisite, with free thumbs and every phalange of every finger clearly defined on the inner side. The right wrist is turned a little more than the left, as if to display this workmanship.

It is baffling, however, to note the freckling on the body when the entire head is almost clear. These imperfections, which vary from light gray to black, show very clearly through the pale complexion tint. They do attest to her age, however.

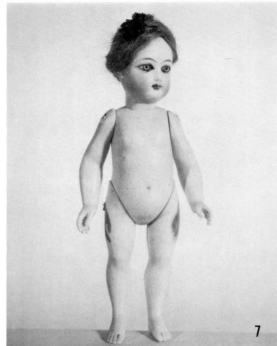

7

7

Her head is large and heavy, with a typical swivel base, so she must be strung like a jointed. The hook from the neck plug is caught in the rubber and then the rubber is pulled through and pegged in the legs. If this is not done, her legs slide up the sides of the body in a disfiguring manner because the pegging holes are at an upward angle instead of being straight through the legs.

She is a most desirable and unusual all-bisque.

No. 8 Truly worthy of the appellation "rare," this 5¼-inch ball jointed doll is incised in the center back but all that can be distinguished clearly is a **B** to the left of the spine. We can only presume that the **TE** was erased in the finishing process because it is like the mark on **No. 10** and is in the same place.

Unlike the following doll, which has rounded forearm tops that fit into the upper-arm cavities, this doll has separate bisque balls which fit between both the arm and the leg parts. In the stringing, these balls and the connecting rubber have been glued into the lower parts of the limbs so they now swivel only in their upper halves. Inasmuch as they went to so much trouble to create this doll, the manufacturer must have had a way of stringing which would leave these balls free, but the secret has been lost.

The irisless eyes are factory set, they have black lid linings and the lids are painted gray. The one-stroke brows are brown. Because the mouth was not definitely molded, the decorators had wide latitude and in this instance both lips are outlined in the rose color used for the center line but the balance of the lip surfaces were not colored, as we expect them to be.

The neck, shoulders, and hips are kid lined, as the French liked them. The open neck is held with rubber doubled over an inside head bar and one piece of the rubber goes to each leg. The wig is silky blond mohair on a gauze cap. The complexion is very pale and all the modeling is good. The legs are long and shapely, the hands are large, and the fingers and toes are well defined, with all the nails carefully outlined with the lip color. The hands are also unusual because she has free-standing thumbs which are under her hands instead of standing out from the palm. These presented a touchy problem for the handlers because, especially in the unfired greenware state, this small digit was very easily broken off. The hands on

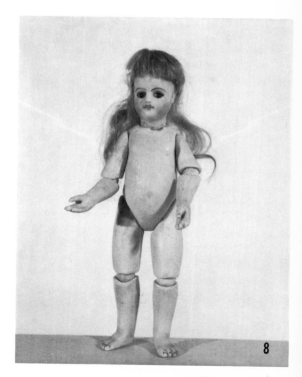

Orsini dolls (**Nos. 283 and 284**), which are so attractive to collectors, posed the same problem in production.

The bisque is old, without any feeling of frailty, and there is none of the sharpness characteristic of German bisque.

No. 9 This 5¼-inch peg strung doll has had her off-center mold lines penciled in for clarity. This is a clue to one of the old French types because unless the body is extremely well finished, the telltale mold lines can be seen on the torso. Instead of being down the sides as they ordinarily are, these are on the opposite sides of the front and back—left on one side and right on the other. It was necessary to use off-center molds in order to open them after the slip had set and still leave the excellent sockets intact in the tender greenware.

Besides a ball head, swivel neck, set blue eyes with pupils, and upper and lower painted lashes, she has the very desirable peg strung elbow joints. This doll has also been seen with straight arms and with knee joints. She was found in eight pieces and is one of the dolls which had bits of linen-like string caught in some of the pegs which had never been removed.

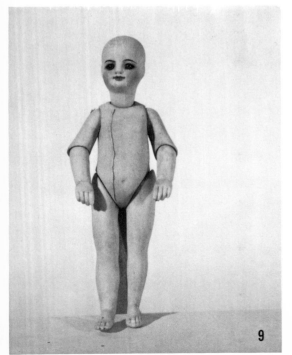
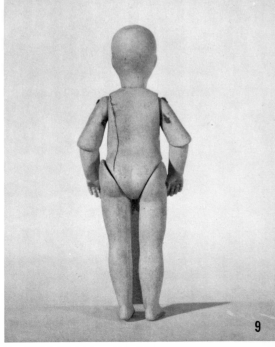

9

9

9 *Author's collection*

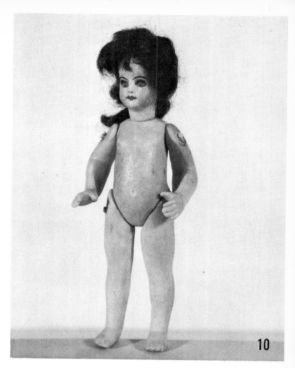

Her long, straight, pretty legs are 3 inches to the hip tops, more than half her length, and this is also characteristically French.

There is a soft, porous feeling to this bisque when compared to other pieces. It is much like the flakey difference between baked piecrust and hard candy. The same quality is noticed at times in old French heads and it very likely is due to a peculiar quality in the clay used in the slip.

Her age and origin are unknown but she is believed to be much older than the average all-bisque in circulation now.

No. 10 Incised **BTE** (a French contraction referring to a patentee) across the back, this 5¼-inch doll has to be accepted as French. Oddly enough, however, this does not prove that she actually was manufactured in France, any more than "Depose" or "DEP." proves a bisque head was made there.

There are many instances among the heads on French composition bodies where the face belonged to and was used by Simon & Halbig, for instance, on untold thousands of their own dolls. These heads could not be doll hospital replacements because there are too many of them available for comparison and the necks are always factory seated to fit perfectly. There is also one example in this collection of a Simon & Halbig face on a head which is incised in back: **S.F.B.J.**, and the head is on the original S.F.B.J. jointed composition body. Since S.F.B.J. was such a late mark, this practice must have continued for many years.

These marks simply indicate that dolls and doll heads were made for French distribution and hence, at least to us, they are French.

Although this BTE doll somewhat resembles the previous doll with elbow joints and the eyes are done like those on the ball-jointed specimen, and all three of them are the same size, she is definitely not of the same quality and it is a good guess that she is later. This is especially evident in the very different bisque.

She has a cut head instead of the older ball type and if she had a cork dome it is now missing. The swivel neck is open and held by a plug with a wire which extends to the hip rubber and the neck hole is kid lined. The head and the features are smaller. She has no eyelashes but her upper lids are painted gray above the black eyelid lining, as women sometimes color their upper lids. It is not very becoming in a doll. The eye sockets are small and the blue eyes are pinhead size, which gives her a squinting stare.

The torso is flat at the shoulders and the arm tops are flat to match. She was wire strung when purchased and there was some question whether the limbs were original because the coloring did not match the torso. However, the hips have full sockets molded in the flanges and the legs have shallow ball areas to match. The bad color matching is simply poor workmanship or low factory standards. The legs are straight and long but they spraddle out. The whole impression is one of carelessness or an amateurish first attempt to do this work.

The hands are rather large and well shaped, which is the French habit with hands, but the right thumb was lost either in the unmolding or in the finishing and the arm was processed nevertheless because the stump of thumb is factory finished.

Although the coloring has to be listed as pale, it is not evenly applied or attractive and the bisque is also of a hard type which does not readily absorb oil color.

When this doll is compared with the others, serious students hazard a guess that the elbow-jointed doll was made in Germany for a French distributor, and the ball-jointed one may have been also. The Germans

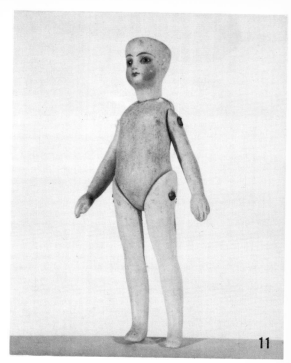

11 *Author's collection*

entered this field early and it is much more likely that their products, rather than their workers, were exported.

No. 11 Unmarked, 4½ inches tall, peg strung and swivel necked, this doll presumably is French because she has more French characteristics than German.

The face is oval, entirely without the fat cheeks the Germans loved. The eye sockets are large in proportion, the blue irises are large enough to extend both above and below the eye sockets and she has both upper and lower lashes. The one-stroke brows almost meet across the nose bridge, as countless French dolls' eyebrows do. The torso has breast modeling, the arms are long and the hands are well formed. The shoulders are flat and closed and the upper arms are flat on the inner sides, like the previous doll's. She also has the long, straight, French legs.

The mottled complexion coat on this doll is difficult to diagnose. The freckling at first appears to be the mildew caused by underfiring and yet she has some of the warts caused by overfiring. So, it is safer to presume that the black spots are foreign particles in the bisque because they do not appear on the inside of the open head and they are widely scattered, the worst being in the head. Like the previous doll too, the bisque did not accept the color well and the pink tone shows as mottled rather than a smooth skin tone.

Nos. 12A-B This boy and girl are beautiful examples of all-bisque manufacturing. Thought to be French because they were among a number brought to the original owner about 1900 by touring relatives, they were packed in boxes marked *France*. Since France had only been a name on a map to the little girl prior to this, she was very much impressed.

Conclusive as this would seem to be, there is ample evidence that "tourist" dolls were made up in France for the visiting public. In some instances these were unmarked but identifiable German heads by Simon & Halbig mounted on marked French bodies and sold in boxes marked *France*. The writer has examined one such doll, cherished as "Grandmother's Jumeau doll" through several generations. This frequently happens because non-collectors do not remove wigs to determine the authenticity of such heirlooms.

12   12

Nevertheless, there were several boxes of these small all-bisques and each box contained several pairs, including a black pair in each box. It is not uncommon to find these black dolls among French exports, as well as quite a few shades of brown, so this memory could be very accurate. Because they so intrigued her playmates who had never seen black dolls before, the black ones were the first to be broken and none of them remain.

Exquisitely detailed and finished, and beautifully decorated, this 5-inch pair are additionally interesting and valuable because they have molded hats. The construction is also unusual.

The mold seams are barely visible down the sides of the bodies because the finishing was so good but, about level with the boy's ear tops, the hat seams are visible. Undercutting would have been the molding problem here and it is very possible that his face and hair were part of the front mold and his neck and the lower rim of his hat were in the back mold, with the top section of the hat in a third piece of the mold. The girl's hat shows no seams at all and could have been entirely separate, with her face in the front mold and her hair and the back of her head in the back mold. This is an instance where the hat truly appears to have been applied.

Added to this, he has a very small Dresden-type air hole in his seat but she has none. If the hat was separately molded and applied, her molds would have been drained through the large head opening.

Although they are of hollow bisque construction, the shoulder areas are at least partially solid, providing rounded channels for the stringing rubber and beautifully molded shoulder sockets for the ball-ended arms. This is the only time such a shoulder has been noted by the author.

The coloring is most attractive. His blouse and her pants are white, his pants and her blouse are pastel blue. His entire hat, the back of hers, both sash fringes and his shirt bow are bright yellow. The slippers are orange and his hat band is green. Both have light brown hair, blue eyes with high-placed pupils, and black eyelid linings. The one-stroke eyebrows come close to the nose bridges and the complexion tinting is very delicate and even. All the ruffling is white and her molded, painted blue necklace looks very much like the Lutin anchor trademark.

Made in France or not, this pair surely deserve the accolade: "French, unless it can be proved otherwise."

No. 13 One of six identical 6-inch dolls billed from France ten years ago as "all bisque Limoges *seconds,*" this is a very poor advertisement for

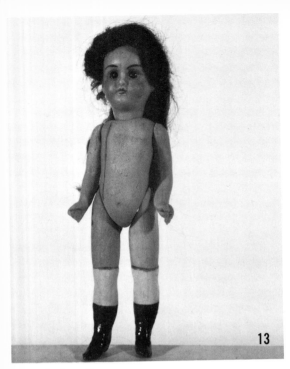

13 *Author's collection*

French workmanship, Limoges or not. It is regrettable that a first quality doll has not been available for comparison in all these years.

The hands are not typical of French dolls and they are poorly finished, with mold lines and mold debris still clinging to them. The open-closed mouth is very poorly painted in a lopsided fashion and it is rough to the touch. The sleep eyes are without irises, an economy measure in this century, and both the upper and lower lashes are in the flesh areas instead of following the eye cut.

Incised on the back of the head:

Petite Français

France

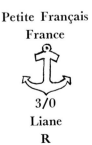

3/0

Liane

R

This is the Lutin mark which often appears on doll heads made of pyro, a substance resembling bisque but lighter in weight and of a yellowish tinge. Pyro can be checked by examining the inside of the head.

Possibly as late as the 1930s, this doll is definitely made of bisque and it very likely is an example of the reuse of old molds. The mold line has been penciled in down the right side of the front for the illustration. Except that the molds were available, there was no reason for the side-opening molds in this instance. There are no shoulder sockets and, to be quite accurate, the arm holes were obviously hand cut, which made them very irregular and not alike in shape.

The arms appear to have been flat on the insides originally, with the heavy stringing loops added to fit the cutout shoulder holes. The same thing is true of the legs because oversize stringing loops fit into the large hip holes.

The use of old molds is further indicated because the doll has the old French stringing loop molded to the base of the swivel neck (see **No. 14**). Close examination also reveals that the high boots were painted over molded lines for the four- and five-strap high bootines found on old dolls.

The most obvious evidence of her late manufacture is the very "high" complexion tint. Whatever the cause, whether it was the available bisque or the paint, French dolls lost their appealing peaches-and-cream complexions long before World War I. Because this bisque did not hold the color well, this doll and her companions were all a very mottled sunburned shade.

Dolls like this raise the question: How should these suspected products from old molds be identified? They cannot be called "reproductions" because that term is reserved for anything made in molds which were taken from old products and this applies to dolls, figurines, and so forth. Unless someone comes up with a more descriptive term, "reissue" with an approximate date seems to be the most accurate.

French-Type

The French-type attract collectors' fancies on many counts. Their faces are sweet and bright looking, the bodies are generally in better proportion than the average German doll. Another attractive feature is the care with which they were assembled. The little swivel necks often fit into kid lined neck holes and, on many types, kid disks are glued to the flat surfaces of the arms, or the arms and legs, where they touch the bodies so that they can be moved without making the typical shrieking bisque sound.

This work could have been done in France. Unassembled dolls very likely enjoyed an import duty easement when entering France from Germany because they provided employment for the French. The work could also have included setting eyes, providing wigs and clothing, and, of course, stringing.

These two nations hated each other and yet, even as with nations today, they had mutual commercial and industrial agreements through economic necessity.

The Franco-Prussian War of 1870-71 was short and disastrous, ending in the capture and exile of Louis Napoleon and the fall of the Empire in France. For at least a full generation after this humiliating defeat, many Frenchmen lived and suffered for only one purpose—revenge against Germany.

Even the children were not immune from this hatred. In the 1880-84 period, M. Jumeau, for instance, included a booklet in each Jumeau doll box. It was in part a sweet note from the doll to the little girl who received the gift and also an amazing diatribe against the Germans and their dolls.

"They are ugly and ridiculous enough, these German babies, with their stupid faces of waxed cardboard, their goggle eyes and their frail bodies stuffed with hemp threads. I [this is the doll speaking] would rather be mute, just as I am, than to have come from my breast, like them, the cry of an animal." This reference, of course, is to the familiar squawker the Germans used instead of the *Mama* and *Papa* string governed bellows the French set into composition bodies.

It is a little surprising to us that this sort of brainwashing of children was still going on in the 1880s, especially since M. Jumeau had been producing his own complete dolls since the early 1870s. But production is futile without accompanying sales volume and there doubtless was a price advantage to buyers of German dolls. Because the French are known to be a frugal race, this was one way to enlist the help of the children in the promotion of French toys.

Advanced collectors differ with novices in the matter of necks on all-bisques which should be called French-type rather than French. Swivel necks are the most desirable but novices generally are taken by the tiny, set glass eyes even in the stiff necks. Advanced collectors look for swivel necks, especially those with built-in stringing loops at the bases of the closed necks.

No. 14 The molded French loop. These required more expensive molds and better finishing than the other types of loop and are easily identified because they always look like the tops of steeple bells. Besides giving the head more flexibility, the loops and the holes make removing the wig unnecessary when restringing, which is an added blessing.

German swivel necked dolls without wooden neck plugs often have holes in the sides of the necks to accommodate the arm rubber which also holds the heads in place. The problem with this arrangement is that such heads will not hold a turned position, but will always face front like stiff necks.

Many of the French-type swivels are peg strung and, while some have painted eyes, most of them have well-painted lashes and glass eyes, both set and sleep. In the smaller sizes the eyes are usually set and are more often blue than brown, without pupils. As the sizes increase, the pupils appear.

They have legs that are another collectors' joy, primarily because of the great variety. Much daintier than the German-made legs, many of them are barefooted but others have textured stockings in vertical or circular molded ribbing and in colors including white, black, brown, gray, blue, and yellow. The shoes are also varied in type and color. Some have high

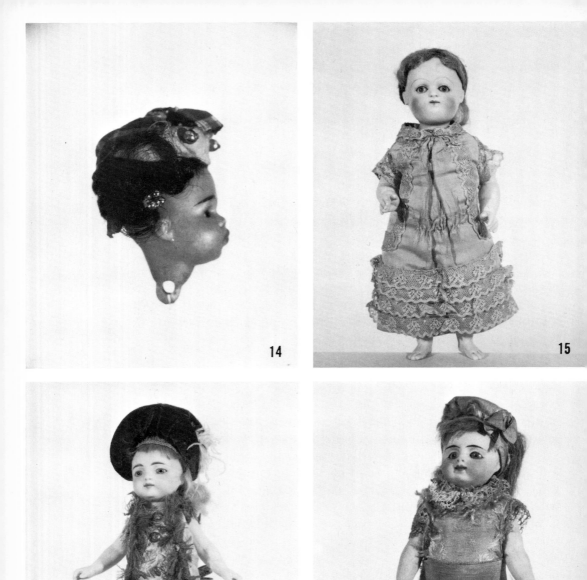

14 Brewer collection; 15 Strong collection; 16 Hilsdorf collection; 17 Author's collection

bootines which come to points on the fronts of the legs, with rubber side gussets indicated. Others have high buttoned boots with four or more molded, painted straps. There are also brown, black, pink, or blue, one- and two-strap slippers, with or without heels, some with bows, and also pumps which can be plain black with a colored bow or such a combination as orange with blue bows and black heels.

These dolls are well decorated and have a becoming flesh tint. The miniature wigs are of straight or curled hair, or mohair done in braids with a center part, or all-over mohair curls which could be regulated in size to suit the doll. Because many of the top cuts in the heads are small, just large enough to permit the setting of eyes, some wigs are on a flat cloth base no bigger than a dime. Others of these wigs have a full cap and a hair length which is most surprising.

No. 15 Unmarked, 7⅛ inches tall, with cobalt sleep eyes with good pupils, upper and lower painted lashes, black lid linings and four-stroke feathered blond brows, this is a quality German swivel head held with a plug; she is peg jointed. She has red eye and nose dots and a dark center line in a rather pale mouth. The complexion is very pale and uniform, and her cheeks are the old, peach color. She is well within the limits of French-type.

All the body modeling is very appealing. Her arms are not alike and her open hands have free thumbs. The legs are very shapely, all the toes are expertly done and there is even a suggestion of arch in her feet. The light blond mohair wig on a fine cap is original and it is done like many of the old wax hairdos. There is a separate fall of hair which was cut to make the bangs, the long back hair originates just behind the bangs, and then the woven hair strands are covered with a ribbon band which is glued in place.

She has to be catalogued "dressed as found" because, while the dark ivory silk dress is delightful, there is no guarantee that it was originally hers. The seams are machine done but all the lace is hand applied and the gathering is hand done. Like **No. 46**, this old dress is flat hemmed down both back openings and then held in place with narrow ribbons tied in bows instead of buttons and loops.

No. 16 This 7¼-inch French-type has closed shoulders and flat arm tops, so she is hip and shoulder pegged and has kid-lined parts. Her set, threaded blue eyes have upper and lower painted lashes and multistroke blond brows. She has a closed mouth with a dark center line and very blunt, Kestner-type lip ends.

Her old blond mohair wig is made like those on many wax dolls, with front bangs and a long back fall which both originate at the top of the forehead. She is slender in the torso as well as in the limbs and she has very blunt, molded-together fingers and short, free thumbs. The five-strap brown bootines with front molded bows and tan soles are unusual, black having been the favorite color. The mid-calf white socks have no ribbing and the bands are blue.

The bisque is very pale and good and all the finishing and decorating, including the "blushing" on the limbs, is excellent.

The French coat-dress with a lace bottom ruffle appears to be original. It is made of ivory sateen with a flowered silk damask front, magenta silk braid and tiny brass buttons. The hat is magenta velvet with an ivory feather.

No. 17 Unmarked, 5¾ inches tall, with a swivel neck which is strung with a plug, this is an extreme example of the long hair. Close-mouthed and peg strung, she has a cork dome, which is typical of good French dolls from the earliest open heads. The sleep eyes are threadless cobalt with pupils and only lower painted lashes. Her one-stroke brows are dark blond. The excellent complexion is not pale but it is very even and slightly pink.

The body and limbs have side mold lines but the arms especially have French characteristics. Most importantly, they are not alike. The right arm is slightly bent and the cupped, very chubby, childish hand is turned in and up. The left arm is straight and the wrist is lifted but the hand is cupped down. Then, although the body does not have molded shoulder sockets, the arms have excellent ball tops. The legs are sturdy and childish and the little pale blue, one-strap slippers have molded front bows, barely indicated heels and yellow soles.

She is very likely "all original" because the odd material in her dress is repeated in her tam, and the narrow ribbons in her hair and on her hat are smaller sizes of the kind used for her sash. Her undies are sewed on, but someone ripped open her dress and chemise in back, probably trying to see if her back was marked since her head is not. Her pale blond human hair wig would be considered "surprising" inasmuch as it touches the floor behind her.

This doll is also interesting because she came in what was said to be

"her original box," **No. 18.** On a small, very old-fashioned label on the box is printed: *Baigneur habillé*. Checking a French dictionary discloses that *baigneur* means "bather, bathing attendant," and *habillé* means "dressed (up), clad, smart, dressy."

At first glance this does not make much sense because if she is dressed as a bathing attendant or a smartly clad bather, French beaches and bath houses must have been something to see. The box fits her perfectly, however, and even the tissue is old and yellow and very different from ours.

This was all very puzzling because, although original boxes are very interesting, few people display dolls in any kind of boxes. Then, quite by accident, the Colemans explained that they have come across advertisements for "bathers" and to the French this meant a doll which could be washed or completely immersed in water without harm. It would not be too good for her pegging, but it could be done. Different languages and different usages because of changing times can stump the best of us!

No. 19 Compared side by side, this and the previous doll are hauntingly alike in spite of their many differences. It is quite possible they were made by the same factory, either at different times or for separate classes of trade.

Across the back this doll is incised 40-3½. She is also 5¾ inches tall, has a swivel head held with a plug in a kid-lined neck hole, a head cork, a blond mohair wig with bangs, set cobalt blue eyes, lower lashes only, one-stroke dark blond brows, a closed mouth, and she is peg strung.

Her hands are very French, childish and rather chubby, but her arms are bent alike at the elbows. She has shoulder holes without sockets and her arms are without the molded ball tops. The legs are very slender and the angle of the hip flange is poor, causing a pigeon-toed appearance because the feet touch. The socks are white with teal blue bands, the molded high boots are gray and have small heels. The soles are light brown.

The torsos are completely different. This doll has a slender, petite body which is accentuated by the typically French coat-dress. The previous doll has a very German, bulging abdomen, and the body is wider and thicker.

They are both French-type but who can tell when or where they were made?

No. 20 The 7-inch swivel neck blonde in the old checkered dress is a lovely all-bisque, incised with a **3** on the head. She is peg strung and her body modeling is like that of the barefooted doll, **No. 21**. In fact, they could very well be the same doll with different legs. The complexion tinting on both is the light, peachy color.

The four-strap black bootines are molded on the fat legs and they have molded pompoms and heels. The white socks have magenta bands. Her light blue threaded sleep eyes have been set and the original wig is pale blond, silky mohair.

Her 5¾-inch companion is incised **1**, her brown eyes are factory set, and she has a two-braid brassy blond mohair wig.

There is some question, however, that a factory would assemble a doll with such a poorly fitted neck, but possibly her original kid lining has been lost through the years. She is peg strung and the beautifully tinted body is peachy pink. The vertically ribbed white socks have blue bands and the molded bootines are lavender with black trim and heels.

No. 21 Incised **2½**, the 6⅞-inch barefooted doll has lovely body modeling for a plaything. Like the two previous dolls, she is hip and shoulder jointed with pegs and her arm tops are flat to fit the flat, closed shoulder construction. She has the same pale peachy flesh tint, gray-blue sleep eyes and her original dark blond cap mohair wig.

The ⅛-inch difference between this barefooted doll and the one in the checkered dress is just the height of the molded heels on the booted doll.

The barefooted type raises the question about shoes. In originally dressed specimens, the ornate silk clothing seemed to be quite out of place with the unclad feet and yet none of these has ever been seen by the author with an original shoe or sock.

All these dolls have almost closed swivel necks, with only a very small center hole for the exit of the rubber from the wooden plug inside the

Plate I.—All-bisque dolls with molded clothes and hair. *(Front row, left to right)* 3½-inch sailor boy (No. 152); 3¾-inch Indian (No. 157); a Negro boy, 3¾-inches tall, with an unusually strung moving head (No. 306); a girl in a bathing suit (No. 156). *(Back row, left to right)* A 7-inch boy in a romper suit (No. 154); a pair of 7¼-inch dolls in the long-waisted clothes popular about 1910 (Nos. 161 and 162); a 7½-inch specimen of the smaller dolls shown in text (No. 151).

Plate II. Half-bisques, one piece to the waist, with bisque hands and feet. The 4-inch boy (No. 3) and the 6½-inch man with the elegant moustache (No. 2) have stuffed brown cloth lower bodies; the 6½-inch lady (No. 1) and the 4½-inch girl (No. 3) have stuffed pink cloth lower bodies. The all-bisque bear (No. 82) can stay in a variety of positions. He is about 3 inches tall when seated.

Plate III. (Left to right) A 5-inch Kewpie (No. 256) with label intact, is a scarce hip and shoulder jointed type; a 4½-inch J. L. Kallus doll with part of the original label (No. 282); another of Rose O'Neill's patents, an all-bisque mulatto girl in the Strong Collection, marked 61 over 17 in two lines on the head, she is similar to No. 22 and is dressed in the same fashion and materials. An 8-inch Heubach doll with the "Smiling Girl" type of face (No. 123) and a 9-inch pegged blonde with a mohair wig (No. 103) which is made of old, very good bisque.

Plate IV. (Left to right) An excellent "Nubian" of fine, low gloss texture, he is 9 inches tall (No. 23); this 8½-inch hip and shoulder peg jointed all-bisque must be an early Kestner (No. 88); the long stockings make this 7½-inch all-bisque doll very desirable (No. 105); a stiff necked bisque of excellent quality (No. 86); this unmarked French-type (No. 17) has a pale blond human hair wig that touches the ground.

Plate V. (*Front row, left to right*) A 3½-inch stiff neck (No. 35); a stiff neck (No. 33) with a tiny metal anchor at the neck; a 4¼-inch pegged swivel (No. 29); this pair may be a bride and groom (No. 28); the companion to the boy at far left (No. 35). (*Back row, left to right*) A 3-inch Flapper's child (No. 292); two versions of the so-called "Amelia Earhart" (No. 290); another specimen of No. 292.

Plate VI. (*Front row, left to right*) A 4¼-inch Frozen Charlotte in fine, old bisque (No. 40); the yellow hat of this pure white bisque doll (No. 63) required a three- or four-piece mold; a Frozen Charlotte 4¼-inches tall (No. 42). (*Back row, left to right*) A 6-inch Old White (No. 72); a 5½-inch child (No. 87) of excellent quality; this Frozen Charlotte is of exceptional weight (No. 44); this Old White is 5¼-inches tall (No. 61); a very unusual man jester (No. 74).

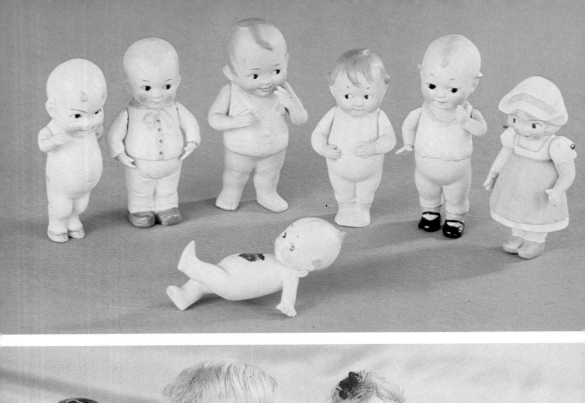

Plate VII. *(Front)* A variation of No. 252, this Kewpie is often found tied to a silk pillow. *(Standing, left to right)* This 4½-inch creature with hoofs, pointed ears, horns, and a tail is "Little Imp" copyrighted by Illfelder. (No. 268); a boy in knit sweater and pants (No. 170); a 5¼-inch Baby Bud, patented in 1915 (No. 266); "Chubby" is No. 169 but without a label; of excellent bisque, he seems to be saying "No! No!" (No. 171); a 4½-inch Dutch girl of excellent bisque (No. 160).

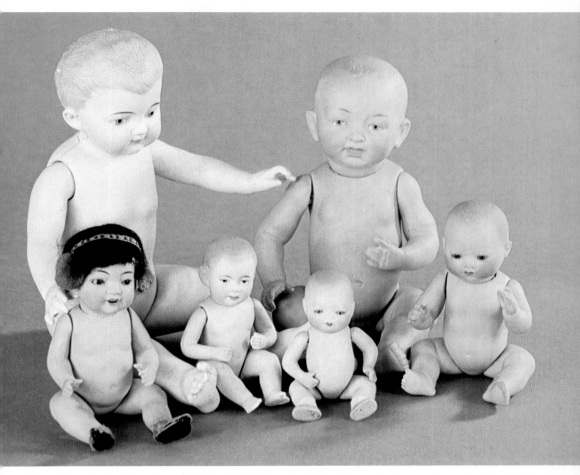

Plate IX. Infants. *(Front row, left to right)* This swivel necked Oriental is 5¼ inches tall when seated (No. 188); unlike most infants, this doll's legs do not spread when he sits (No. 133); a Bye-Lo Baby with slippers (No. 274); this 5¼-inch infant has a high complexion tint (No. 186). *(Back row)* Sometimes identified as "the 13-mold infant," this is a beautifully detailed doll 9⅝-inches tall when seated (No. 184): a swivel head (No. 185).

Plate VIII. *(Front row)* This characteristically French doll has the mold line penciled in. She is 5¼-inches tall with very desirable peg strung elbow joints (No. 9); another French doll (No. 10). *(Back row, left to right)* A 7½-inch stiff necked Kestner with original mohair wig (No. 96); this 8½-inch blonde with brown sleep eyes is marked Simon & Halbig (No. 112); a very desirable and unusual French all-bisque (No. 7); this 6⅞-inch barefooted French-type doll has lovely body modeling (No. 21).

Plate X. (Front row, left to right) A 5½-inch Oriental of very fine quality (No. 26); with extremely small hands and feet, No. 24, dressed; a peg strung Oriental, 4⅛-inches tall (No. 25). (Back row, left to right) 6¼-inch girl is dressed No. 108, with beautifully molded and painted hair, this 9-inch doll shows painstaking workmanship (No. 124); a dressed No. 100, hip and shoulder peg jointed and an excellent specimen; this swivel neck blonde is a lovely French-type all-bisque (No. 20).

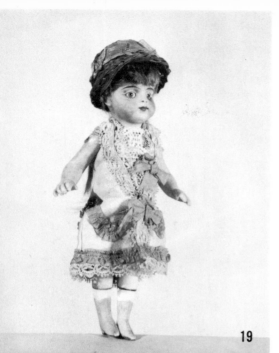

19

20

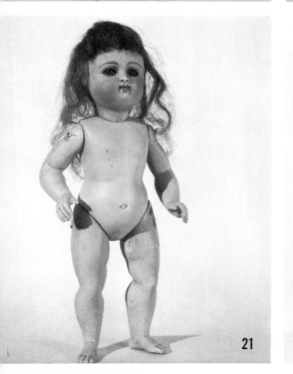

21

22

19, 20, & 21 Author's collection; 22 Brewer collection

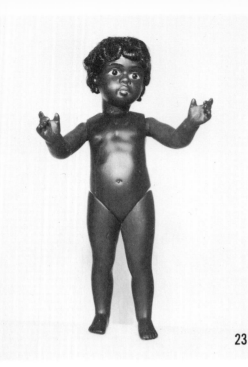

23

24

25

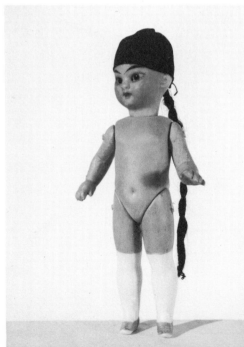

26

head. Usually the doubled rubber passes through the hole in the plug and is held in place by a small nail or part of a nail astride the top of the plug hole because they are too small for plugs with hooks.

French-type or not, they are doubtless of German origin. The dainty, widely spaced, multistroke eyebrows, the sleep glass eyes, and the beautiful bisque which is superbly finished and decorated simply scream, "German!"

Among the barefooted, long-legged, so-called French-type with swivel necks, various colored dolls appear in every shade, generally with set glass eyes without a colored iris.

No. 22 The mulatto boy whose head was used (**No. 14**) to illustrate the French-type neck loop is 5⅞ inches tall and incised on the head **61** over **13**. The same numbers, side by side, appear on the leg flanges. An even, golden coffee color, he has irisless eyes and black one-stroke brows. The nose is very broad, the thick, pursed lips are bright red, and the mouth is closed.

All the modeling is very good; he has excellent hands, arms that fit into molded shoulder holes, and good, sturdy legs. The head has an open top and the curly black mohair wig is on a cardboard dome.

His gingham loincloth and wound-about hat are in excellent taste. They are both made of carefully folded bits of colorful cloth which are held by pins inserted in gold beads a little larger than those around his neck. Because the sewed-on leather shoes are handmade, the presumption has been that he was dressed by a meticulous collector somewhere along the line. However, there is a similar but larger doll in the Strong Collection dressed in the same material and it also has handmade shoes.

No. 23 This pitch black 9-inch specimen is an excellent "Nubian" illustration. He is loop strung with rubber and has a fine, low gloss texture. The finishing, especially in the hands and feet, is extremely well done. The wig is good quality mohair on a cap and the mouth is closed.

A German production trick was observed on a very similar doll with an open mouth. To give it the appearance of an open-closed mouth, a piece of velvet was inserted back of the teeth. The dull back of the velvet almost exactly matched the lip color and the ruse was not discovered until the doll had to be restrung and the wig was removed. It frequently pays dividends to check an open-closed mouth doll with a plain pin.

No. 24 Incised **2/0**, this open mouth doll is 5½ inches tall. It is peg strung and the modeling is not as elaborate as that of the black one. The hands and feet are very small, quite out of proportion, and the color is a soft brown. The original wig is curled black mohair on a cap.

No. 25 Peg strung, this Oriental is 4⅛ inches tall, and of excellent quality. It is tinted a warm, golden yellow and the irisless eyes are set. Strangely, this one has a long, blond, human hair queue set into the hole in his ball head. It is undoubtedly someone's little restringing joke.

His machine-made kimona is red cotton trimmed with twisted metallic cord, and his shoes seem to have been cut from laminated cardboard with pasted paper instep straps. It would be difficult to say whether this is original dressing, although it is quite appropriate, because other Orientals owned during the years have had a great deal of paper trimming in such authentic and complicated costumes that they could not be other than original.

No. 26 Another Oriental of very fine quality, 5½ inches tall. It is tinted a deeper color but has the same almond eyes and ball head. The high white socks are ribbed and his molded, heelless slippers are painted pale blue. The long queue is of black mohair and the original cap is sateen.

A similar doll in the collection of Mrs. Margaret W. Strong came with a note attached which reads: "Wee Ting, San Francisco, 1904." The note is held with a rusted pin to a cotton kimona which looks original. Whether we can accept this as a proper name or the date of this doll is anyone's choice. It is very believable, however.

ぐ 8

Dressed French-Type

Dolls in their original clothing interest all collectors and the small hip and shoulder jointed boys and girls with set glass eyes are very desirable. Because they are so appealing, they cause a great deal of discussion among both collectors and dealers but almost everything about them is guesswork at this late date.

They can be found in several sizes under 6 inches and they have both swivel and stiff necks. The swivel heads are generally of the pegged variety and the stiff necks are thought to be a less expensive contemporary type because, while they are wire strung, they appear to be the same kind of decorating and they are equally well dressed. In fact, it is impossible to tell them apart without trying to turn the heads.

For want of a better name, they have come to be identified as French-type although the author has never examined any which carried a French mark. Their arms are both alike and the hands have German rather than French proportions. The vertically ribbed socks with blue bands and the heeled black slippers are like those on countless German dolls, and the little swivel necks have a base hole instead of the molded French stringing loop.

And yet, in many ways, they *look* French. They have long, straight, slender legs, faces which are less round and "healthy" than the German image of childhood and the set glass eyes, in both blue and brown, are not a recognizable German type. The small mohair wigs, both curled and straight, are made with more care than most small German wigs. The painted upper and lower lashes are similar to those on large, marked French dolls and the brows often almost meet across the nose bridges, which was a French decorating habit.

The decorating causes a great deal of speculation. Many people, including the author, think these are German dolls which were assembled, had their eyes set, and were dressed in France. If they were made to order for French specifications, experienced German decorators could have copied anything set before them.

The clothing, always imaginative and attractive, comes in an amazing assortment. Some of them are in what passes for provincial costumes, with starched cotton lace shawls, aprons, and hats; others look like Dickens' characters in quaint fitted coats and felt hats; others are Russians in muffs, belted coats, and high furlike caps. Many brother and sister pairs in children's clothing are still found in elderly ladies' estates, tucked safely away in mint condition with other sentimental valuables.

Twenty years ago the author saw one 3-inch pair in Russian costumes which were said to be in their original container—a decorated papier mâché Easter egg, complete with gold paper lace and tiny flowers. The story was that they were brought home by a great-grandfather who had occasion to visit the Czar's court in the 1800s. He said the adults received beautiful jeweled gifts in elaborate eggs and the children received these little dolls and other small toys in various-sized eggs.

Through the years a few have been seen in exquisitely handmade clothing which was very dainty and elegant but these were doubtless the products of specialty shops or private doll dressers such as collectors patronize today. As a general rule the clothing appears to be factory made because sewing machines are involved in what is obviously professional workmanship. The material is always good and appropriate, even though it is only cotton, wool, mercerized cotton, or bright colored felt. The dolls have a chic air about them which an amateur could not achieve, even when they are in simple attire.

It is the construction which has kept this clothing in such good condition through the years. The lace trimmed pants are often made of lightweight buckram and many of the little skirts are completely lined with the same material. To eliminate raw edges and any sign of hemlines, the material was sewed together, turned inside out and then carefully pressed so that a narrow margin of the dress material can be seen on the under side below the lining. When lace, soutache braid, or ribbon was used, it was sewed in place instead of being glued; all the findings are in miniature—buckles, belts, emblems, and the like, and while the buttons are beads, they are hand done and caught into the basic costume, the trimming is sewed on the hats and the hats are sewed into the wigs.

All of this seems to eliminate the possibility that these were dressed as a home industry in France. The sewing machine made all kinds of factories possible when it was invented in 1846 but even in such an advanced country as the United States sewing machines did not become standard home equipment until after the turn of the century. Before that many dressmakers brought their sewing machines with them when they moved into a home to outfit the family for the coming season. Added to this, the French did not like to take work into their homes, even if the "factory" was just a workroom in their employer's house. It is also very difficult to believe that the owners of these pretty little dolls allowed them out of their sight for wigging and dressing purposes.

In spite of this lack of definite background, they are avidly sought and great pride is taken in them.

No. 27 No collector would deliberately undress one of these dolls but this 5-inch specimen has lost her clothing and serves as a model for the others. She is peg jointed, the set glass eyes are cobalt blue with upper and lower painted lashes, and the one-stroke brows, which almost meet, are brown. She has a very definite dimple in her chin, which is lost in the smaller sizes, a nicely modeled childish body, and fairly good hands which would have been improved by better finishing. The long, straight legs have mold seams down the center front and back. The high white socks have blue bands and vertical ribbing, the two-strap, heeled slippers are black with tan soles. The original light blond mohair wig is of excellent quality and is made on a cloth cap, with a band of knotted red tape across the head from ear to ear.

The body is quite pale in coloring and the head is slightly more intense, which is understandable because they were not done by the same decorators.

Rather than endlessly repeating the standard specifications for these dolls, only their differences will be noted in the descriptions. All of them have set eyes, with only the color varying; all the eyebrows are one-stroke in shades of medium to dark blond; the swivel necks have upper and lower painted lashes and the stiff necks do not. All the boys (just as in real life!) have yellow-blond pencil curls and the girls have straight to barely-curled almost white mohair locks.

All the bisque is good and so is the decorating; some of the shoes have two painted straps and others have only one, with the depth of the painted counters being the variable and this can be seen in the pictures. None of these slippers have molded straps or outlines, so the decorators could do as they pleased, within reason, of course.

No. 28 Left: 4¼ inches, pegged swivel with brown eyes. She has buckram pants with lace, a lined purple mercerized dress, white organdy apron, and shawl collar with lace edge. The bonnet is white buckram with the same lace, and tiny waxed flowers tied with narrow white silk ribbon decorate her bonnet and her neckline.

Right: 4¼ inches, pegged swivel with cobalt eyes. The swallowtail coat is of blue-gray wool with raw edges and the long pants are golden yellow mercerized material with a diagonal woven pattern. He has a white sateen shirt with a high collar and silk ribbon bow tie, a flowered cotton vest, and the same waxed flower tied with silk ribbon on his lapel. The mustard yellow felt hat has a half-inch crown and a quarter-inch brim, with a front buckle and a silk ribbon band with flowing streamers down the back.

Could he be a bridegroom? Perhaps. His companion may be the bride. We are inclined to forget that white was not the bridal color until comparatively recently and there was a time when brides wore fancy bridal aprons and fancy bonnets instead of veils and bouquets.

No. 29 A 4¼-inch, pegged swivel with cobalt eyes. The pants are lace-trimmed buckram, the lined lavender mercerized dress and bright yellow apron are trimmed with purple velvet ribbon. The bonnet is tied on with very narrow cotton tape and, like the the collar, is buckram with lace trim.

No. 30 This 3¾-inch pegged swivel with bright blue eyes has no painted lashes. The felt suit is red with white soutache trim on the dickie and has a white mercerized square sailor collar. His matching felt cap is trimmed with gold cord and brown button beads like those on the suit.

No. 31 Much the worse for moths, this 4¼-inch boy is a pegged swivel with cobalt eyes. The blue-green coat looks like wool challis and so does the pink vest. He has a lace neckerchief, blue bead buttons, and ivory pants with pale blue mercerized stripes and white silk knee bows. The brimmed black felt hat has a silk band and a metal buckle.

No. 32 A pegged swivel, 4¼ inches tall, with cobalt eyes. She has a starched cotton petticoat, starched white cotton blouse, and white pleated

27, 28 & 29 Author's collection; 30 Millar collection

31

32

32

33

31, 32 & 33 Author's collection

peplum attached to her belt in front. The red wool skirt is trimmed with black velvet ribbon and she has a red silk neck bow.

She is also pictured from the back because her gauze based wig is in such good condition. This style of hairdo, with a top bow and a bow in the middle of the long hair, must have been a style in France for children because it has also been seen on very large dolls with long human-hair wigs.

No. 33 Left: a 3¼-inch wire strung stiff neck, with blue eyes and the only one in the group with red lid lines. His once-white outfit is made of outing flannel and has a brown leatherette belt and a machine stitched neck scarf which drapes down the front and the back. The undecorated matching hat is also machine stitched.

Right: a 3½-inch stiff neck, wire strung, with dark blue eyes. She has lace trimmed gauze pants and the suit is navy blue and white felt with gold bead buttons and a tiny metal anchor emblem decorates the neck. The skirt trim is white soutache braid, machine sewed, and the shallow crowned matching navy felt hat has a white silk ribbon pompom in front.

No. 34 Left: a 2½-inch stiff neck, brass wire strung, with light blue eyes. She has a gauze pants with lace trim, white lace cap sleeves on a dress of machine embroidered edging which is a little on the wild side. The scallops are bright red and the stars and fruit are navy blue. The yoke and shoulder straps are pale blue silk ribbon. The front brim of the straw hat is also trimmed with blue silk ribbon festoons.

Right: a 2½-inch stiff neck, brass wire strung, with irisless black eyes. She has the same clothing but her dress scallops and star and dot design are done in dark blue, while her shoulder straps and yoke are pink silk ribbon and there is pink silk ribbon on the front of her hat.

No. 35 Left: a 3½-inch stiff neck, wire strung, with cobalt eyes. His dark green felt suit has a bright red collar and gold bead buttons. The little crown hat is also red felt with gold cord trim.

Right: A 3½-inch stiff neck, brass wire strung, with cobalt eyes. She has a sleeveless, lined, navy blue dress with a metal anchor trim at the neck and a bright red felt cape with gold bead buttons. The machine stitched hat is also red felt.

No. 36 A 1½-inch stiff neck, brass wire strung, with black eyes. Collectors generally are not too fond of dolls dressed in black and especially not in a small size but this appears to be original. The pants and tiny blouse were

34 & 35 Author's collection

white voile and the skirt is a black basket weave mercerized material. The trim along the hem is bright red silk stitching and the blouse buttons are clear glass beads. She has a white silk ribbon sash, black silk ribbon shoulder straps, and a little black lace cap. Her wig has a machine stitched center part and a tiny braid hangs down her back to the knees.

No. 37 This 3½-inch stiff necked, pegged pair are from another maker. The left arms are bent at the elbow, the legs are shaped at the knee so the calves appear fat, the shoes are one-strap bootines and the set blue eyes are the type known as "pop." These have had their wigs replaced but this crocheted clothing is found on many stiff legged German dolls. This is difficult handwork at which European women excel, the clothing is always sewed on the dolls, and it always fits extremely well. Even more puzzling than these suits, however, are the crocheted boy and girl outfits on the tinies like **No. 199** because they are so detailed and yet so small.

No. 38 A 3½-inch stiff neck, with irisless black eyes, brass wire strung. This pair is not of the quality of the previous dolls and, although they are

36, 37 & 38 *Author's collection*

machine dressed, there is no proof that the clothing is original. The wigs are little pieces of raw cotton on paper bases, held on the heads by glued bits of lace to represent bonnets. The legs are a German length in proportion, entirely lacking the French slenderness of the others.

The brass wire can be checked in her legs and his arms but, if they were anything at all, they were competition for the other, finer types.

Frozen Charlottes

There is no need to repeat the long story or the poem which says these oldies were named after a vain girl who froze to death on her way to a dance rather than wear her outer clothing. They are generally stark naked.

Collectors seem to be more interested in their construction, often not realizing that unless the arms are molded to the sides, all or part of them had to be applied. In some the complete arm is applied at the shoulder, but in others the original mold contains stumps of arms somewhat short of the elbow and the forearms only are applied at the cutoff. This accounts for the occasional differences in the position of the hands or the twisted arms.

No matter how good the workmanship, the application seams can almost always be found because there seems to have been no compulsion to make any secret of it. Pincushion tops frequently have many application seams but they are more carefully finished as a general rule and more difficult to detect.

Even though most of the very good Frozen Charlottes are hollow, there is very little reference material available in English about their manufacture. Sometimes a trained ceramist can detect filled pouring holes in the feet or in the head but the work is so well done collectors often cannot be sure, and yet we know that the unset slip had to be poured if they were molded in that manner. There is always the possibility that the very old ones were pressed into the two halves of the mold, sealed at the seams with moist slip and allowed to set to the handling stage. Some of the old specimens in this collection are so thin, however, this latter process seems a precarious manufacturing method.

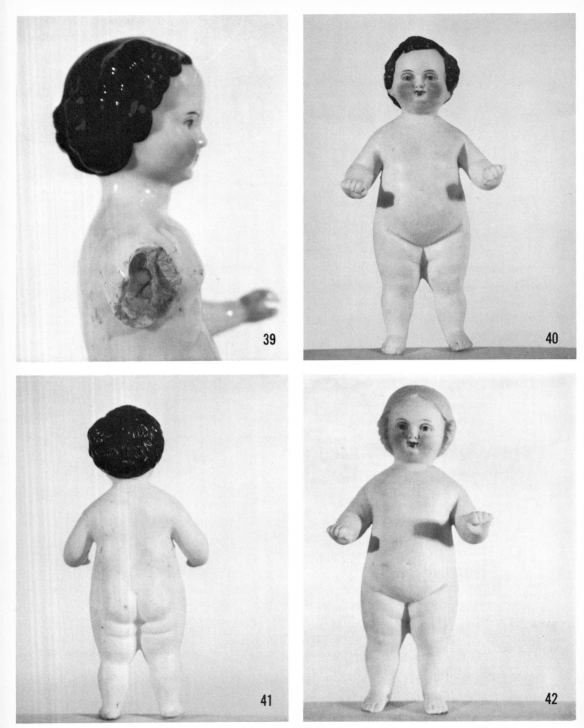

39, 40, 41 & 42 *Author's collection*

No. 39 This broken china sample illustrates the unglazed, roughened under surface of the shoulder area inside the remains of the upper arm. This roughness is undoubtedly the drippings from the slip used to attach the arm to the rather large shoulder.

Collectors also ask about the round holes of varying sizes found in the seats of some of these dolls. They are sometimes called "Dresden-type" or "pouring" holes and this practice has apparently arisen to make it absolutely clear that the word "hole" does not mean that the doll is at all damaged or broken.

Professional ceramists tell us that gases form within these closed bodies while they are firing and the holes permit these gases to escape. They further suggest that very likely all Frozen Charlottes had such holes but that some firms may have closed them before the decorating process, and the plug of clay fired satisfactorily along with the decorating. Ceramists also say that the holes could have been in other parts of the body, such as the shoulder area, and that is why we cannot detect them now.

At any rate, a good Frozen Charlotte is neither more nor less valuable because it does or does not have a visible gas hole.

No. 40 Without a hole, this pink, 4¼-inch, boyish looking doll is an excellent specimen in fine old bisque. The painted blue eyes have high pupils, dark blond lid linings, and red lid lines and eye dots. The brows are also dark blond. The unusual dark brown hair, which has the gloss mentioned in the Parian section, is molded from a part and, although there are no forehead brush marks, the hair has excellent all-over comb marks in the short ringlets.

The German legs are short and the calves are thick but in this small size the proportions are not unbecoming, and the closed hands and well-defined feet are very good.

No. 41 illustrates the funny, baggy seats which are found on many of these dolls in both bisque and china.

Through a group of dolls which had been in one English-American family until 1965, several of these dolls came into this collection in china. Everything was in pairs, as the two little sisters had left them, except a 1¾-inch pink-toned china of this type which was securely tied in a wooden antique medicine box. On the inside of the box lid, in childish printing was "Dolls — 1856." The first printing was not too well done, so, in the same printing, the figures were repeated — "1856." A 3⅜-inch pair in white china were also in the group and in all of them the baggy seat is very pronounced.

None of these chinas is of the quality of the bisques but the date helps us to place this type in time, even if we just say, for safety sake, the 1850s.

No. 42 Perhaps the little sister of the previous doll, because the bodies are exactly alike, the bisque is equally as good and the complexion tint is much paler and girlish, this 4¼-inch doll is delightful. She has the same blue painted eyes with high pupils, blond lid linings and brows, red lid lines and eye dots, and red nose dots.

Her very light yellow hair has excellent comb marks from a center part and vertical curls all around the head with the same good comb marks. The childish, round face is less vivid in coloring than the boyish doll and she has the same closed fists and baggy seat without a hole.

No. 43 Also without a seat hole but not nearly as well done as the two previous dolls, this 3¾-inch specimen has painted blue eyes with high pupils, blond lid linings and brows, but there are no red eye dots or lid

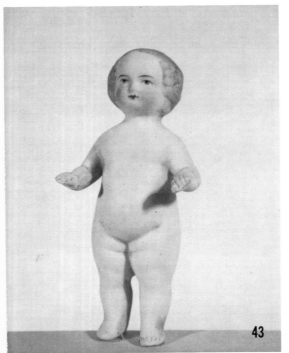

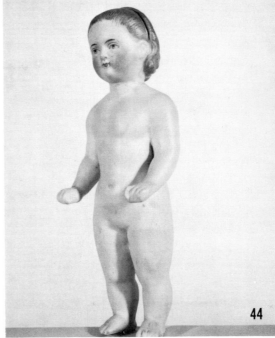

43

44

43 & 44 Author's collection

lines; and yet she falls well within the era when these were common procedure. The lids are not molded and the nose is very flat.

The poorly done hair is light blond without comb marks and the vertical curls are not well defined. The bisque is old and good and pure white, with only a touch of color in the cheeks. The mold debris on the hands and feet indicate poor workmanship but the question remains unanswered: Is she later or just a cheaper edition of the other girl? Unless the mold was wearing out, the answer tends toward *cheaper.*

These dolls sometimes have painted blue garters with front bows and gold painted slippers, but they seem generally to be an added decoration on the dolls with the poorer finishing. Inasmuch as finishing was a more expensive operation because it was more time-consuming, this is logical competition because the few quick brush strokes did attract attention and children would desire both kinds.

No. 44 With a molded and painted "Alice" band across her pretty head and closed fists, this 6⅞-inch girl is an excellent specimen even though her left hand has been repaired.

She has painted blue eyes with high pupils, dark blond lid linings and brows, red lid lines and red eye and nose dots. Her very yellow hair has forehead brush marks, good comb marks over the entire head and excellent broken back curls. Her cheeks are merely touched with color.

She is made of excellent old white bisque, she is of exceptional weight, her features are very good, including the exposed ears, and her hands and feet have well-defined digits.

The Alice band is sometimes thought to be later than the other hairdos and the baggy seat is gone, but she has the blond lid linings instead of the later, almost universal, black, so she is early. She has a seat hole.

No. 45 This unmarked 5⅞-inch Parian-quality hatted Charlotte is made of very sharp and glossy white bisque. The painted blue eyes have high pupils, red lid lines and black lid linings; the one-stroke brows are blond. The ear tips show below the excellently molded, short, taffy blond curls; the cheeks are bright pink; the small, tight mouth is red. She has pretty closed hands with cupped fingers.

The pink hat has a painted rose band around the shallow crown and a molded bow with streamers down the hair onto the shoulders. There is no sign of application except where the arms were added to the shoulder caps, so this hat was molded. The face, front hair, and hat brim appear to have been in the front mold; the back of the hat, the hair, and the bow with streamers in the back mold.

The dainty dress covers her fine-ribbed white socks with molded top bands. The boots are royal blue with white soles.

No. 46 Because she has shoes with heels instead of bare feet or flat-soled boots, plus black instead of blond lid linings, this beautiful doll is classified after the others. Of Parian-quality with a barely perceptible flesh tint, she has a low "squash" pompadour as well as a wide molded band with broken back curls, very good comb marks over the entire head and brush marks across the forehead. The large painted blue eyes have small, high pupils, red dots and lid lines, and, as noted, black lid linings. The one-stroke brows are dark blond, her pretty open hands have free thumbs and raised fingers.

The tight little mouth is brick red and the fat German cheeks are the old peach pink, but unfortunately the left one was smudged before the firing. She has no seat hole.

She is not balanced to stand alone, perhaps purposely, but from the knees down, including the soles of the shoes, she is highly glazed. The white socks have raised, overlapping scalloped tops with purple painted bands with loop and dot trim. The heeled shoes are intense grape lustre with yellow soles.

She is the most appropriately dressed doll of this type the author has ever seen. She has a fine white cotton, lace-edged shift with a scoop neck drawn to the proper size by an enclosed tiny cotton tape. The beautiful little dress appears to have been made from a fine doily, perhaps one that fitted into a dresser tray, rather than from a handkerchief. The method is very ingenious.

The straight lace edges were overlapped and sewed to form a new lace design down the center, and the front piece was cut with kimona cap sleeves which have a slanted top seam allowance. The two back pieces were cut from matching areas of the material in such a manner that the insertion met the mitered front lace at the underarm seams. The backs have the same cap sleeve cut, of course. The neckline and sleeve edges were handkerchief hemmed and lace trimmed. The back closure is from two narrow lengthwise hems and is held together by loops over tiny cloth-covered buttons so that the material is not piled up bulky and double.

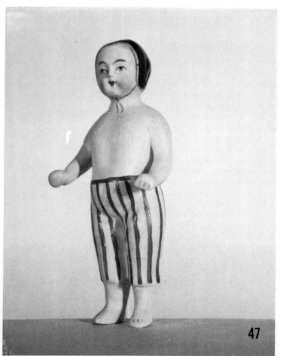

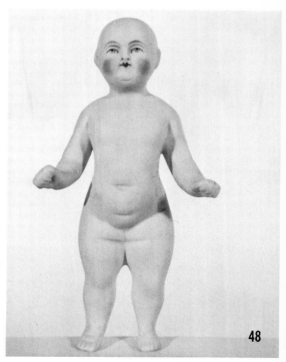

45 Hilsdorf collection; 46, 47 & 48 Strong collection

The dressmaking is hand done and so is all the work on the minutely embroidered original doily, so the whole effect is light, dainty, and delightful.

No. 47 Pure white and of very sharp, fine quality, this unusual Frozen Charlotte is 3½ inches tall. In proportion, the painted blue eyes are large, with large high pupils, black lid linings, and dark blond, one-stroke brows. The little mouth is dark red.

The molded bonnet is glossy black with a narrow blue band all around. The blue ties, with a bow under the chin, are freehand painted. Only the bottoms of the pants are molded and the bright red stripes are painted over the bare body with the baggy seat. He has clenched fists and bare, flat feet. No attempt was made to hide the addition of the arms and they look like molded shirt sleeves. He has no seat hole and is of such a thin shell of bisque that he echoes if touched with a fingernail and shrieks when rubbed.

No. 48 Almost Oriental looking because of the wigless ball head, this 4⅛-inch baggy seat is such a deep cream color that it adds to the illusion. At first glance it appears to be made of something other than bisque but the color and texture must be the result of an early attempt at complete complexion coating. The very attractive peach tone which came later must have been this creamy tint with rose or pink added.

The painted eyes are blue with such high pupils they seem to be ready to roll back into the head, and have red eye dots and lid lines, black lid linings, and one-stroke blond brows. The nose dots are as bright as the tight, puckered mouth and the cheeks are bright dabs of color. This particular doll must have been made in a very new mold because all the modeling is very deep.

A duplicate in the Strong Collection is 8 inches tall. In both dolls the arms were molded to the length of short sleeves and consequently, because the addition of the arms was easier, there is none of the distortion which happened sometimes when the entire arm was added.

No. 49 Of exceptionally fine quality in every respect, this 3½-inch hatted boy is a beautiful specimen. His eyes have blue iris rims around tiny intaglio pupils, black lid linings, and red lid lines. The one-stroke brows are dark blond and the deeply molded mouth is painted in two sections, leaving a hairline white center.

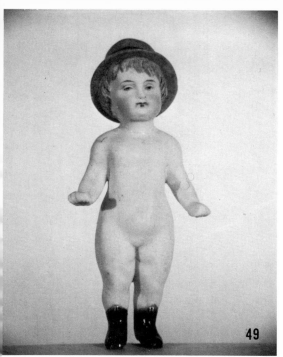

The ash-blond rim of hair under his hat is well molded into boyish wisps and it is all deeply comb marked. The flawless complexion tint is the old, soft peach color. The boots are almost heelless, with pointed fronts and raised tassels. They are painted a shining dark brown with the top rim and the tassels done in gold.

There are no signs of mold seams in the light brown hat or its brown molded band, which has a flat side bow. Since the seams are visible in the middle of the upper arms, there is no reason to believe that hat seams would have bothered anyone. In such a case the answer is always thought to be that the hat was applied. It is logical in this instance because there is such a deep pitch to the brim that it would have caused undercutting.

Once in a while such a guess can be checked out and this is one of those instances. Unfortunately his neck had been broken and, when he was taken apart for a better mend, it was possible to see into his head. If he had been molded with the hat on there would be no demarkation between the rim of the head and the hat. In this little boy there is a sharp channel between the two pieces, so we are sure the hat was applied.

No. 50 These bonnets are solid, and the doll on the left is doubtless the oldest. She is 2⅝ inches tall, has painted pupils only, blond brows and straight, comb-marked blond bangs. There is a small bow molded into the peak of the bonnet and there are tiny molded gathers on both the upper and the lower sides of the brim, with a painted red trim on the front only. This matches her painted shoes, which have molded front tassels. In back the bonnet has a ribbed crown with a molded, mitered band, but it is undecorated.

The 3⅝-inch center doll has painted blue eyes with high pupils, blond lid linings and brows, and a fluff of molded blond curls on the forehead. The bonnet is excellently molded on both the upper and under sides, with a rounded crown which has a wide molded band. The entire bonnet is a light shade of opaque pink and the band is yellow.

Although her feet are not well finished, they are more detailed and later than the previous doll's. She has horizontally ribbed socks with a red band

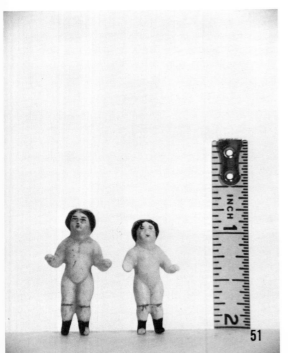

51 & 52 *Author's collection*

below the molded top line and her slightly heeled shoes are done in what looks like the bright gold used on dinnerware.

The 2⅜-inch duplicate on the right is exactly like her big sister except that her bonnet is a soft, dull shade of blue and the band was not picked up in yellow.

None of these dolls has any complexion coloring but all of them have pink cheeks.

Because some people collect for differences as well as desirability and beauty, the record would not be complete without some of the following little oddities, all of which are solid and only two of which are marked.

No. 51 Only 1¼ and 1⅛ inches tall this pair with black hair, which is vaguely molded to represent vertical sausage curls, are lightly complexion coated in a cream color. They have black brows, lid linings, and pupils, little black boots without heels, and blue top bands on flesh-colored socks. The amount of body modeling on these tiny things is surprising—spinal columns, for instance.

No. 52 Three blondes, only one of which has her features left. They are from the left: 1⅜, 1¼ and 1 inch tall. The amount of modeling on these is surprising too, including curls and waves in the hair, tassels on the boots of the largest one, and spines down all the little backs. The smallest one has her arms safely molded against her chest.

No. 53 These two, with entirely different black hairdos, are 2¼ and 2⅜ inches tall. The one on the left appears to have some kind of "squash" arrangement and the other has vertical sausage curls. The one on the left has only one eyelid lining and one pupil left but the other was more fortunate.

The second doll has different arms and her boots are bright red. The toe of the right foot was broken off in the factory but it was painted nevertheless.

No. 54 The mark on the center back of the 3-inch doll with the bonnet is raised and much more difficult to read than incised marks. Whether it is 408 or 108 cannot be determined and there is what appears to be a small T below the figures.

The bonnet is unusual because it is molded to represent the knitted type of hood which falls in a small shawl about the shoulders and even the small string bow is molded under the chin. The peaked top has a molded flower in the center. It is barely touched with color now, although it may

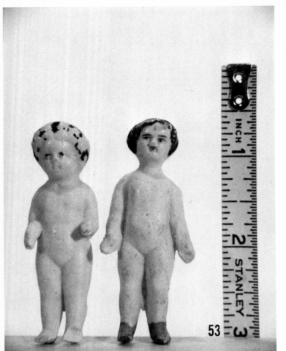

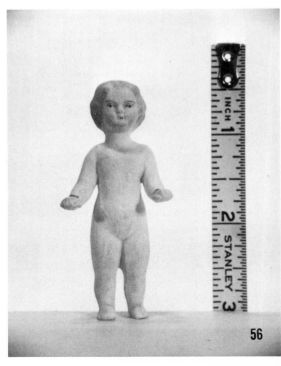

53, 54, 55 & 56 *Author's collection*

have been completely painted originally. The short bangs on the forehead are comb marked and painted yellow. She has bare, very short feet and fairly good hands molded to the body. Her brows are dark blond and she has pupils only.

Her 2¾-inch companion hasn't a vestige of color but was definitely a girl because the hair in back is molded into quite long vertical curls. The molded shift has a great deal of detail, including the banded V neck, a collar in back, and fullness in the garment.

The complete hand is merely a stump without modeling, the debris was not cut out between the legs, and during either the greenware handling or the firing her feet bent up so far that she is a heel-walker.

This type of molded clothing was much more common on small china dolls than on all-bisques and generally they are found with their painted detail in good condition.

No. 55 These three have ball heads but entirely different arms. The 2⅛-inch girl on the left has the remains of a professionally made fringe wig and in the center back there is a large incised **E**. Her heavy brows are brown and she has only pupils. Her feet have the familiar molded boots with front tassels but the unbroken foot was painted green only up to the tassel. Her seat is baggier than the others.

The center doll is 2⅝ inches tall and her only distinguishing feature is the peculiar kind of string molded around the tops of her short boots and tied in knots in front. She is either very early or an inexperienced attempt at molding because the sides are entirely flat, without any body roundness. This flatness extends up the sides, across the shoulders, up the neck, and over the head.

The third doll, 2 inches tall, is a far better piece of workmanship. Even though the protruding hands are only unmodeled stumps, the tiny feet have toes indicated.

No. 56 This 2½-inch girl appears more often in china than in solid bisque. She has blond hair molded from a center part into curls over the ears and broken curls in back. Her little hands are closed fists like those on **No. 44**, and across the top of each wrist there is a gold band. She cannot stand alone because of her small feet.

Her complete arms are attached at the shoulders; she is well finished for the type. The decorating included red lid lines, blond brows, and black pupils and lid linings.

No. 57 Collectors do not ordinarily think of these pretty children as Frozen Charlottes but "immobile" is a term better reserved for dolls frozen into some position other than standing.

All incised on the back between the arm tops, from the left they are: 3⅜ inches tall with brown hair, incised 1; 3¾ inches tall, the same hair in blond, incised 2; and 3½ inches tall, with a different hairdo, also in brown, incised 1. Each has a very small seat hole, blue eyes with pupils, black lid linings, dark blond one-stroke brows, and red nose dots. The arms were added at the shoulders.

The doll on the left is almost white, the center one has a very pale complexion coating and the third one is slightly pinker. The two with forehead curls have very good ringlets in back; the one with bangs has excellent comb marks all over the head and just slightly curled wisps. All the bisque is very sharp and old, the finishing and decorating are very good, and the bisque "cries" at a touch.

These dolls appear to have been made by the same firm that made the pot-bellied infants, Nos. 177, 178 and 179.

No. 58 Only 3⅞ inches tall, and with a shell so thin that she is transparent in places, it is a marvel that this little doll has survived.

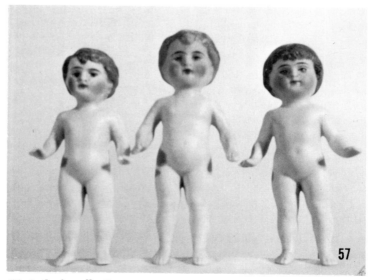

57 Author's collection

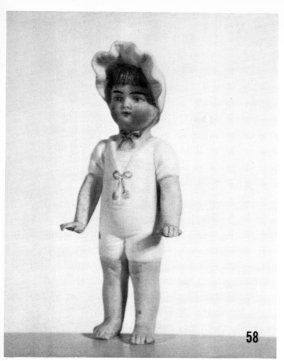
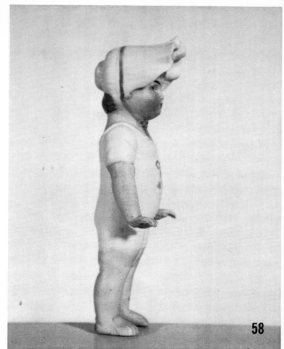

58 *Strong collection*

And she is a doll, not a figurine, because she is in no way prepared to stand by herself. If all Frozen Charlottes were made of china, she would have to be classified as "an immobile bisque" but she is properly identified as "a bisque Frozen Charlotte bonnet."

Late enough to be incised **8/0** across the shoulders, she is made of sharp, good bisque which was well modeled, finished, and decorated. The modeling is especially fine because her bonnet has an excellent and unusual shape with good detail, her little sleeves have shaping, and her suit decorations stand up from the body. The hands and feet are very good, and even in the back she has seat, knee, and ankle ridges. The bonnet bow is molded and painted blue like the ribbon across the hat and the molded bow on the suit.

Her blue eyes have high pupils and black lid linings, the one-stroke brows are brown, the complexion is only slightly mottled and it is so evenly spread that it suggests trouble with the oil color in the firing. Her dark blond hair is well comb marked.

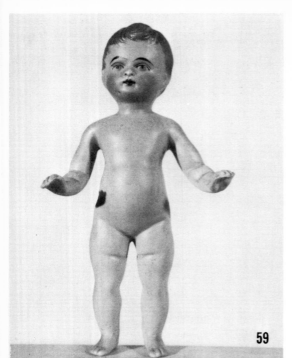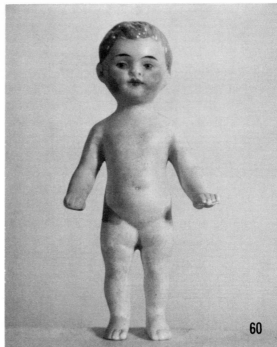

59 Whitton collection; 60 Author's collection

No. 59 This 5⅛-inch lad has good modeling, painted blue eyes with high pupils, black lid linings, red lid lines and nose dots, and one-stroke dark blond brows. The hair has very good comb marks from a center crown with a raised front lock. The bisque is old and good, the complexion coating is a medium shade, well padded and slightly glossy.

This boy and his brother, following, are unmarked and without seat holes and both have bright yellow painted hair. Both stand alone.

No. 60 Little brother, 3½ inches tall, has the same specifications except that he does *not* have red lid lines or comb marks. His hair is molded in raised wisps, not ringlets. His complexion is very dull and peach toned.

Both of these have arms added at the shoulders and the slip seems to have been drained through the feet.

Old White

The very old, pure-white type is rather difficult to find in the more desirable kinds. Families did not consider these small dolls important, so while they carefully saved the papier mâchés, the chinas, and the bisque headed dolls, all-bisques were lost in the confusion as each generation cleaned up after the other.

Often of quite good quality, the Old Whites have wire-jointed arms and legs, or frozen legs, and they are not marked. The molded hair is yellow blond in most instances and the painted eyes are blue except in the small sizes which have only painted pupils. These are undoubtedly German because so many have hairdos and limbs resembling those of the Frozen Charlottes.

The smaller sizes have solid bodies but it is puzzling to determine just where the hollow bodies start. Tapping, hand hefting, or weighing two sizes on a postal scale will help in the decision if it makes that much difference to the owner. To establish the hollow bodies, a thin wire can be inserted into the torso through the arm or the leg stringing holes.

Several general classifications divide them: hip and shoulder jointed with bare feet; shoulder jointed with molded boots which have heels and may be with or without front tassels, both in plain bisque and with a china glaze on the boots; shoulder jointed with bonnets and heeled and tasseled boots.

No. 61 Hip and shoulder jointed with brass wire, 5¼ inches tall, this doll has flowing, light blond, molded hair with a side part and good comb marks. She has dark blond brows, red eyelid lines, blue eyes with high-placed pupils, her lower eyelids are molded in the bisque, and there are black eyelid linings. The body shows good modeling which is not often found in later all-bisques except for those which are considered to be French-type.

She has good, wide open hands and pretty feet with well-defined toes, slight arches, and excellent heel bones. The quality of the bisque is very good and slightly glossy.

No. 62 Although her face is marred by minute imperfections in the white bisque, this charming little 5⅛-inch girl is hip and shoulder jointed with brass wire, has blue painted eyes with high pupils in molded eyes, red lid lines, and black lid linings. She has good, open hands and dainty feet with good toe modeling, slight arches, and good heel bones. The body modeling is also very good.

Her most charming feature, however, is her delightful and rare hairdo. With all-over, fine comb marks, her pale blond hair appears to be brushed back from her face with a slight center part and is topped with a dark blue molded bow with streamers down her crown. Across the back the hair hangs in vertical curls, each excellently molded and comb marked.

No. 63 This 4½-inch hatted doll has body modeling and molded hair similar to that of the previous doll and is made of pure white bisque. In this smaller doll the kneecaps are more pronounced and the hands are more cupped, but both dolls have the same protruding heel modeling.

Because the face is small, this doll has no painted irises and no red eyelid lines but both upper and lower lids are molded, the pupils are painted, and there are black eyelid linings. The well-done hair is light brown and so are the one-stroke brows.

The yellow hat, marked to represent straw, with a flat, molded lavender-colored flower in the center front, presents a molding problem. From marks on the brim and smudges on the band, this set of molds must have been in three, or perhaps four, pieces. It definitely was not applied as an entire hat.

No. 64 Only 3¾ inches tall, with center-parted dark blond hair, this is another good specimen. The hair is flat on top with three rows of sharply defined back curls and there are excellent comb marks in both the top hair and in the tight curls.

Her brows match the hair color, the blue eyes have high pupils with red eyelid lines and the upper lids are well molded. The body modeling is in good proportion but not elaborate. The hands are not as good as some

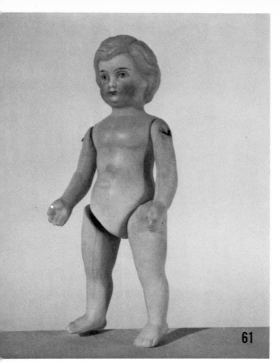

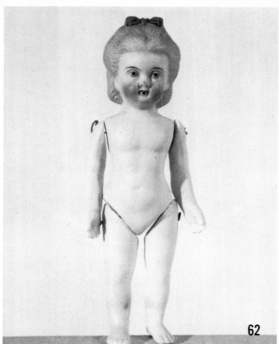

61

62

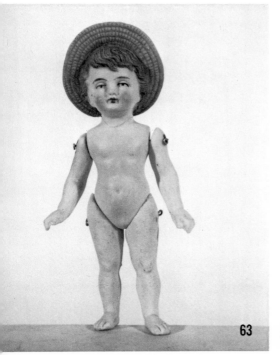

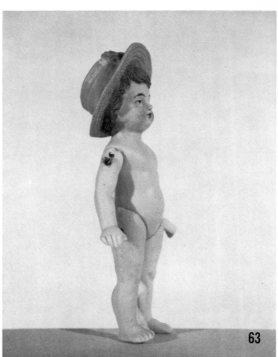

63

63

61 & 63 Author's collection; 62 Strong collection

but much better than ordinary, with the fingers indicated on both sides of the hands and with thumb cushions in the palms. The feet have molded midcalf socks and undecorated, heeled boots. The white bisque is very good.

No. 65 The dressed doll is 4½ inches tall and quite inferior to the four specimens of Old Whites listed above, although she is a good doll of the type. Her center-parted hair has comb marks in the short vertical curls but the coloring is taffy rather than the pale yellow of the better types. The brows are dark blond, the blue eyes have high pupils, and there is only a blond top eyelid line because the eye molding is very poor. The body is common, the hands are almost closed fists and the bare feet have no modeling at all and are too small. Yet, with all these shortcomings, she is a desirable doll.

Her companion, not quite 4 inches tall, has vertical curls molded from the forehead wave but with few comb marks. Her face decorating is the same but of poorer quality. She also has the closed fists but there is some indication of toe modeling in her feet.

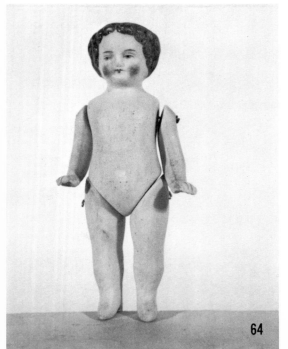

64

65

64 & 65 Author's collection

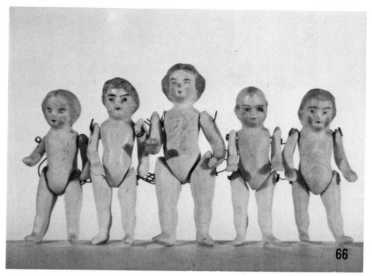

66 *Author's collection*

No. 66 The group range in size from 2¼ to 2¾ inches and incised marks appear on two of them. The girl on the left is incised in the center back **280** over **5/0½** and the boy, second from the right, is marked **11 77**, with perhaps some other number in the center which is too blurred to be read.

The hairdos and all the workmanship are poor, due in part to the small sizes. The center doll, however, is a small size of the undressed doll in figure **No. 65**, although the larger one is not marked. Oddly, she has upper eyelid lines but no eyes.

The boy on her left is unusual, even though one pupil appears to give him a black eye. Tiny tufts of hair molded on his forehead, above each ear, and at the nape of the neck set him apart from the others. He was not an infant, however, because he is the only one with tiny molded heels.

All of these dolls in the Old White category are wire strung and yet some of the wire is not brass, even in those thought to be original.

No. 67 An unusual Old White, this girl is incised in back **1240** over **4** and she is 4⅞ inches tall. She has blue eyes with high pupils and dark brown lid linings and brows.

Her light blond hairdo is rare. A circle of comb-marked curls rise out of a part across her head, falling forward over her forehead and going

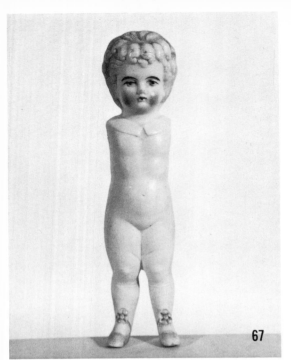

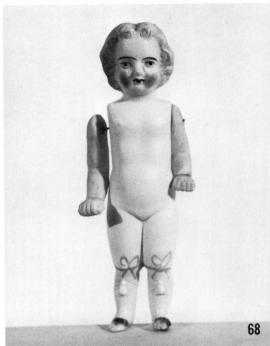

67, 68, 69 & 70 *Author's collection*

back to the mold line, as shown in the illustration. Two excellent curls line the temples, leaving her ears exposed. The back of the head is covered with small ringlets and she has three short neck curls. Because of the high hairdo, her molding was interesting.

She was made in a two-part mold. The entire flat shoulder area was in the back mold because the seams show a very definite forward curve at the bust level, completely avoiding the stringing hole which, of course, made it one piece and much stronger. The front mold also has another curve which starts at the side of the ankle and puts all of the front of the slipper, with the molded instep flower, also in the front mold.

She is hollow, the bisque is fine, very white, and heavy; there are still some signs of the baggy seat. She has a good circular molded collar with a raised button in the center front, socks molded to the knees with very fine vertical ribbing and top bands, and flat blue slippers with a six-petal flower molded at the ankle and painted pink.

The black edges of the stringing holes indicate that she was strung with wire and this doll is well worth a pair of custom-made arms by a modern ceramist who specializes in such work, even though we will have to guess at the type—a plain curved arm with a closed fist.

No. 68 Stiff legged and 5 inches tall, this doll is incised in large figures on the back 240, and below that, 4. The hair is well molded, center parted with forehead curls and broken curls in back. It is the common taffy color and the decorating is intense, giving her a harsh appearance. Her brows are dark brown, the entire eyes are painted blue with a large, high pupil, and her mouth is deep red.

The body modeling is fair, she has closed fists but the fingers are also indicated on the under side, and the well-proportioned arms are incised in back 3, instead of the 4 one would expect. The boots have a good china glaze, the tips are gold washed and the tassels are high and clean. Her painted garters are blue.

No. 69 The group of four dolls with stiff legs range in size from 1½ to 5 inches. The largest is a duplicate of the previous doll but without the garters. It is incised 240 and 4 but the arms are not marked.

The next size, 3½ inches tall, is incised 240 but her size number is 0′2. The two smallest are incised only with size numbers too blurred to be read. All four have tasseled boots, but only the largest ones are china glazed and it was apparently a dipping process because the soles are also glazed.

No. 70 Truly an anachronism in this day of ball points, this little pen-wiper is proof positive that ladies young and old followed the instructions we see in old magazines which started: "To make a thoughtful and appreciated Christmas present, secure a little doll about three inches tall. . . ."

She is one of these little hip and shoulder jointeds (although the stiff legs were also used), 2½ inches tall and her skirt is 3 inches in diameter across the base. Twenty-eight 2-inch squares of felt in black, purple, and pink were cut diagonally, folded in half, and arranged in a color pattern. The points were fastened around her waist under the pink ribbon sash. A thread was run through the raw edges in two places to keep the skirt intact—obviously doing a good job. A gathered bit of lace forms her modest collar.

No. 71 Shoulder jointed, 2⅜ inches tall, this fellow is the only one left of half a dozen factory-dressed bandsmen or possibly soldiers.

His suit is made of bright red paper and was cut in four parts—two sleeves, a sleeveless coat, and a straight bottom piece. This straight piece was glued on first and tucked between the legs in front to look like trousers. The coat, which overlaps in front for a good purchase, came next and the sleeves were added last. Gold stripes were painted around the collar, the cuffs, and down the pants legs. Gold buttons were painted on the double-breasted front and fringed white paper epaulets were added at the shoulders to hide the juncture of the sleeves and the coat.

Bonnets

No. 72 These two, which have a dull finish, are an even whiter and finer grained bisque than the other Old Whites.

The largest, 6 inches, is incised 6 in the center back. Her 4½-inch companion is incised 3, indicating a ½-inch size variation. The torsos have flat shoulder areas and the arms are flat on the insides.

No. 73 These range from 1¾ inches to 4 inches tall. Originally all of them had a wash of blue color on their boots but time and play have worn most of it off all but the smallest doll.

The largest is incised 160 and below that 1. The next size is 160 and 0. The one-armed is 162 and 3; the smallest is: 6' and 6. Because she is so small, the mark on this doll may have been split up for factory inventory purposes and to those workers it could have meant 6⅙ and that would

71

72

73

71, 72 & 73 Author's collection

mean model **160**, because her bonnet is the same as the others, and **1/6** because she is the sixth size below **1**.

It should be noted that the doll marked **162** has a different bonnet. It is quite possible that at this plant **160** indicated bonnets to the workers and the last figure pinpointed the type because **162** is not a greenware error. There was a special mold to put that dent in her bonnet and one wonders what bonnet variation **161** had.

The bonnets are nicely molded in back as well as in front but all the decorating, including the hair, is in front, with the backs a chaste white. The rims offered great possibilities to the decorators and they range from pure white or solid colors to splashes and dots of one or more colors. The boots sometimes match the bonnets, sometimes they are in a contrasting color, but never show any signs of rhyme or reason. The painting is so crude it could well have been the work of children.

There are molded bows in the bonnet peaks and under the chins, and in the larger sizes the chin bows are quite thick. Consequently there are no neck or chin indentations at all, which helped mightily in the unmolding. With the chin bows entirely filling the neck areas, they stand up from the chests from $\frac{1}{8}$ to almost $\frac{1}{4}$ inch and only their front surfaces are painted.

The pair in picture **No. 72** are different from the others in two respects. They have painted blue irises and black pupils, while the others have only pupils. They also have painted knee-high boots and the boots have heels.

CR **11**

Men and Women

Men all-bisques are comparatively rare and their place in the doll world is not clear. We only know that they are quite old and, of course, very desirable.

No. 74 This 5½-inch specimen is apparently a jester of some kind, judging by his clothing and his gleeful expression. The neat holes all over his head and body are a complete mystery. At first glance he appears to be a puppet of some kind, with the holes intended for manipulating strings. A close examination voids this theory for several good reasons.

First of all, there is no practical way to string him, even in a factory. Secondly, there are six holes in his cap and cap band and yet his neck is stiff and the four holes in his front neck ruffle would simply obscure his face if they contained strings. Thirdly, there is a hole in each thigh and on the inside of each calf but there are no matching holes in back for the strings to be pegged. The final analysis is that these holes are simply there for added decoration.

Hip and shoulder jointed with pegs, his arms are known replacements but closely resemble arms seen on similar dolls. The pure white bisque is of excellent, sharp quality and the modeling, the molding, and the finishing are so good that the jacket and tights actually appear to be added to the figure. The work is almost flawless.

The cap trim, midriff bow, leg bands, and shoe bows are royal blue. The ruffled vestee, the heeled shoes, and shoe soles are bright yellow. All the paint is glossy.

The face has a fine complexion coat, the eyes are blue with high-placed pupils, and all the hair, including the brows, is a soft brown. There is another round hole in the center of his mouth and he has a long, Pinocchio nose.

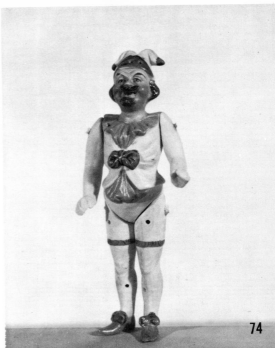

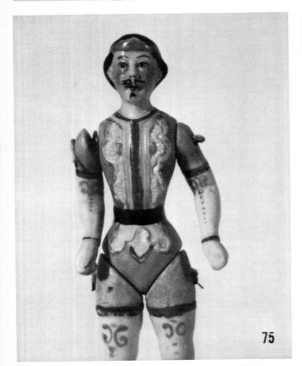

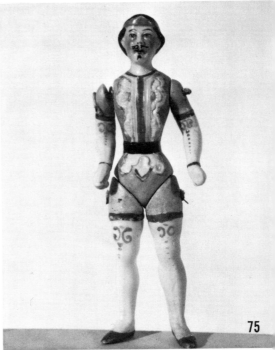

74 Author's collection; 75 Goldfinger collection

No. 75 Another man, perhaps a highwire acrobat or circus equestrian performer because he is wearing the ballet type shoes common to these artists. He is also peg strung, but has black hair.

This fellow is quite a peacock. There are heavy, braidlike molded designs down the body and across the abdomen and the illusion of a suit was created by painting and trimming the body but leaving the molded designs white.

The main portions of the suit are pink. There are orange bands around the neck, down the front, around the upper arms and the wrists, and around the pants legs. The molded crown is orange and so are the slippers, which have white soles. To add further to his glory, there are blue bands inside the orange ones around the neck and down the front, and around the design across his middle, and the same blue was used for the tattoo marks on his arms and legs.

His featuring is very good, his hands are complexion coated, but his legs are white as tights would be.

No. 76 Shoulder jointed with pegs, this $4\frac{7}{8}$-inch ball-head lady is also unusual and in many ways resembles the much later Gibson Girl figurines in molded underwear which have the delightful little mohair wigs with pompadours and braided top buns.

This doll has painted blue eyes with high pupils, black lid linings, and red lid lines and eye dots. She also has red nose dots, one-stroke blond brows, and a nice complexion.

The Old White bisque is excellent and the modeling is in elaborate detail. All the creases in the clothes, back and front, are very natural and the ruffles on the pant legs have molded scallops and the details of embroidered lace. The stockings have alternating wavy and straight horizontal lines to indicate hand knitting. The pointed-front boots are dark brown with black top bands and they have heels and tan soles. All the underwear trim is dark blue.

Unlike the later, mass-produced dolls, all the finishing and decorating was done with care and she is balanced to stand alone.

No. 77 Perhaps this 6-inch hatted lady should be called an "almost all-bisque" but, since she is so unusual and she was offered for inclusion in this volume, she was gratefully accepted.

She is very old and, within the limits previously explained, deserves to be classified as Parian-quality.

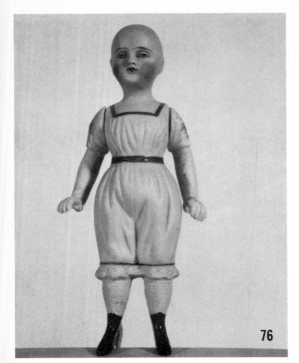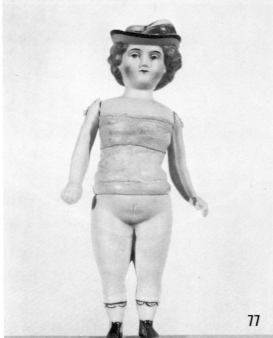

76 Strong collection; 77 Brewer collection

Shoulder jointed with large pegging holes, she has painted blue eyes which have high pupils, black eye linings and red lid lines; the one-stroke brows are brown. Her painted yellow hair is well done in good waves all around the head and there are some comb marks. Her hands are cupped but they are not alike because the right one cups down and the left one cups and also turns inward.

She is fascinating to examine because the mold lines are visible and very different from those on other hatted dolls. In this one only two molds appear to have been used, causing a jog in the mold line on the top of the hat. Instead of adding all or part of the hat while she was greenware, the molded feather was included in an odd cutoff which turns sharply forward in the front mold. Because the brim bends up all around instead of down or straight out, the undercutting problem must have been solved.

The hat is painted gray, with a black band and black rim bindings, while the feather is glazed grape lustre. The feet are glazed to the tops of her molded, scalloped socks, which have a plain grape-colored design painted around the tops. The shoes, with barely indicated heels, are finished in grape lustre with very pale yellow glazed soles.

Both the shoulder and the hip sections have molded rims into which the kid body can be wired. Inside the kid section there is a large, fairly soft spring which not only holds the two sections apart and the doll upright but also gives her some possibility of motion.

Delightful specimen!

Swayers and Nodders

Some collectors do not consider swayers and nodders play dolls but some of them are excellent all-bisques. They apparently were toys for children as well as collectible items for adults and they were revived in this century as dolls, both in bisque by the Japanese and in composition by American manufacturers. Because many collectors have never had an opportunity to examine truly beautiful old specimens, two of each are included here for reference purposes.

The swaying figures move forward and back because wire loops are attached to the tops of the pedestal legs and a wire at the waistline passes through these loops to hold the two pieces together. The loops are reversed when they are to sway from side to side and a wire goes through the body from front to back.

No. 78 Like old dolls, this 5⅛-inch girl has painted blue eyes with high pupils, red lid lines, black lid linings, and red nose dots. The one-stroke brows are dark blond like the hair, and the mouth is in two parts with a white center.

Her hair is quite beautiful, so the back is also shown. Molded off the face, the shoulder-length curls fall from a center part and are held in back with a molded black band. The entire hairdo is comb marked—vertically down the hair through the waves and horizontally across the curls.

Her rose-pink dress has an excellent bottom ruffle with a magenta trim line, gold waist cord with molded tassels, and a gold trim line at the neck. There is a narrow scalloped trim molded inside the scoop neck which was left white and there is a hole through the closed right hand for a few feather strands. The complexion coat is even and good.

She has pantalettes and flat boots with molded front tassels completely

78

78

done in bright orange. The top of the base is green and brown to represent grass and earth and the bottom rim is dark brown.

Like the doll which follows, she is stamped on the underside of the base with a dark blue anchor mark:

No. 79 This younger, smaller girl, 4¾ inches tall, has painted blue eyes with high pupils, black lid linings, and red eyelid lines and nose dots. Her complexion is even and good. Her brows are a very yellow taffy color to match the childish curling hair which is well molded up off her face and ends in a curled up roll across the entire nape of the neck. Her mouth has no center white line.

Like all little girls of her time, she has a white pinafore. The light pink dress has a slightly ruffled bottom but is without any painted trim line. There is a gold band around the pinafore neck and her little cap sleeves are pink like the dress. Flowers fit into her hand hole.

79

80

80

81

79, 80 & 81 Strong collection

She has the same pantalettes and feet as **No. 78**, but the entire top of her base is green.

No. 80 A 3¾-inch child, this white nodder has a 2¾-inch body which seems to be a variation on the swaddling clothes theme. The eyes are blue with pupils, black lid linings, and pink lid lines; the brows are dark blond. The molded hair in front is pale blond.

The molded ribbons around the base are painted lavender with dots of gleaming gold trim. The entire edge of the white cap, the back stand-up collar, and the front edge are trimmed with gathered lace which was dipped in slip and applied. Under her chin there is a flat, pink bib.

This particular doll nods for a surprisingly long time, apparently because of her excellent engineering. The second illustration shows the rather heavy metal rod which is held in her neck cavity by wooden pegs and the lead balance weight. Of course, these dolls are always hollow, like bells, and the metal rod which pierces her neck rests in square and deep shoulder holes which are in the front body mold. Since such a weight would crack the bisque body if it struck the body while in motion, the length of the rod is calculated to provide a short stroke inside the body. The deep shoulder holes hold the head better than those on most nodders.

No. 81 A 3-inch seated lady, this nodder has a 2⅛-inch body. The eyes are blue with pupils and black lid linings. Her brown brows match her short, molded, comb-marked hair.

The dress is a pretty shade of clear pink overshot with gold dots and coral stars which are also gold trimmed and she has gold bands on her sleeve ends. The dress detail is most elaborate, with a coral ruffle around the apron front which is finished in back with a molded bow and long streamers. The neck is a molded kerchief with a deep point in back above the bow. The white hat is some variety of mob cap because it has a gathered brim and a ruffled front on the crown. It is pink trimmed, including a pink flower which forms the top.

This doll has a large bisque ball on the end of the neck rod and shallow shoulder holes to hold the neck rod.

Both **No. 80** and **No. 81** are made of very clear, old, sharp bisque. All the workmanship is excellent.

They are too old to be marked, of course.

$\backsim$ 13

Animals

Many all-bisque collectors are not aware that hollow, wire jointed animals also were made at different times during the popularity of bisque. Many millions of frozen animals were made during the bisque era but the wire jointed ones are especially interesting.

No. 82 This old bear is a very versatile and amusing toy. He is well balanced and will hold many positions without support. Only 3 inches long and 2½ inches when standing on all fours, his decorating is done in black—pupils, eye linings, and mouth.

To collectors he is interesting for another reason and that is the bisque from which he is made. All the dark spots and streaks are impurities in the slip and they appear to be bits of metal or some type of slag which melted in the high firing process.

Early collectors used to tell stories they heard from immigrants about their childhoods in the dollmaking areas of Germany before 1900. One of the jobs the children had, they said, was to work the slip after it had been strained to remove the large particles of foreign matter which came in the clay. Small, sharp pieces passed through the sieve holes, however, and the children found them with their fingers by puddling through buckets of slip.

Be that as it may, it was those tiny, undetected particles that caused the "beauty spots" and the "freckles" on fine old china and bisque pieces. Because they were heavier than the supporting clay, these disfiguring bits penetrated until they were stopped by the hard surface of the plaster of Paris molds.

Unfortunately, the molds for dolls generally stood with the heads down and this meant that these bits finally rested in the face and in the molded hair of the dolls. These spots are rarely ever seen on the inside, even if

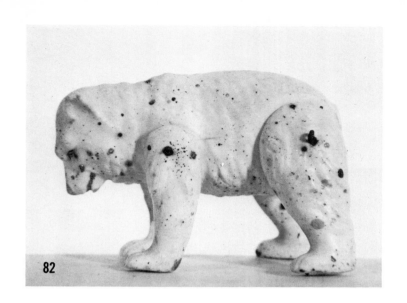

82

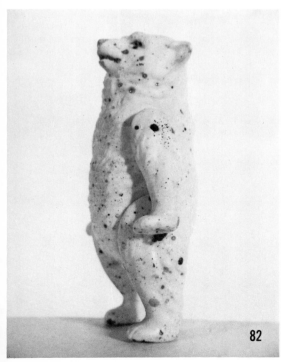

82

82

82 Author's collection

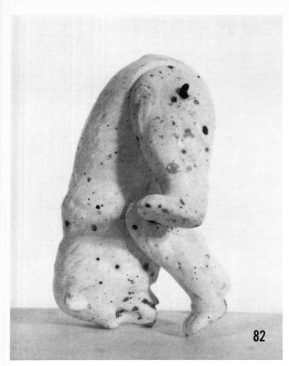

82 *Author's collection*

the face is badly marked. One wonders how many of them are undetected under the black painted hair and if this isn't the very best reason why so many of them are black.

This particular little animal was a happy solution to waste problems. The markings are so generously scattered all over the body, this slip must have been dregs in the buckets from which the top, clearer slip had been carefully poured off. Made of waste or not, this bear is cherished in this collection not only for his own charm and age but also because he was a gift from a friend.

Incidentally, this is "sharp" bisque. That is, it has a hard, brittle feeling when rubbed. Old bisque buyers used to grade bisque by rubbing it quickly with their fingers until they established what they called "the cry of the bisque." There is an almost tin-like sound to old, sharp bisque when it is rubbed and this is entirely missing in objects made of the technically compounded modern slip.

The ability to judge bisque is acquired in direct proportion to the amount of bisque handled and the time and study devoted to the subject. There are many qualities of old bisque which can be graded from very good to very poor because of the variations in the slip and in the manufacturing processes. Many of the existing pieces were made for specific markets—wealthy, middle-class, and poor.

The grade often depends on the amount of finishing the articles were given and the thoroughness of the bath after the sanding, because the slip in many instances was almost the same. The good basic workmanship, plus the excellence of the decorating, determine the grade of the piece.

In some areas of this country, very thin, sharp old bisque is called "Irish" and nobody knows why. Very good quality is called "French" and the next classification is often "German." Very poor quality is called "Oriental," even if the object is not marked "Nippon" or "Japan." Because these are territorial whimsies, none of the terms is proper (especially the word "Irish") unless the word "type" is added, as German-type, French-type, Oriental-type.

The biggest hurdle in judging bisque is to bear in mind that types and qualities changed, whereas our own personal preferences do not. Because of our prejudice, because it does not appeal to us, the fact is not changed that an object can be an excellent and even an unusual piece for its type.

No. 83 Although the exact period is unknown, this excellent old dog, 2¼ inches high at the ears and 2⅜ inches across the base, is incised on the back of the body **Germany** over **787.** Her puppy is incised **Germany** across the back of the body and 4 on the back hip; it is ¾ inch high and 1⅜ inches long. Both have pour holes in their bases and even the mother dog's meets the old requirement, "no larger than the tip of a little finger."

The modeling is very good, with tufts of fluffy fur indicated and comb marks to add to the illusion. Both have molded mouths outlined in black; the mother has black lid linings and pupils; the puppy has only pupils.

Two clues may help date them. First, although they were properly fired and the color does not flake, the pretty brown tinting appears to have been done with a spray gun. Second, they would have to be classified as collies.

The spray gun was a late decorating tool. Then, too, the Germans were quick to capitalize on anything popular in the United States and Albert Payson Terhune (1872-1942) made the collie famous through his novels *Lad* in 1919, *The Heart of a Dog* in 1926, and many others. Since we have to guess, these are very likely from the late 1920s.

Doll collectors buy these small animals for display with their all-bisques but bisque animals also enjoy the entire collecting attention of people

 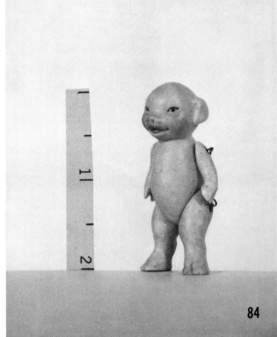

83 Author's collection; 84 Strong collection

not interested in dolls at all. There are many Japanese animals available, some of them very good examples of this type of work, but the old German ones are the most desired.

No. 84 Much, much later, perhaps in the period immediately after World War I, this cute little pig has **Germany** incised down his back. There was a vogue at one time for dolls with animal heads and this is one of the hard-to-find samples in bisque. He is 2 inches standing and his pink cheeks and smiling pink mouth are well done. He has just black pupils and lid linings and the over-all fired complexion is very adequate.

Unlike the old bear, **No. 82**, this fellow cannot stand on all fours because the front legs, even though the feet are properly cloven, are short, like arms. Many general collections contain composition dolls which are much larger than this but the pig heads are on standard bent-leg baby bodies or bodies with long, thin, human legs.

Old Stiff Necks

Old stiff necked bisques, generally unmarked or marked only with numbers, are very desirable on many counts.

No. 85 Peg strung, 3⅝ inches tall, and very much resembling a jointed version of the Frozen Charlotte **No. 48**, this doll has the same dusty complexion coat in a deep cream color, the tightly closed and slightly raised fists, good feet with ankle and heel modeling, and most of the baggy seat marks. The large black spot in the lower left leg is a piece of slag or metal which came to the surface in the molding and fused in the firing. None of the old bisque is clear like the later type.

This is as good a place as any to remind collectors NOT to pick at these spots in the hope of removing them. In the first place, they help us to identify old dolls. In the second place, the removal will either leave a hole, which must be filled and can never be color-matched, or the picking can cause the immediate area to break.

She has painted blue eyes with black lid linings and high pupils, blond one-stroke brows, red nose dots and a ball head.

The arms and legs are not hollow and there is a good chance that the body is also solid. For its size it is heavy and the stringing hole through the base of the body is a channel with no opening in the torso.

No. 86 In this 7-inch doll the bisque is excellent, the limb and body modeling is detailed in the same manner as some of the finer Frozen Charlottes. The head is pure German, with attractive pale blond molded hair. The partly exposed ears and the tiny, different curls molded close to the center part are indications of its age, even if there were no others.

But there are others. The eyes are glossy bright blue with slightly above-center pupils and white highlight dots. There are eyelid lines done

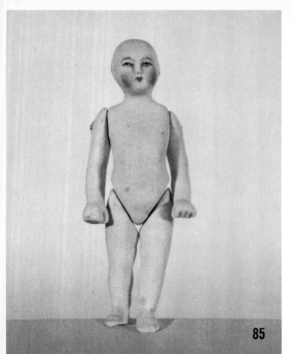

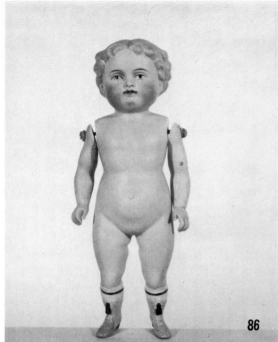

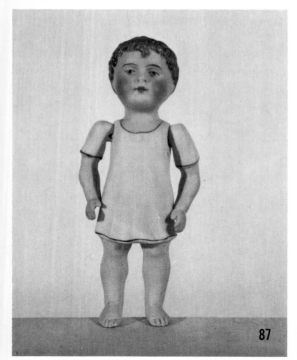

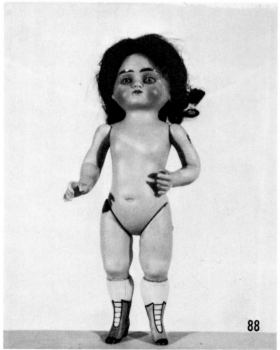

85 & 86 Author's collection; 87 & 88 Strong collection

in the cheek color instead of the red found on chinas and the small mouth has a dark red center line like many of the fine old shoulder heads. The all-over complexion tint is a soft peach which is also very like the creamy color of many of the French-type.

In this type the peg strung arms are flat on the inner sides at the top to match the perfectly flat, closed outer surfaces of the shoulders.

The fat, childish lower legs are not in good proportion, which is typical of German dolls, but they are most appealing. The knee-high white socks have a very fine molded vertical ribbing and top scallops; the molded bands are painted a subdued green. The detailed bootines are glossy pink with black front tassels and heels, and light brown soles.

Collectors are amused by what they call the "fat fannies" on many of these old stiff-legged dolls. The reason is very obvious on this doll because both rear cheeks and one back curl are roughened from contact with the floor of the kiln or the wire of the basket. This 3-point balance kept her entire back, as well as her pretty legs and feet, from being marked during the firing.

No. 87 Incised **772.3** across the hips, this 5½-inch child with a molded shift has been classified with these dolls because he is in no way related to the much, much later Candystore dolls with molded clothes and hair. This type of garment is more like those on many china Frozen Charlottes.

Shoulder jointed with loops which fit into excellent shoulder sockets in the torso, he has painted blue eyes with high pupils, black lid linings, and one-stroke dark blond brows. The all-over tightly curled molded hair is done in glossy yellow with dark shadows between the curl crests. He is nicely balanced to stand alone and his hands and feet are very good.

In fact, he is completely beautiful. The bisque is of excellent quality, finished to perfection, and although the pour holes in his feet are filled, they are barely visible. All the trim, at neck, sleeves, and bottom of the shift, is in magenta color, and where the hemline would ordinarily be in a dress there is an incised line of tiny depressions representing stitches.

A smaller duplicate in the author's collection is 3⁷⁄₁₆ inches tall and is incised **722 3/0**. A mathematical reduction from **722.3** to **722 3/0** indicates a steady decrease of approximately 6/16 inch between sizes, with no size marked **722.0**. This span includes only six sizes and gives us some idea of the tremendous number of molds required to keep production rolling because there had to be many molds in every size. (See page 5.)

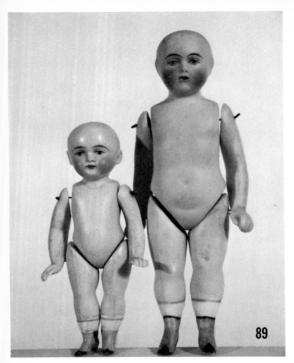

89 Author's collection; 90 Strong collection

No. 88 There is no way to prove it but this 8½-inch hip and shoulder peg jointed with set glass eyes must be an early Kestner product.

The threaded blue eyes are German, with upper and lower painted lashes, red eye dots, and glossy, feathered brows. The breasted body is well done and the arms are quite different, with good ball tops and partially cupped hands which have free thumbs.

Her fat legs are kid lined at the hips and the white knee socks have vertical ribbing and blue bands. Her tan bootines have rubber gussets indicated at the sides and they are outlined in black, with black tips and heels, and tan soles. Her original dark brown mohair wig with a white, machine-stitched center part is on a cloth cap which eliminated a dome over the small open top of the head.

Her cheek color is vivid but becoming, and all the finishing and decorating is good. She is made of good, old bisque and the complexion coat is the old peach color rather than pink.

No. 89 Hip and shoulder jointed with brass wire, the larger doll is 5⅛ inches tall. She has the old body modeling and the same enclosed shoulders to fit the flat arm tops. The eyes are painted blue with high pupils, red eyelid lines, and black lid linings. The dark blond brows are one-stroke. The finishing and the complexion tinting are both very good and she is made of old, excellent bisque.

Her fat legs have white socks without molded ribbing but with blue top bands. The gray boots have rubber top gussets indicated in black and the top rims, sole edges, and toe tips are also black. The soles are tan rather than yellow.

Like the doll with molded underwear, **No. 76,** the old ball head required a wig but moths were so fond of the mohair, it is almost impossible to find one with an original wig.

Her 3¾-inch companion is also jointed with brass wire, has the same eyes but without the red eyelid lines and she has an *almost* ball head. There is a small hole in the back head mold and a few hairs from a push-in wig still cling to the opening.

This little doll's boots are blue instead of gray and the tops of her white socks have rose bands. The tops, the tips, the guessets, and the heels are black and the soles are tan.

Her complexion coating is very pale but she is made of the old "greasy" bisque which never loses its soft gloss even when it is soiled.

No. 90 Unusual because of her molded mob cap and hair, 9 inches tall, hip and shoulder jointed with pegs, this is an excellent specimen.

She has painted blue eyes with high pupils, molded lids with black linings, red lid lines and eye dots, and one-stroke brown brows. The puff of blond hair which leaves her ears exposed is beautifully comb marked and her pink cap with molded front bow is well modeled, finished, and decorated.

Like many of the better dolls, her arms are not alike. The left arm is bent and the cupped hand turns in, while the right arm is turned over and the hand turns down. One thumb is free standing and the other is only partially clear of the hand.

The body modeling is more trim than some of the previous dolls and the arms have ball tops which are not as good as those on later dolls. She also has a fat fanny and amazingly thick legs—German to the nth degree. The white socks have molded vertical ribbing and blue bands; the high black bootines have two straps, heels and tan soles.

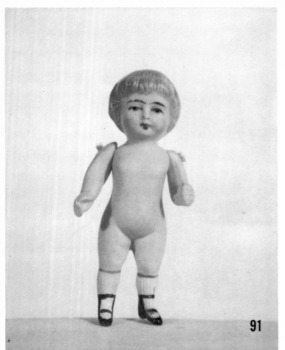

91 & 92 *Author's collection*

The bisque is excellent, the complexion is pale, and she is beautifully balanced to stand alone.

No. 91 This 2¾-inch miniature with blond hair belongs to the same family as the previous and the following dolls. The molded, comb-marked bangs extend from the crown of the head like those on the well-known china and bisque shoulder heads known as "Highland Mary." In back and over the ears the head is covered with good molded ringlets.

The tiny breasted body, with the baggy seat associated with the older dolls, has an excellent soft peachy complexion, good molded shoulder sockets, and ball tops on the pegged arms. The fat legs have vertically ribbed white socks with blue bands and the two-strap, heeled bootines are brown with tan soles.

She has painted blue eyes with large pupils, black lid linings, one-stroke brown brows, and there are tiny red nose dots but no red lid lines because of her size.

Unfortunately the right arm is missing but the left one is bent at a right angle even in this miniature.

124 § *All-Bisque and Half-Bisque Dolls*

No. 92 These three dolls with painted bootines are another version of the same doll and they measure, from the left, 3, 3¾, and 5½ inches; all have uncut ball heads and have heeled black, pink, and brown bootines, respectively.

The largest and the smallest are the oldest and have peg strung arms with ball tops which fit into good shoulder sockets. Although they are not marked, they are two sizes of the same doll and a variation of the dolls with the mob cap and the molded hair immediately preceding. Both of these are made of the same fine bisque with a low gloss.

These two also have the even, soft peachy complexion tint and all the finishing and decorating is good. They have blue eyes with high pupils, black eyelid linings, and brown one-stroke brows, and the larger doll has red eyelid lines and eye and nose dots. The white socks have blue bands and molded vertical ribbing; the two bootine straps are also molded. Each has a blond mohair wig on a cloth cap; the largest was removed to show the good ball head.

The center doll is one of several of the type in the collection and she is a much later issue because she is incised with a stock number and a size in two lines on the back: 2120 and 0 1/2. The bisque is fair but the finishing and decorating are both much poorer. The head has been cut out on top for a push-in hank wig, the very inferior arms are flat and wire strung. The blue eyes have no pupils and both the lid lines and brows are dark blond, a decorating speed-up and not age in this instance. There is some evidence of vertical sock ribbing, the pink boots are painted but not molded, they have no heels and the soles are pink.

Another 3¾-inch specimen has blue molded one-strap shoes with blue soles, socks with fine molded vertical ribbing and a good top band, above which there is a painted pink trim. She is shoulder jointed with brass wire and has a push-in wig. Incised in two lines on the back, 0 1/2 and 2120, she has brown lid linings and brows. The eyes are well molded but have only painted pupils.

Still a third type in the group has the same specifications, but with pink shoes with pink soles and is incised in three lines on the back, **Germany** 0 1/2 and 2120, so they were made over a long period of time.

No. 93 A 6¼-inch specimen of the same dolls, this one with black bootines. She is also unmarked but has a cut head instead of the ball type. It is interesting that her excellent blond mohair wig is made like the molded

93

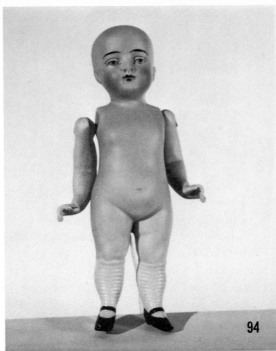

94

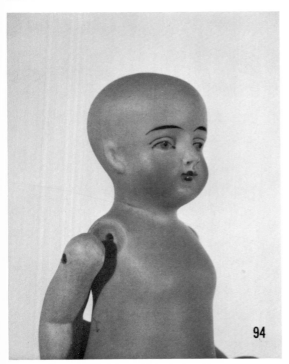

94

95

93, 94 & 95 Author's collection

doll's hair, with bangs extending from the crown. She is dressed as found in old, feather-stitched white silk.

No. 94 This 5⅝-inch ball head is a later vintage and there is an incised circle in the top of her head to guide the cutters if she was to have a push-in wig. She has every sign of being a Kestner.

The pegged arms are worth special notice. Although the mold seams are visible down the sides of the body, she has molded arm sockets in her torso and good molded shoulder balls on the arm tops.

Because the elbow jointed bisque, **No. 9,** had a swivel necked head and moving legs, the torso was molded separately and offered very limited areas for the molder's fingers to get a purchase for unmolding. This is the reason for the off-center torso mold in that doll. This German doll, with molded head and stiff legs was much easier to pull from the mold and to handle as greenware. Because of the added body area, it was possible to use the front and back molds and still preserve the arm holes.

The bisque is excellent and there is a gloss to all her feature painting, including the brown eyebrows, the blue eyes which have no highlight dots, and the two-piece mouth which is very similar to the type on many shoulder heads and some chinas. The red eyelid lines and the black upper lid linings are also very glossy, along with her high, pink, circular molded ribbed socks and the one-strap black slippers with heels and yellow soles.

Enamel is a glossy and opaque medium and some of these glossy colors are not enamel, but it is possible to add gloss to the china paints used in this kind of decorating. Very likely that was the method used here because she is without doubt a quality product. This type of painting was abandoned in many of the later, mass-production operations.

The complexion tinting is very uniform and only a slightly deeper tone than that on the early dolls, but it is still basically the creamy peach color.

Her stiff legs are also in better proportion than those on the dolls previously illustrated, even though the body has less modeling. Unfortunately she is not properly balanced to stand alone, probably because the toes of her slippers were trimmed or rubbed too much in the original finishing and lost the necessary thickness in the soles.

No. 95 With the same fine closed arm sockets as the previous doll, and also unmarked, this 8¼-inch specimen is another quality product. She is also a wonderful example of the problems encountered in attempting to

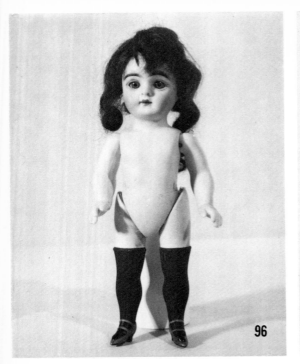

96 Author's collection; 97 Brewer collection

place all-bisques from the same company, let alone from the same general period, in the proper order.

She is much the same doll BUT: Her head was cut around the incised circle so that her deep blue glass eyes could be set. She has upper and lower painted lashes and black linings on the upper lid rims. Her reddish brown eyebrows each required seven carefully placed brush strokes. She is peg strung in both the arms and the kid-lined legs. Her knee-high shirred socks are blue and the one-strap slippers with good heels are brown with deep yellow soles. In this doll only the slippers are glossy, even though the eyebrows appear to be in the picture.

The bisque is very good and all the workmanship is excellent. The human-hair wig on a cloth base is too full for such a small doll but it fits perfectly and may have been made for her or bought especially for her but, in the countless dolls owned and examined through the years, original wigs have been mohair almost without exception. The biggest reason why so many of them are missing is that moths delight in destroying them.

No. 96 Stiff necked and loop strung, 7¾ inches tall, this doll is incised

307/9 high up on the head rim. The arms have fine ball tops which fit into good socket rims, not complete sockets.

Her sleep blue eyes, which have been set, have fine upper and lower lashes. The high black stockings, besides being vertically ribbed, are dotted with tiny molded holes added to the texture. The yellow, two-strap slippers with medium high, black heels and black pompoms are quite pointed.

There is no doubt that this is another Kestner. Her closed mouth is shaped and painted like a Kestner, her original mohair wig is a color associated with wigs on large Kestner jointed dolls over a long period. It is a bronze rather than brown color, very unlike any natural hair color, and it seldom fades.

The bisque is beautiful, the workmanship is all very good, and all of it is in keeping with the place Kestner occupied in the doll field.

These dolls raise the old question: Are dolls without heels older than those with heels? In all-bisques this obviously does not apply. Shaped heels caused more problems than flat soles in the production line and, of course, they added to the decorating time and the manufacturing costs.

No. 97 Marked in two lines on the head **164 5/0**, this 4½-inch hip and shoulder loop jointed, stiff necked Negro boy is an excellent, soft, chocolate brown finish. The irisless glass eyes are set, with one-stroke black brows; he has a closed mouth, red nose dots, and a black mohair wig on a gauze cap.

While he was on loan for picture taking, the wig came off and it was discovered that he has a little plaster dome no larger than a dime. It was Kestner who used these, of course, as well as the neatly curled little wigs on cloth caps.

The red and white gingham suit and red cloth hat are both machine made in a factory. To the author's knowledge, there is no evidence that Kestner did this type of dressing, so the assumption is that the doll was made for, or sold to, one of the many nameless firms which did dressing only.

German
Swivel Heads

No. 98 Glass-eyed swivel heads with molded hair are not common and this one, with a black band encircling her head, is especially nice. She is 8 inches tall and unmarked.

Hip and shoulder jointed with pegs, she has set brown eyes, upper and lower painted lashes, red eye dots and one-stroke dark blond brows. She has a small mouth with a dark center line and the lip color was used for the dots in her childish, rounded nose.

The painted blond hair is beautifully molded from the forehead curl to the wide V down the nape of the neck, all with nice comb marks. The narrow black band is molded, not just an added, painted decoration, and her ears are partially exposed. The bisque and workmanship are excellent.

The thumbs are molded to the open, well-done hands and they are larger, and in better proportion, than the average German hand. The white socks have a herringbone vertical ribbing and they end at mid-calf with rose bands. The two-strap black slippers have heels and tan soles.

No. 99 Uncommon, to say the least, this 10-inch, knee jointed specimen is most attractive. She is undoubtedly an early Kestner because the remains of her plaster dome can still be seen around the cork replacement. She is hip and shoulder pegged, the head is marked only **1111** below the top cut in back and she has a kid-lined neck.

In order to permit the knees to bend as they do, there are large, flat "bend" areas on the bases of the thighs in back, like those on the backs of thighs on good German jointed composition bodies. These areas are incised like the head, **1111**. Small holes in the tops of the lower legs allow the rubber and crossbar to be dropped into the lower limbs. Wide slots in the backs of the knee balls carry the rubber when the knees are bent.

The sleep brown eyes have black lid linings, upper and lower painted lashes, and four-stroke dark brows. The dark mahogany mohair wig is old but may be a replacement.

The fat cheeks and closed mouth with a rose-colored center line are typically Kestner. Although the arms are bent alike, the right hand is tightly molded into a fist and the left hand is completely open, with a free thumb. The pale bisque is excellent in both quality and weight (she weighs 13 ounces) and both the finishing and complexion padding are the finest.

The five-strap bootines are gray with black heels and sole edges, there are molded front bows and the soles are tan. The fine-ribbed white socks have a narrow magenta line below the molded scallops which form the tops.

The old, long waisted dress is made from tan, red, and blue striped cotton and there is a pleated petticoat ruffle attached at the waist. She has a red velvet hat and purse.

No. 100 With set, threaded, cobalt eyes, this hip and shoulder peg jointed doll is another excellent specimen. It is quite possible that she was made

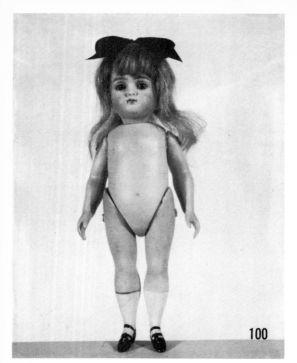

100 Strong collection; 101 Hilsdorf collection

for French distribution because there is a hole directly above each ear through which her hair ribbon passed to hold on her little cork dome and beautifully made light blond mohair wig.

She is 8½ inches tall, marked **192** over **4/0** on the back of the head and she has upper and lower painted lashes with dark blond brows. The neck and limbs are kid lined.

The body is paler than the head or the limbs but she is by no means a "put together" doll and this is a factory fault. She may have been sold dressed, in which case this would not have been noticed.

The arms are very pretty, with free thumbs and very slender fingers on excellent hands. The white socks have vertical herringbone ribs and blue bands, one of which is poorly done. The legs are nice and long and the two-strap heeled slippers are black with tan soles.

Her mouth is squared off in true Kestner style on the right side but on the left end the brush slipped and this has never been seen before. She is also the only doll examined with a freehand letter incised on the leg flange; the letter is **K**.

No. 101 Undoubtedly another Kestner, this pretty 8½-inch unmarked swivel neck is strung through forehead holes, with the knot under the front of the wig. Her plaster dome is intact, she has kid-lined parts and is hip and shoulder jointed with pegs.

She has an open mouth with two small teeth and pierced ears, both features which are not common in all-bisques. Like many good dolls, her arms are not alike; the right one is fairly straight but the left is decidedly bent. Her right hand is open with a free thumb and fingers molded together, while the left hand has a free thumb and forefinger but the other fingers are cupped.

Her threaded gray-blue sleep eyes have been set, she has upper and lower painted lashes and feathered brows. The old blond mohair wig with bangs and a back fall has a good cloth cap.

There are excellent ribs and blue top bands on the socks. The five-strap bootines are yellow with black gussets, trim, sole edges and heels, and they have yellow soles.

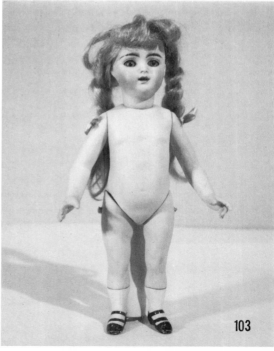

102

103

102 & 103 Author's collection

The bisque is old and very good. The little dress is cotton.

No. 102 Also pegged, 7⅜ inches tall, with **7** incised on the head, this doll has closed shoulders and flat arm tops. Her head is made of excellent greasy bisque, her complexion is pale peach, and her weight is very good. She has nose dots, and the pink mouth, with flat outer ends on the upper lip, has the Kestner dark center line which is so attractive.

She has sleep brown eyes with upper and lower painted lashes, black socket linings, and red eye dots. The dark blond brows are of six overlapping strokes. The excellent original blond mohair wig is on a good cloth base and she has an original Kestner plaster dome.

Her pretty hands have partly free thumbs, each finger is defined on both the upper and under sides, her tiny fingernails are all outlined and the knuckles are dimpled. Her shapely legs are like the previous doll's but the white socks have plain vertical ribs and the narrow magenta band is molded ⅛ inch below the top edge. The slippers have only one molded strap, good front bows, completely black heels, and deep yellow soles.

No. 103 Incised **31** over **23** on the neck, this 9-inch pegged blonde certainly looks like a remake of **No. 100**. The open mouth has only two upper teeth but their poor placement certainly argues in favor of an early attempt at this highly advertised novelty. Her complexion tinting is very pale and creamy and she is of the old, exceptionally good weight.

The sleep blue eyes have upper and lower painted lashes, the eye sockets are lined with black, and she has glossy, brown, multi-stroke brows.

Her torso is thicker, her legs are shorter, and the flanges are less oblique than those on the previous dolls but the red-banded socks have the herringbone design and the two-strap slippers are the same design with lower heels and wider, more childish proportions. The nice old blond wig may not be original but it is good mohair, the proper size, and very becoming.

She is not as pretty as many of the other dolls but being pretty is not always a doll's most desirable feature. She is a combination of old and new features which makes her most interesting.

No. 104 This unmarked little girl is 4 inches seated. She has a swivel neck and is peg jointed at the shoulders. At present she is strung with a wire V but she has top holes in a good ball head and could have been strung like the Belton-type. The old wig is short blond mohair.

The set cobalt eyes have black lid linings, upper and lower painted lashes, red eye dots and one-stroke dark brown brows. Both arms are bent

but only the right hand has a free thumb. The bisque is old and good but the head is slightly higher in color than the body and arms.

The black boots are high and glossy, with the fronts painted to a high point; they have tiny heels and brown soles. The fine-ribbed white socks have blue bands.

Why is she seated? Nobody knows but she is frozen in a good sitting position, as shown in the illustration.

No. 105 All-bisques with long stockings are very desirable and much sought after. This pair of sisters, 5⅝ inches, incised **2/0**, and 7½ inches, incised **2** are good examples.

German markings within the same factory often differed greatly from one type to another and any comparison between plants is impossible. We have come to believe that single incised size numbers are older than combinations of model and size numbers but we could be wrong. As collectors we use these model numbers as a means of identification but this was by no means the intent of the manufacturer. Incised marks were for the guidance of the workers in assembling parts for stringing, for boxing, for inventorying and for price classification in shipping and billing.

In this particular case, for instance, all of the large doll's parts are also incised 2 but only the leg flanges on the small doll carry the figure. Her arms have a pair of single strokes under the stringing loops which look like an unfinished Roman numeral II but that is all.

These two have beautifully molded legs, the hose are brown in a vertical molded pattern, and the shoes are orange and yellow respectively, with molded bows which are painted blue, and they have black Cuban heels. Another doll in the collection has these same shoes but they are black with blue bows.

All three of the dolls with these legs have closed necks with stringing holes low on each side rather than the molded bottom loop considered French. Except that they are loop strung instead of pegged (and this could have been considered an important "new" feature, we must remember) and have this neck difference, these little German dolls meet all the

106 & 107 *Author's collection*

other requirements for French-type on casual examination. Collectors are happy to overlook these small items. French buyers would have dismissed them also, one feels sure.

No. 106 This little 5 incher, incised only with a small 4 high on the head, is shown for two reasons. She may be an earlier or a special version of the two dolls which follow and her costume is typical of those which millions of all-bisques wore years ago.

The floppy hat and two-piece dress are loosely crocheted of fine cream-colored baby wool, all the edging is crocheted in shining pink silk thread and pink silk ribbon was run through alternating stitches completely around the hem and it also forms a sash at the waist, a hat band, and a hat bow. In her day she was the personification of all-bisque glamour. Mothers, grandmothers, and aunts enjoyed making us this kind of finery, and it is still very appealing today.

She has set brown eyes with black socket linings, long upper and lower painted lashes, one-stroke brown brows, and red nose dots. Her very light blond mohair wig is original and done on a pink cloth cap.

All her other specifications are like the following.

No. 107 This pair, one 5 inches, incised **310** over **4,** and the other 7 inches, incised **310 . 9,** have the same face. This is an instance where we feel that the 310 is the face identification and the 4 and 9 are the sizes.

They have bright yellow, glossy socks with an all-over pattern like window screening. The glossy black slippers have molded pompons and Baby Louis heels. They have closed necks with side stringing holes and pale coloring but their joints are not kid lined. Like the previous dolls, they are loop strung but would be accepted as French-type.

The fact is, however, they are German and very likely Kestners. They are of beautiful bisque, the mouths and eyebrows are very Kestner, and they have original wigs which are miniatures of the wigs found on many types of Kestners.

Because they have no country of origin, they could have been sold anywhere as French, and this is especially true if the distributor handled them from a French address.

Because of this closed neck with side stringing holes, descriptions of all-bisques should be explicit because the implication could be taken that they have end loops, which would be unfortunate. There is an inclination to include everything possible as "French" but the French used the end loop even in very late, nondescript manufacture, so it cannot be taken as an indication either of age or quality. It was just a French peculiarity.

It will undoubtedly be noticed that in these pairs sometimes the larger head is the prettiest and sometimes the smaller one is the beauty. This happened in all kinds of heads and often accounts for the buyer's disappointment if a doll is ordered by marks without personal inspection.

Many things caused these differences. Sometimes it was the decorator's lack of skill and sometimes heads sagged or widened in the firing. There are doll faces which are much more attractive in large sizes and others that are prettier when small.

In the **No. 105** dolls, the rather high cheek bones and full face are more appealing in the larger size. But in the **No. 107** pair, the face appears to be more oval and much prettier in the small size.

The following three dolls are peg strung, glass eyed, swivel necked and very desirable. These are often called "French-type" also, but serious collectors always classify them as German, which they surely are. They appear to have been made for the American market because of the very popular Mary Jane slippers, which are still classic footwear for little girls.

All are incised **31-32** over **15** on the backs of the heads, all of which are ball type.

In a comparison of German jointed head marks with all-bisque marks, a 15-inch closed mouth, pierced ear head came to light in the collection with the same method of identification. Close to the head cut the figures **32.26** are incised in rather ornate type. This doll is a jointed Kestner and also has a childish, pensive face very similar to the appealing faces of these three.

Even though they have less body modeling than previous specimens and they are thicker and more childlike in the torso, they would have appealed to American tastes, and still do.

Identically marked, they are shown for several reasons.

No. 108 This 6⅛-inch brown-eyed girl has perfectly matched parts. The arms and legs are incised **31-15** and the same mark on the shoulder of the torso was blurred in the finishing but signs of it are still there.

No. 109 Blue eyed and blond, this doll and her parts are similarly marked, but her legs apparently shrank in the firing and are not as large at the hip sockets as her sister's, so she is ⅛ inch shorter.

Nos. 110 and **111** Also blue eyed, this doll has head, torso, and arm

108

109

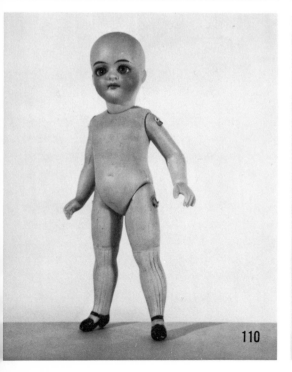

110

111

108, 109, 110 & 111 Author's collection

markings like the others, but her legs are replacements and the high stockings and one-strap slippers with molded pompons are from an earlier type.

She presents a good example of the problems encountered with substitute legs. They fit beautifully at the hip sockets for size but they spraddle out when pegged. Like human beings, all-bisques normally have a very good center of balance from the head through the heels and they do not do this.

Her clothing hides this fault to some extent, **No. 111,** but she would be much prettier and more valuable with her own legs, which had a different angle at the flange. The ribbed stockings are light blue and the slippers are black.

Because of faults like this, collectors should be wary about dolls which are offered for sale unstrung because it is impossible to hold all the pieces together the way the pegging does. And for the same reason, it is wise to think twice about buying dolls whose clothes are securely sewed on.

The last doll and the brown-eyed one (**No. 108**) have much larger eyes than the blue-eyed one in the petticoat (**No. 109**). Since the sockets did

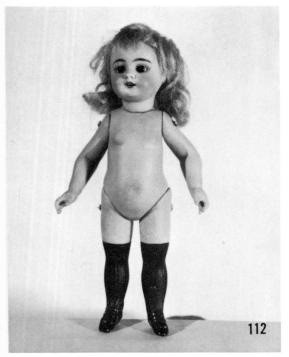
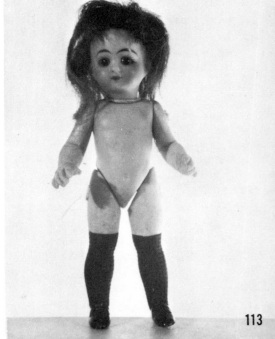

112

113

112 & 113 Author's collection

not sag or elongate, they obviously were simply cut a little smaller in the blond and the eyes were then fitted to the fired holes.

There is a factory error in **No. 108** which is not often seen in dolls of this high quality. The rim of one sock is blue, as it should be, and the other rim is brown in front like the shoes and blue only in the back.

All of them have small center neck holes and are strung like jointeds with wooden neck plugs.

No. 112 This 8½-inch blonde with brown sleep eyes, painted upper and lower lashes and an open mouth with four very even teeth is more than pretty. Her high, vertically ribbed black stockings (of nightmare memory to the children upon whom they were inflicted in real life up through the early 1900s) and brown two-strap slippers with molded bows and heels are not her most important features by any means.

She is marked! Distinctly incised in her head is **886** over **S 5 H** and an exact duplicate formerly in the collection eliminates any possibility of a Simon & Halbig head from a small jointed doll having been substituted.

She has her original blond mohair cap wig on a cardboard dome, and so did her duplicate. She presents a puzzle in that her coloring is definitely high, which we presume to be late, but she is peg strung, which is not.

One who handles dolls constantly with keen observation learns to recognize manufacturers' oddities, weaknesses, standards, and general workmanship—or at least they should learn. This **886 S H**, for example, has a typically shaped head for this firm. It is a variation of the old slanted crown cut which followed after the ball heads—the entire front of the head is one mold. Because of this, in these dolls, the foreheads rise and curve back well past the normal hairline before reaching the cut.

No. 113 Only 4 inches tall but undoubtedly a miniature of the **886 S H**. The head shapes, the slanted cuts, all the body modeling, and the high color are alike. Both have kid-lined neck holes, flat upper arms for peg stringing, long, black, patterned stockings and brown shoes. Even the coloring of the shoes is the same rich reddish brown.

The differences are: In the large doll an open mouth, sleep eyes, blond wig, and heeled shoes. In the small one, closed mouth, set eyes, brown wig, and flat shoes, all of which are logical changes because of her size.

No. 114 Oval faced, with a slightly breasted body, this little girl is 4 inches tall, has a closed mouth and set, blue glass eyes with upper and

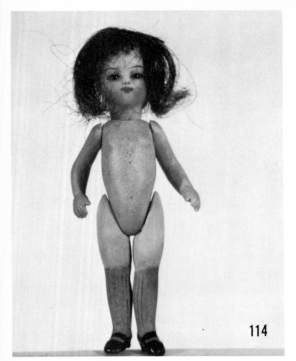 

114 Author's collection; 115 Brewer collection

lower painted lashes and red eye dots. She is unmarked but she has many indications of being experimental.

Her hip construction is different. Instead of having diagonally cut hip flanges, the cut on these legs is molded with a setback lower edge. The base of the torso fits into these ridges and this makes for a good stance because the torso weight rests on these edges.

Hidden, and very uncommon, the method of stringing is inside pegging. Instead of holes through ball tops on the arms and legs, this doll has ball tops with inside openings in them. The balls fit into the shoulder and hip holes with great precision and the rubber is pegged into the open holes so that it is invisible from the outside.

This evidently was not a successful experiment. These dolls are difficult to find, indicating that not too many of them were made and, having been found, they are very difficult to string. As a high-speed factory operation this method would have been thoroughly impractical and costly.

She has vertically ribbed gray stockings and one-strap heeled slippers of luggage tan color. The bisque is very good and much less brittle feeling than the average German doll's, and her complexion tinting is even and rather pale.

No. 115 Not as old as the others but one of the most avidly sought of any all-bisques, this 6-inch knee and elbow jointed swivel goo-goo is a darling.

Incised on the head **112** over **3** and on the back **112   2** over **Germany**, she is also incised **3** on the arms and **111.3** on the legs.

She looks like another Kestner.

The blue-gray sleep eyes (a color that Kestner never tired of using both in paint and in glass) are side set in unusually good goo-goo style and they have upper and lower painted lashes. The one-stroke brows are brown; she has a tiny watermelon mouth, red nose dots, and her original blond mohair banged wig on a pink paper cap. The spread hands have rouged backs, the socks are white with blue bands, and the one-strap slippers have slight heels and the old black painted line around the soles.

The torso has only slightly molded arm sockets but very deep leg sockets; the rubber goes through the limb parts to be fastened into holes in the rounded tops of the lower legs and the lower arms.

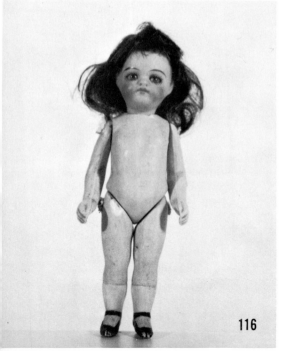
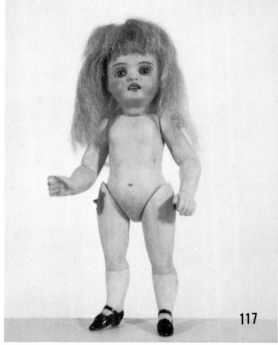

116 & 117 Author's collection

The bisque is very good, the complexion tinting is very even and all the workmanship is top quality. The consensus is that these were prewar dolls and they must have been fairly expensive items for department and toy stores because none of the collectors who have them now can remember having them as children, although they remember many of the other dolls quite clearly.

No. 116 This little pegged swivel is 3¾ inches tall and her mark is oddly incised. She has **31** high on her head, **0** at the base of the neck, and **31/0** over on her left shoulder. The arms show **31** on the upper inside areas; the legs have **0** on the flanges. Her head is strung with a crossbar in the head, the two pieces of rubber going to the arms.

Her body modeling is very good, she has set blue eyes with both upper and lower lashes and dark blond one-stroke brows. There is good vertical ribbing in the blue-banded socks and she has black one-strap slippers with heels and tan soles. The brown human-hair wig is a replacement. The bisque and all the workmanship is good German.

No. 117 With an open mouth and two upper teeth, this pegged swivel with a kid-lined neck still has her little Kestner plaster dome under her especially good light blond mohair wig, with a cloth cap. She has set dark blue glass eyes with upper and lower lashes, dark blond one-stroke brows, and red nose dots.

The slightly breasted torso has a somewhat potbellied shape, there is a faint crosshatch pattern on her blue-banded white socks and her one-strap black slippers have molded front bows, heels, and yellow soles. She is well made, has excellent hands, and the complexion is very even and rather pale.

Actually, she is a bundle of contradictions. Because of the open mouth we would not normally expect her to have this body shape, a kid-lined swivel neck, pegging, the pale coloring, or the very good hands. Mr. Kestner had many ways with dolls, there is no question about that!

16

Gebruder Heubach

The first clue in any attempt to establish the origin of unmarked dolls is usually something small. In these little novelties it was the hands, and the system worked backward.

Rather similar to the hands of Kewpies, they have one difference—the center and ring fingers are molded together but they still have the so-called "starfish" appearance which Rose O'Neill must have noticed in babies and added to her Kewpie creations.

As dolls with these hands accumulated, it was noticed that the color was high, indicating manufacture after the 1910 period. It is caused by a heavy coating of the henna colored complexion paint and it was very deliberately done. It is difficult to pad the color down to a lovely, even tint and this color speeded up production without leaving the dolls with an unpleasant mottled appearance from hasty padding.

Other Kewpie characteristics were also noticed. They have, for instance, side-painted eyes with highlight dots of relief white and small, thick, upper eyelashes. Some of them have one-stroke upturned Kewpie mouths and others have molded-together stiff legs and, to prove their difference, feet molded to points so that slippers could easily be added. All these things at first simply classified them as "Kewpie competition."

Then two dolls came along with **MADE IN GERMANY** stamped in a double-rimmed circle on the feet. The name Gebruder Heubach came to mind instantly because this mark is often found stamped on completely incised Heubach articles of all kinds, as well as on known Heubach pieces which have only incised stock numbers.

A minute examination of all the dolls disclosed that they are all made of excellent, sharp, German bisque. With the exception of the Orientals, they have intaglio eyes with relief white highlight dots. This was reassuring because it was a favorite manufacturing process of the Heubach firm in both doll and figurine heads. Ordinarily they painted a rim of color around the intaglio indentation but in this instance they followed the lead of the O'Neill charmers and painted oversized pupils only. And, while old Heubach dolls do not have painted lashes, they did begin to appear in their dolls with the advent of open mouths.

We know from existing records that Kewpies were manufactured by every German firm that could accept an order, which accounts for the difference in quality, coloring, and finishing in any given group of Kewpies. A comparison of these little dolls with all kinds of Kewpies leads to the conclusion that it would be a safe guess to include Heubach among those firms. These little dolls are more imaginative and in a wider variety but they are "kissin' cousins" to Kewpies and they are so closely related for one reason—American money.

Nos. 118 and **119** Collectors are always delighted with brother-and-sister pairs and these seem to be. Both 4½ inches tall, her slippers are light blue to match her nicely molded hair bows and his slippers are a deep henna which was obtained by using the complexion color full strength. He has a watermelon mouth and she has a rosebud, his ears show and hers are covered. Her feet carry the printed stamp.

No. 120 This Oriental's foot is stamped. He is also 4½ inches tall; the complexion coat is a warm, golden yellow and the hair is a shining black. His cap is decorated in soft pastel colors of pink and green and the molded slippers are also pink. Other specimens have other very attractive color combinations.

One of these boy dolls in the Strong Collection has the characteristic hands, a decorated cap, and a queue, and also a triangular paper label in excellent condition pasted on the front. There is no indication that the label has been tampered with, so it is presumed to be original.

The center triangle is white with a small red printed figure which looks very much like a devil, and **GERMANY** printed in red across the base. This is surrounded by a bright yellow border in which is printed, in each of the two upright sides, the word **CHIN** and across the base the word **BABY**. There is also another, outer, narrow plain red border. (It is too small to photograph satisfactorily.)

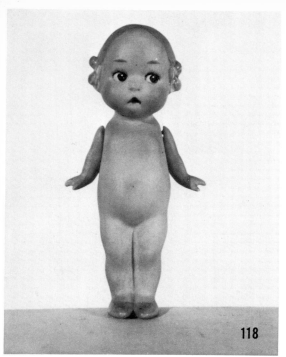

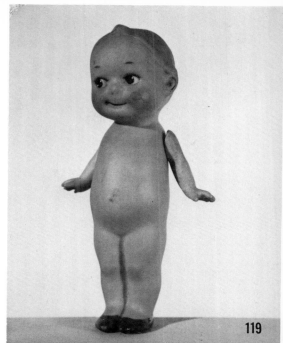

118

119

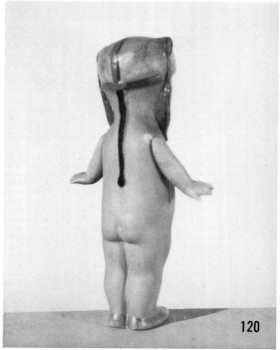

120

120

118, 119, & 120 Author's collection

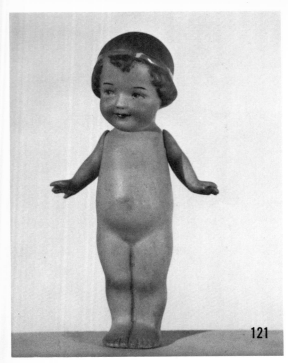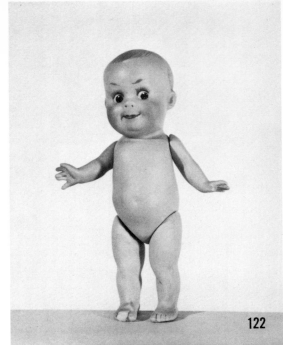

121 & 122 Author's collection

So, at least this kind of Oriental has a name, "Chin Chin Baby," and he is made in Germany.

No. 121 Very few collectors see this 4⅝-inch doll without remarking on her resemblance to the well-known "Heubach Smiling Girl." The band in her hair is glossy pale blue, she has 80 incised in her feet, and her complexion-matched arms are original and have the little star fingers.

It is very unlikely that one German firm would infringe on such an unusual head design as this one, especially since it was used by Heubach on dolls, both shoulder heads and swivel necks, and also on many of their figurines.

These suspected Heubachs should not be confused with the "Queue San Baby," Orientals made by Morimura Brothers, even though they have the same hands, sometimes the same feet, and otherwise closely resemble the German dolls.

Collectors have been puzzled about the Queue Sans. Because their quality is superior to that of the average Japanese doll, some have felt that they

148 § *All-Bisque and Half-Bisque Dolls*

were made in Germany. Even without the Morimura material from Elizabeth A. Coleman, which is quoted in the Japanese section of this book, labeled dolls in both Mrs. Strong's and the author's collections settle the question once and for all: the Chin Chins are German; Queue Sans are Japanese.

It is difficult to pinpoint and explain but, with a German doll in one hand and a Japanese sample in the other, there is a great deal of difference between them. The typical good bisque texture in the German dolls is not at all matched in the Japanese type. As a matter of fact, they do not feel like Japanese bisque, either. Whether it is the complexion paint, which filled up the pores, or a different bisque compound than that used in later dolls, the color of the Queue Sans is dense and smooth but that of the Chin Chins is clear, light, and typically sharp to the touch.

No. 122 Hip and shoulder jointed, this 5-inch toddler has all the distinctive features of the other small dolls. His mouth is oddly pursed, his color is paler than any of the others (he may have been earlier), and he has tiny tufts of molded hair in front, over the ears, and in the center back. Inasmuch as there were also sit-down Kewpies, he seems a logical addition to this series. His starfish hands are very good.

No. 123 While all this recording and speculating about these small dolls was going on, this unmarked, 8-inch doll with the same "Smiling Girl" face came along, and it was immediately noticed that she had the same star hands and they were very pronounced in this size. To those of us old enough to remember, she is typical of the large all-bisques which were carried in department and specialty stores and for which we longed and prayed with unholy desire. Some of us remember having jointed dolls with similar heads which we now know were Heubach but which to us were just *different* from the typical German Christmas dolls we found under the tree in many sizes.

Her complexion coat is not as good as old Heubach products but it is satisfactory and the head is beautifully done. She has side-painted eyes with slight brown irises and highlight dots, one-stroke brows like the hair, and a very pretty mouth, but the hair is her most outstanding feature. Molded in a childish, slightly curled cut, the base coat was done in a dull blond color and darker blond paint was skillfully applied over it to simulate carefully combed hair. The molded circular hairband is bright blue.

A duplicate in the Strong Collection has brown hair with a bright orange hairband.

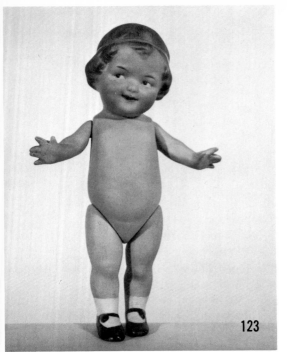

123

124

124

125

123 Author's collection; 124 & 125 Strong collection

Both have white socks with crosshatch molded patterns and their glossy, one-strap, heelless slippers are luggage tan with molded side pompons on the straps.

No. 124 This 9-inch doll has always attracted a great deal of attention, even in the enormous collection housed in Margaret W. Strong's private museum, but it was not classified as Heubach. Besides having the star hands, it is the only one with an incised mark, **10490** over **3**. Such four- and five-figure numbers in the same kind of print are frequently found on completely marked Heubach pieces.

She has intaglio pupils with relief white highlights, both Heubach features in piano babies and dolls. Even more than that, she *looks* like many of the charming, turned-head children Heubach produced in such great numbers and sizes—the Dutch girl, for instance, which can be found both sitting and standing both alone and together with her Dutch brother.

Like the others, this doll is hip and shoulder jointed with excellent loops which fit into precise holes, and she is well balanced to stand alone, an uncommon feature in hip jointed all-bisques. Her hands and feet are in much better proportion than most German dolls of any manufacture. The irises are light brown, she has black lid linings, red eye and nose dots, and one-stroke gray-brown brows. Her open-closed mouth has one lower and two upper teeth showing. The white socks have vertical molded ribbing and the dull, dark tan, flat-soled slippers have high molded center bows.

Her beautifully molded and painted hair is just delightful. The base coat is a dull gray-brown like her brows and then a darker coat was applied so skillfully that it gives the illusion not only of careful combing but also of highlights and additional curl. This darker coat is glossy and, starting with brush marks on the forehead, covers the entire hairdo with practiced ease. The molded bows are glossy lavender-pink and a molded, painted band goes around the back of the head from the two ear bows—in America early in this century the band ran across the tops of little girls' heads between bows like these or rosettes of ribbon.

The bisque is excellent, the weight is very good, the workmanship is beautiful Heubach quality. The complexion coat is a medium tone but Heubach never did make pale, frail children. Her body, with a change in the shoe-strap decoration, was used for the Smiling Girl which seems to prove that this doll with bows was the earlier edition.

No. 125 Although her bob with bangs is a much more modern hairdo, this 8¾-inch girl has the same body and shoes as the girl with the three molded bows.

In this instance the base coat of the hair was a dull sand color and the brush-marks treatment was dark blond. She does not have the brush marks on her forehead, however. The eyes have shallow intaglio pupils with highlights and brown iris rims and, of course, she has the star hands.

She was photographed in the dainty, machine-made underwear which is like that on the girl with three bows. This girl also has a dress exactly like the one on the previous doll, the only exception being that the pink shoulder ribbon is modern and obviously a replacement. Both dresses are voile-like material with small sprigs of colored flowers and the same lace spans the waistline.

Since they came from different sources at different times, there is a great temptation to believe that they were sold dressed. It is doubtful, however, from the records available to us now, that this work was done by Heubach. It is more logical to assume that they were very special items in shops which catered to what was then known as "the carriage trade."

The Gebruder (Brothers) Heubach firm of Sonneberg is dated by the Colemans from 1820 in Lichte, Thuringia, although their trade address was always given as Sonneberg. They were still listed in directories at the beginning of the twentieth century and that would cover the production period of all these dolls.

So, until positive proof can be uncovered one way or the other, this series with the odd little hands can be considered Heubach with more certainty than usually results from these detective jaunts into the past.

17

Goebel

No. 126 Swivel necked, hip and shoulder jointed with loops, this little Dutch girl carries the uncommon all-bisque mark of an old German firm, W. Goebel of Thuringia. This does not necessarily mean they did not make a great many all-bisques, but they certainly did not mark them.

The blue eyes have slightly intaglio pupils and black lid linings, and the short bangs and eyebrows are dark blond. The bisque, the weight, and the finishing and decorating are all very good. The short molded socks are blue and the one-strap black slippers have very low heels.

Her most outstanding feature, aside from the mark, is the Dutch cap. The white front band is molded into a ribbed band and, at half-inch intervals, is further decorated with small, incised, 7-petal flowers. It also has a horseshoe or "covered wagon" molded back panel with a molded band to hold the neck gathers and the top and back have been flocked with a very fine brown material.

There is a good chance that the next two dolls are also Goebel products, later than the Dutch doll which carries the factory marking. They are incised with numbers instead of the crown and initials and they were classified as products of the same factory long before the Dutch doll came up for comparison.

The bodies are all alike, with unusual knee depressions in horseshoe shapes; fat modeled on the insides of the legs is uncommon; the feet are the same; and in these glass eyed ones, the eyes are so large that almost none of the white shows. There is also a flaw in the workmanship which we seldom find from such experienced firms as Kestner, for example. The

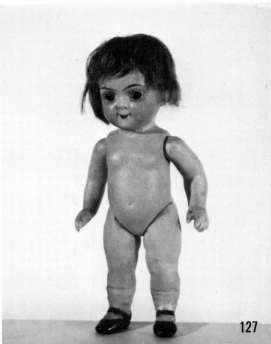

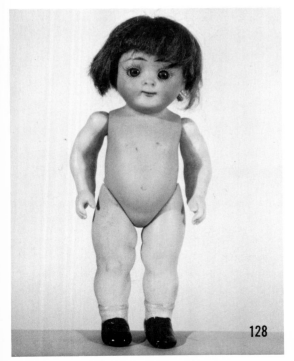

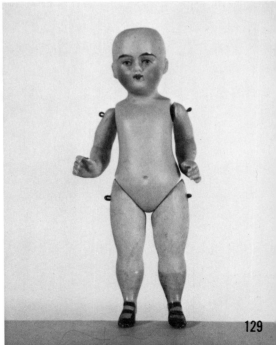

126 Strong collection; 127, 128 & 129 Author's collection

Dutch girl and **No.** 127 have yellow soles but the black paint does not stop neatly at the edges of the soles. Instead, it is smeared very carelessly over the sole and the bottom of the heel.

It is quite possible, of course, that these were made under contract for a distributor and the Goebel name was deliberately eliminated.

No. 127 Incised on the head **401** over **16** and 6½ inches tall, this one has brown sleep eyes with upper and lower painted lashes and wavering brown brows. The mouth has a deep lower lip in a watermelon shape and the complexion coating is very high on very glossy bisque. The original light brown mohair wig is on a cloth cap with a cardboard dome. The molded low socks are the same glossy blue with blue bands as **No. 126.**

No. 128 Incised **217** over **16** on the back of the head, this one has blue sleep eyes which have been set, the same upper and lower painted lashes, and one-stroke glossy brown brows. The mouth is a paler color but it is a lip added to a molded watermelon shape. The complexion coat is pale and the very good bisque is without the high lustre of the previous doll.

Because of the lower incised number and the better color, this one may be the older and the incised **16** may indicate it was made for the same buyer. All this guessing worries some people but we have no other way of accumulating information about these little dolls. Eventually, if we make enough notes, some of this guessing may turn into facts.

These blue socks are the same odd shade, very glossy, and with darker blue bands, and they are molded lower on the ankles, like the Dutch doll's. The shoes look like an attempt to create oxfords, or "low cuts" as they were frequently called, but they are painted over the same molded one-strap detail as on the other two dolls. In this instance the soles are painted completely black, which solved the careless decorating on the others.

The wig belongs to the previous doll but it is quite possible that this one had a short wig, or a Buster Brown cut with bangs, in an attempt to create a boy.

Collectors of pincushion tops are more familiar with this old mark than are all-bisque collectors. The firm had every right to be proud of the beautiful pincushion ladies with a great variety of hairdos and it is quite possible that to them the all-bisque doll business was nothing more than "pot boiling" which kept the factory busy all the time, gave them ample opportunity to train decorators, and provided additional income.

130 *Author's collection*

Kling

In *Dolls, Makers and Marks,* page 44, Elizabeth A. Coleman lists the Kling firm of Ohrdruf, Thuringia, from 1863 through the Bye-Lo heads in the 1920s. "They made all porcelain dolls, both the so-called 'Frozen Charlotte' type and jointed all porcelain dolls especially in smaller sizes," the book states.

Nos. 129 and **130** These are two of those "all porcelain" dolls incised on the top of the head with the famous Kling mark, known to all collectors as "a K in a bell."

Both dolls have the word **Germany** in the old script incised on the backs of the bodies and individual numbers under the trademark. They were so beautifully finished the numbers are difficult to decipher but appear to be 5'0 15 on the 6-inch pincushion and 9'1 11 on the undressed doll.

This is the type of construction collectors have come to consider as "old" because only the very tops of the heads are cut out for eye setting and/or push-in hank wigs such as the pincushion still has. The blond mohair is professionally dressed in two long braids down her back. Both are strung with brass wire and the bodies are not only wide at the hips but also slightly potbellied.

The undressed doll has blue, horizontally ribbed socks and black, two-strap slippers with heels; the pincushion's socks are black and the slippers of the same type are jade green.

These dolls pose a problem.

Even though they have **Germany** incised on their backs, we must remember that, out of sheer pride of workmanship, some German firms marked their products before it was required by law.

These are of such excellent quality it is safe to say that they belong in the 1890-1900 range. Competition became so furious after 1900 that this type of excellence fell by the wayside.

Limbach

The trefoil, or clover leaf, incised on the backs of the following two dolls is familiar to collectors in many fields. It appears on the black haired bisque shoulder head commonly known as "The Irish Queen." Apparently the mark was mistaken for a shamrock somewhere along the line and in many areas the aloof lady with the decorated shoulder plate and the blue bow across the top of her rather elegant hairdo still carries the title. Collectors also peer hopefully at the bases of pincushion tops for this mark, although in the small space available on these collectibles the clover leaf is frequently malformed.

The story of this firm is very complicated and is explained in detail in Coleman's *Dolls, Makers and Marks* on page 27. These dolls are evidently some of the porcelain dolls and "bathing children" advertised in 1897. This pair have a mark which differs from others given for the firm, so it should be added. Each is topped by a number but the basic mark is:

No.131 Incised across the top of the mark P.85.0, 7½-inches, hip and shoulder jointed with wire, there is a 1900s feeling about this doll, so the firm must have continued in operation into the twentieth century or sold their molds and rights to a firm which remained active.

131 & 132 *Author's collection*

The molded bob is a bright yellow, the bows are blue with a slight glaze. What appeared to be spilled glaze on the cheeks was nothing but colorless nail polish, however, because a careful application of polish remover whisked it off. She has painted blue eyes with very high pupils, black lid linings, and light brown one-stroke brows. The white socks have vertical ribbing and blue bands; the one-strap, heelless slippers are brown.

The finishing is not well done and the complexion coating is very mottled, especially on the legs. The bisque is good and the weight is excellent but the workmanship is shoddy.

No. 132 Incised across the top of the mark, **P. 23,** this 5½-inch toddler may be later than the larger doll. Also hip and shoulder jointed with wire, the molded hair is washed carelessly with brown and the small blue bow on the right side is molded into the hair rather than standing free. She has blue eyes with high pupils, black lid linings and brown one-stroke brows.

The vertical ribbing is almost gone from the blue banded socks and the brown slippers have slight heels. One molded strap was not painted and not noticed on inspection. The bisque and the weight are both good but the finishing is poor and the complexion coating is only fair—much better than the larger doll's but not high German quality.

No. 133 Incised in three lines on the back **8675**, the clover leaf, and **GERMANY** in a straight line, this infant is included here with his similarly marked sisters. He is 5½ inches lying as flat as he can, he sits 4⅜ inches and has a 5-inch head circumference.

The neck is unusual. At a casual glance it looks like a flat cut swivel with an inner rim like the Putnam Bye-Lo Baby (**No. 273**) or the Averill "Bonnie Babe" (**No. 280**), but it is an adaptation of the French molded loop. There is a ⅛-inch molded set-back which rests on the neck hole in the body and in the center of this there is a molded round plug ½ inch long. The bottom portion of the plug narrows to half its width and there is a left to right stringing hole through the base.

Like **No. 180**, this fellow's leg holes are cut into the lower abdomen but he is not potbellied. Unlike most infants, however, his legs do not spread out when he sits. In fact, he can sit *on* a chair, or sit *up* because he

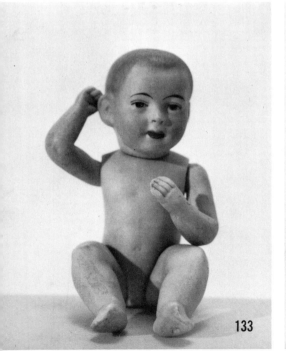 

133 & 134 Author's collection

balances on his flat seat and his heels but when he is on his back his legs stay up in the air.

Hip and shoulder jointed with good loops, he has slightly intaglio pupils, gray irises, black lid linings, red lid lines, and one-stroke brown brows. His dark blond hair is only slightly molded. He is well finished and the complexion is not too high, but the bisque is heavy and dull to the touch, without the early sharpness.

S W C

No. 134 Whether this could be a Strobel & Wilkin doll is open to debate and anybody may join in. Instead of having the superimposed **S** over the wide **W** which is given as two of their marks in *Dolls, Makers and Marks* (page 71), this little girl is marked in a straight line across the head **S W C**, and above that there is the figure **12**.

Using logic rather loosely, there does not seem to be anybody else who used those initials in the pre-World War I period and she could have been made to their order by Kestner, especially judging by her legs.

She is 4½ inches, hip and shoulder jointed with loops, and has an open mouth with molded teeth which are most interesting. After the mouth was cut along the edge of the lower lip, a knife or some serrated tool was used to cut the teeth through the entire thickness of the face and, consequently, under magnification they look like the teeth on a thick file.

She has painted dark blue eyes with black lid linings and overly large pupils, which were carelessly done, and one-stroke blond brows. The excellent dark blond mohair wig is original and it is on a good cloth cap. It has a machine-sewn center part and the hair is professionally done in two braids wrapped around the head. This is another hairdo little girls used in the early part of this century, especially in summer.

She has vertically ribbed white socks with dark blue bands, and one-strap black heeled slippers with tan soles. As usual, the torso is better complexioned and not mottled as the arms and legs are, with the legs the poorest.

18

King Kestner

Because this book abounds in suspected Kestners, and, in the author's opinion, the beautiful Frozen Charlotte **No. 46** may be one because the hands so closely resemble a style that Kestner used for many years, a chapter about this famous firm may seem ridiculous or redundant, depending on your point of view. But it isn't, really. So many collectors and dealers have such fixed notions about what is and what is not a Kestner, the generally accepted late types should be given their special place.

In *Dolls, Makers and Marks*, Elizabeth Coleman gives 1805 as the starting date for this firm in the papier-maché-toy field and the founder is said to have been "one of the first doll makers to have his own establishment." This certainly places the firm among the early practitioners in the doll industry.

There is also some interesting background material on this family. On page 43 the book states, "Johann Daniel Kestner, Jr. succeeded his father. The firm of J. D. Kestner, Jr. expanded with the erection at Ohrdruf, Thuringia, of a porcelain factory under the name of Kestner & Co. where the firm was able to make their own china and bisque doll heads. As far as is known, Kestner was the only German doll maker who made entire dolls (heads, bodies, etc.). . . . Kestner was one of the firms that made Kewpies when they came out in 1913 and Bye-Lo heads and all-bisque dolls in the 1920s."

It is unfortunate, but very likely unavoidable, that Miss Coleman does not mention the year in which the son took over from the father.

These stiff necks, ranging in size from 10½ inches down, have variations of two different stock numbers, but they all have many Kestner characteristics. It is truly amazing how many dolls this manufacturer put on the market through the decades by the simple procedure of maintaining quality features and switching combinations.

All the painting is very uniform and good Kestner quality. The glossy, multistroke eyebrows are like those found on so many identifiable dolls and infants from this firm. All have upper and lower black eye linings, but only some of them have painted upper lashes. This is not a factory error because they undoubtedly originally had "real eyelashes" which Kestner often advertised.

All the sock patterns were retained and interchanged at will but the shoes advanced with the times. All are hip and shoulder jointed with excellent sturdy loops and all the incised marks are high on the head.

No. 135 This husky 10½-inch boy is incised 150 over 6. His blue sleep eyes have only lower painted lashes. The shirred blue socks have no top bands and the one-strap black slippers have heels, molded front pompons, and strap buttons.

There is a 9¾-inch girl in the collection like this boy. She is a girl simply because she has a long, light brown mohair wig on a gauze base instead of a short one. She is incised 150 over 5, and her socks are pink without top bands.

No. 136 Incised 150 4, this 9-inch girl has her original, very light blond mohair wig with the familiar gauze base, but it is over a replacement cardboard dome. The light blue sleep eyes have been set and have only lower painted lashes. The high pink socks are vertically ribbed with deep rose top bands; the one-strap black slippers have heels and yellow soles.

These three dolls with the same stock number, 150, indicate that there was a ¾-inch difference between the sizes, so the others would be: 8¼ inches, 3; 7½ inches, 2; and 6¾ inches, 1.

No. 137 Incised x 150 4, this doll is also 9 inches tall and she has blue sleep eyes with both upper and lower painted lashes. The high pink socks are vertically ribbed with magenta top bands. Her heeled black slippers have unusually wide painted bands and yellow soles. The brown human-hair wig may or may not be original.

No. 138 Incised 208 over 8 and 8¾ inches tall, this doll has brown sleep eyes with painted upper and lower lashes. Her vertically ribbed socks are white unpainted bisque with blue top bands and the one-strap, heeled black slippers have yellow soles. She has what appears to be an original brown mohair wig on a gauze cap.

135

136

137

138

135, 136, 137 & 138 Author's collection

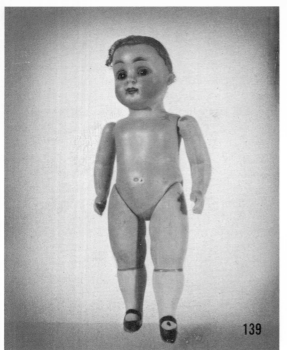 

139 & 140 Author's collection

No. 139 This is the same doll in the next smaller size. She is incised **208** over **7** and is 8 inches tall. This also indicates a ¾-inch size differential so there was a 9¾-inch size between the big boy and girl, and 8¼- and 7½-inch sizes between 4 and 1, so size 1 must have been 6¾ inches.

The fancy, glossy, colored socks on the two largest dolls could have been an added feature for a different price range. Most of the litttle Candy-store dolls from Kestner have plain white socks with blue bands which are very attractive. This design speeded up production because the shoes did not have to dry before the socks could be painted or vice versa.

All the bisque is very good and so is the finishing but the decorating on the boy and the two wigless girls is superior to the other two—a mass-production variable. Several things could be responsible for the trouble in the skin tone, which is not uniform—some trouble with the bisque in a later production period, a fault in the paint, or inexperienced decorators, for instance. There is no way to be sure. All the production standards were high, however, as evidenced by the nicely filled pour holes in the soles of all the shoes.

Four of these dolls, as well as **No. 105**, the doll with the yellow shoes and long hose, have another peculiarity which may help to identify other suspected Kestners—all but the 6¾-inch specimen have heads warped out of the round shape.

In some, the warping is so bad that the top opening is oval, **No. 140**, but it does not disturb the face. It does affect the narrow shelf rim extending around the top of the head which should hold the wig. In the small, unwarped head, the wig rim is complete around the head, as shown in the head on the left in **No. 141**. In the others this rim is gone entirely or extends only from ear to ear in the back, as on the right in **No. 141**. Perhaps this is the reason that none but the boy has a cardboard dome and all the wigs are the more expensive type with a gauze base, such as the gauze still clinging to the one doll's head, **No. 139**. The wigs on gauze could be firmly glued to hide the warping entirely.

Modern porcelain dollmakers in America would discard these dolls, although it is very doubtful that one person, working alone, would have such a problem repeatedly. The warping could have occurred if the green-

141

141 Author's collection

ware was unmolded prematurely or was handled before it reached the proper leather state, or it could have been caused by poor heat circulation in some areas of the kiln. It seems more likely, in mass production, that the kilns were at fault because we know there was great difficulty in controlling the heat. One does wonder how many fired dolls never found their way to the decorators at all, however, if these were considered "passable."

It is rather evident that the self-styled "King" of dollmakers in Germany did not let anything which could be covered by a wig bother his output. After all, they were only toys!

The pieces of wood set in plaster inside these heads are nothing more than backstops for the sleep eyes. Some idea of the haste with which they were assembled can be gained by studying these little bars. They worked in almost any position and that is where they are—in almost any position.

It is always very satisfying to a doll researcher when proof of all the pondering, comparing, measuring, studying, and worrying comes along.

No. 142 Apparently in mint condition, because she has a perfect Kestner label, this girl has her original reddish-brown mohair wig with red ribbon bows and no signs of wear from play. This is the late Kestner label without the pendant streamers which are so often found stamped on kid-bodied Kestners.

Incised **150.1** up at the head cut, 6¾ inches tall, she is hip and shoulder jointed with good loops. The brown sleep eyes have "real" upper and painted lower lashes. There are four teeth in the open mouth, which has the squared-off Kestner ends on the top lip, and she has nose dots. The blue socks with dark blue bands are vertically ribbed by rows of small dots between the ridges and her one-strap black shoes have heels and pouring fill-ins in each sole.

The complexion tinting is satisfactory, although the legs are slightly deeper pink than the torso and arms, and the well-molded hands are nicely finished. The original wig, with the center part machine sewn in white, is on a gauze base. The wig is supported by a cardboard dome which rests on a complete rim around the head.

Since this head is not warped, the question naturally arises: Is that why she wears a Kestner label? This blue, red, and gold label would appeal to a child and it seems odd that there should be no signs of labels ever having been on dozens of these dolls which have been examined. The warped heads are common enough but, if they once had labels, they have long since disappeared.

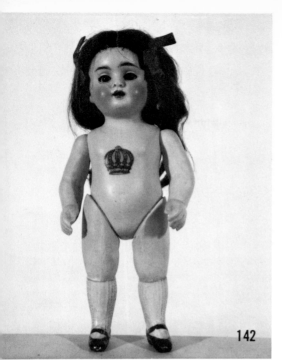

142

142

143

142 & 143 Author's collection

No. 143 Another open mouth Kestner with the sawed teeth which were molded. This one is 4¾ inches and incised on the head in two lines **257** and **12**; the arms are marked **12** and the legs are **150** on the flange, and **3** on the inside of the thigh. The rather poor arms for this firm (and because of the figure 12 they must be original for this doll) fit into very good shoulder rims in the torso.

The legs could be "seconds" from the firm's own dolls, hence the **150** mark. While the white socks have blue bands and are shirred, and the brown two-strap slippers are the ones with black bows, heels, and sole rims, the calves of these legs have lost their roundness and are quite flat from the knees down.

The torso is very good. It has an excellent flat ridge around the entire back of the head on which the dome rested, and the head is not warped. The eyes are blue with pupils and black lid linings; the one-stroke brows are dark blond. The complexion coating on the legs is as good as that of the torso and only the arms are mottled.

It is interesting that in the 1908 Butler Brothers Wholesale Catalogue they say: "Our four houses buy and sell more dolls than any other in America." They list quite a good selection of these Candystore types under the heading: "Solid Bisque Dolls" but describe them in the text as: "real bisque hollow dolls." Instead of "hip and shoulder jointed," the terms now used, they describe them as both "free arms and legs" and "jointed arms." We now use "jointed arms" to mean dolls with elbow joints.

They list these dolls in several kinds and in three main sizes: 3¾-inch at 38 cents a dozen; 4½-inch at 42 cents a dozen, and 6-inch at 75 cents a dozen. In the descriptions to the storekeepers there is an added note: "Big Dime Doll" with another size at 79 cents a dozen.

Inasmuch as the prices generally ranged from 10 cents to as much as 39 cents each in the candystores, it is now possible to understand the great patience those proprietors showed—for a profit. Unhappily, many of these little dolls did not last a week.

On page 236 of the same catalogue, Butler Brothers illustrate an all-bisque with the word "Kestner" printed across her chest in white against the skin tone. This was undoubtedly for the benefit of storekeepers who were familiar with the other Kestner lines. The headline above this little doll says: "The genuine. Made by the king of doll makers." Mr. Kestner was never shy. He was also the man who called his dolls "Royal."

The Kestner sizes, prices and descriptions are:

3¾ in. jointed arms and legs, curly wig, natural glass eyes and features, fancy painted shoes and stockings   Doz.   87¢

5¼ in. stout, natural moving glass eyes   Doz. 2.10

5¾ in. ½ doz. in box   Doz. 1.80

7 in.   sewed wig   Doz. 3.95

9⅜ in. sewed curly wig, double ribbon bow tying; real eyelashes   Doz. 8.40

At least in the eastern section of the country, anything over 6 inches appeared only in small towns with the Christmas toys, although they could be purchased year round in large department stores in New York, Philadelphia, and other cities, and thus came to us as awe-inspiring birthday presents or gifts from visitors.

ℳ **19**

Molded
Clothes and
Hair

German dolls with molded clothes as well as molded hair have an almost universal appeal which even extends to people who are not collectors. Many of them are made of rather sharp bisque, but some types were allowed to set to only a very thin shell, which gives them a hollow sound when handled. The quality would have been improved in many of them if they had been more carefully finished but they were mass produced and, for what they are, they make a valuable contribution to a collection.

Believed to be among the oldest of this type are those with daintily ruffled one-piece underwear trimmed in either pink or blue. Very few of them are incised as to origin unless they are later issues of a previously popular doll. Those that are marked, however, prove the contention that they are German.

No. 144 Incised 6 on the torso and all the limbs, the large, 6¼-inch specimen is strung with old brass wire. The hair is very pale blond with fairly good comb marks and the complexion is pale. The brows are glossy brown and the blue eyes with centered pupils have black lid linings and red lid lines; the trim is blue. With the exception of the arms, the finishing and decorating are both well done. The shoulders are closed and the tops of the arms are flat.

Faint mold lines down the outside of the legs in the back and down the inside on the front indicate that the complete bows and the toes were in one mold, while the heels and insides of the legs were in the other half.

The distressing hollow sound in this doll is exaggerated because oval holes, ⅝ of an inch long and ⅜ of an inch wide, mar the inside tops of the leg flanges. The extra slip was poured through these holes, of course,

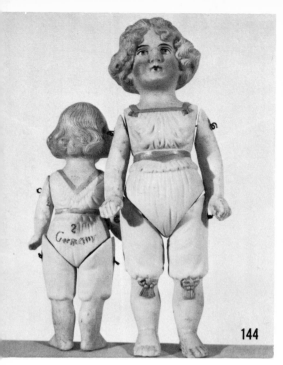
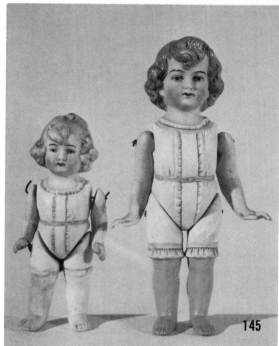

and they did not bother to fill them because when the stringing wire was new and tight, the disfigurement did not show. At these holes the extreme thinness of the bisque can be seen.

Her 4¾-inch companion is incised 2 on the inside leg flanges and torso but across the rounded seat in back the word **Germany** has been penciled in to show the crescent shape. This doll shows signs of being a later issue for additional reasons and may have been among the Candystore dolls before World War I.

Although the painting is the same, the complexion color is much higher and the comb-marked hair is yellower. Her trim is done in glossy rose color and she also has brass wire. The oval pour holes in the legs are large in proportion to her size.

The backs as well as the fronts of these dolls show the same detailed modeling of the underwear and painting of the trim, which is not true in many other specimens.

No. 145 Very likely from the same original period, perhaps the 1890s, these dolls appear to have been made by a different firm. The hair of the larger, 5½-inch girl is beautifully modeled with overlapping curls and comb marks, as well as good, deep blond decorating. The hair and all the trim, which is rose, is glossy. The blue eyes have high-placed pupils, black lid linings, and red eye lines; the brows are brown.

She is a quality product of her type and all the workmanship is excellent. The torso has molded shoulder sockets, the tops of the arms have molded shoulder balls and the lifted hands are unusually well modeled and finished. Her complexion tinting is pale. The legs are darker because one was broken and they had to be retinted when she was repaired.

This doll has a nice, substantial feeling indicative of all-bisque quality. She is not a thin shell and her leg tops are completely closed and well finished. She is hollow but she does not echo at the slightest touch.

The 4-inch companion is not a duplicate of the larger doll and very likely she is a later issue, even though she is not marked. Her trim is blue.

The hair is a different style, painted a dull, pale yellow and without

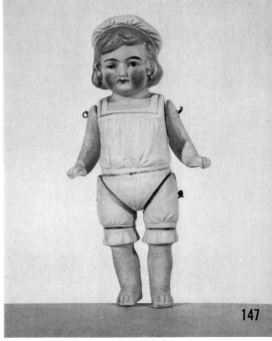

146 Brewer collection; 147 Strong collection

comb marks. The red eyelid lines are gone, the pupils are centered in the blue eyes and only one eye has a black lid lining from speeded-up mass production. The shoulder socket was eliminated, a small ruffle to fit the shoulder was added and the arms were flattened to fit the changed construction. The pretty hands have been replaced with a very common type and both the finishing and tinting of the limbs are inferior to the other doll.

No. 146 Unmarked but obviously from the same maker as the previous dolls because it has the same underwear, this 6½-inch doll is shoulder jointed with hard wire. As the picture shows, the feet tip up through an error somewhere along the line, and she cannot stand alone.

The blue painted eyes have high pupils, black lid linings, and red lid lines. The well-done curly hair is pale yellow, the brows are dark blond. The complexion coat is rather mottled but not too high in color. The suit trim and tam o'shanter pompon are glossy rose.

Although this doll is a very satisfactory weight and the arms are in good proportion, she does not have the good shoulder sockets and arm tops of the larger hip and shoulder jointed specimen.

No. 147 Hip and shoulder jointed with hard wire, this 5¼-inch child has the previously illustrated crescent **Germany** in the seat, along with the figure 3, which is also incised in plain sight on the backs of the legs. It was undoubtedly made by the firm that made the other dolls.

The mass-production processing was not as good, however. The eye painting was not too accurate, so one pupil with blue rim is larger than the other, and the one-stroke dark brown brows do not match very well. The cheeks are very bright and the complexion is quite pale. The molded hair is yellow and all the trim is in rose.

This torso is better than that of the other dolls because the pour hole was in the top of the cap and the hip flanges are closed. But there are large, gaping holes in the inside tops of the legs and another large one mars the inner side of the left upper arm.

The large, flat shoulder areas seem to have been designed for arms with puff sleeves, which would have been more attractive. These arms are original but they are small.

No. 148 This may be the little brother of the last doll. He is 4⅜ inches tall and is incised on the seat with the crescent **Germany,** and in the dip of the crescent the size number appears: **2½.**

The suit modeling on these two is extremely good but modeling had to be done only once whereas trimming and decorating was a never-ending task. His trim is blue and with the exception of the back of the collar, extends around the back. His specifications are like those of the little girl except that his complexion is mottled.

It is difficult to classify all-bisque infants by age because so many of them are unmarked but those with old-fashioned molded clothes at least hint at their age. The subject of infants in the all-bisque world is taken up in a later chapter but these belong here.

No. 149 With a molded ribbed suit of knee-length underwear and a molded, shaped bib, this unmarked fellow may be before 1900 because those of us who were shopping in the years before World War I would have considered this an anachronism.

He sits 3½ inches tall and is 4½ inches when stretched out. He is hip and shoulder jointed with hard wire and has painted blue eyes with high pupils, black lid linings and red nose dots. The hair is a light blond wash, with only a small top lock molded. The complexion is pale.

The amount of detail is surprising. There are molded turned back cuffs, molded button closure down the back of the suit, and the bib, which is trimmed with a line of medium blue, comes to precise points in the back. The fists are closed but the arms are not alike and he has the raised big toes found on almost all identifiable composition baby bodies by Kestner.

No. 150 Also hip and shoulder jointed with hard wire, this boyish looking infant sits 3½ inches tall and is 4½ inches stretched out. He has painted blue eyes with high pupils, black lid linings, dark blond brows, and red nose dots. The hair is a blond wash without any molded detail.

This shirt is also well done and it appears to be a later type of baby attire. The painted neckband is medium blue and there is uncolored white "embroidery" above it and fine tucking molded below it.

To collectors of small immobile dolls, or figurines if you prefer, this doll will undoubtedly bring to mind the series of kneeling and sitting children whose clothing is very similar.

The complexion coat is slightly higher than that of the previous doll, the arms are not alike but the hands are open, and the raised toes are the same.

Collectors feel that these may have been old general-store and department-store dolls, prior to 1910. Like the author, some of the collectors had

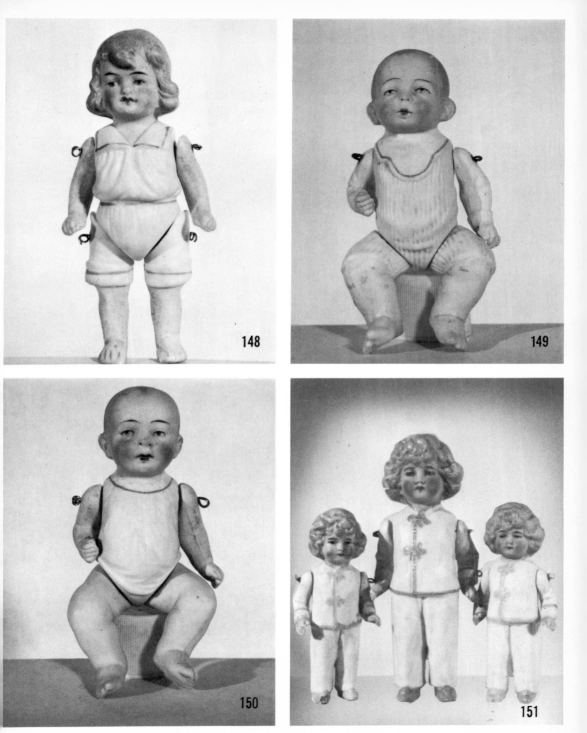

148 & 151 *Author's collection;* 149 & 150 *Strong collection*

a passion for these dolls even as children, and they had their own money to buy them, but they do not remember these at all. Our all-bisque infants were pinker and quite nude but also entirely sexless.

No. 151 These three in blue-trimmed pajamas are in two sizes, 4 inches and 5¾ inches, of the same doll and there is also an excellent 7½-inch size in the collection. Unmarked, with light blond hair which shows no comb marks, they have flat shoulders and arm tops and the same high complexion tinting as the later dolls. The brows are light brown, the eyes have black lid linings only, and the pupils are centered. There are faint signs of vertical stripes in the suits to indicate pajama cloth but the fairly good finishing process wore off much of the pattern.

They are substantial to the touch and quite sharp, and the excess slip was poured from the back molds at the tops of the heads. A round, filled-in spot in the crown of each head catches the experienced eye but it is very well done.

No. 152 In a sailor suit, without marks, 3½ inches tall, shoulder jointed

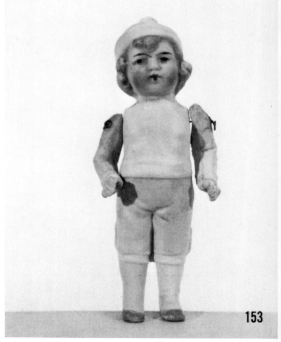

152

153

152 & 153 Author's collection

with hard wire, this is another excellent little doll. The modeling and finishing are good, the molded hair is blond, the suit is bisque white, and the trim is pale blue.

Butler Brothers Wholesale Catalogue for Fall 1908 lists these dolls in a bordered display box as follows:

"SAILOR BOY" BISQUE DOLLS

Big Value   5 and 10 centers

F4072—4⅛ in., flesh tinted faces hands and legs, painted features and hair, white costume and hat, blue and pink painted trimmings, shoes and socks. 1 doz. in box. Per dozen, 41¢.

F4074—5⅝ in., as F4072, jointed arms and legs. ½ doz. in box. Per doz. 78¢

The largest one examined, the hip and shoulder jointed mentioned above, was the same fine bisque and workmanship as the small one in this collection.

To this generation it seems truly incredible that a wholesale house could make a profit on such a beautiful little item at these prices but it is quite understandable that they measured to the eighth of inches in setting prices. It was common practice for such large importers to pay their own shipping and customs charges and if that were true in this instance, and Butler Brothers was a very big firm, the German porcelain works must have sold these dolls for pennies, boxed.

Such specific instances certainly add credence to the German immigrants' stories about working conditions, starvation wages, and child-labor practices in Germany.

No. 153 Shoulder jointed with hard wire, this 4¼-inch boy with a molded white cap, sweater, and high stockings has blue pants; his molded hair and flat shoes are yellow. He has large pupils with narrow blue rims and dark, one-stroke brows.

He is cute but the workmanship is shoddy. He has mold debris in his hands, unfinished mold lines, and rather poor decorating.

Listed in Butler Brothers 1908 "Santa Claus Edition" Catalogue, he came in assorted dozens with the little Sailor Boy and they were 48 cents per assorted dozens. That price certainly explains the statement to storekeepers at the top of the page: "The profits are very satisfactory." Because the

154

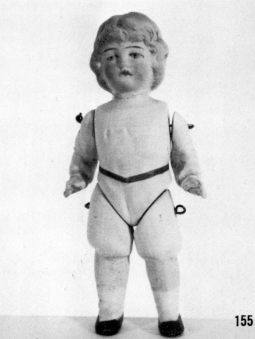

155

156

157

154, 155, 156 & 157 Author's collection

Sailor Boy is so much better quality, Butler Brothers undoubtedly made up those "assorted dozens" themselves.

Clothing helps to date many of these dolls and the hairdos on those without molded clothes serve the same purpose—for what it is worth, of course. When new styles in children's clothing became established here, new dolls had to be modeled and working molds had to be made in Germany. It has been estimated that this process took about a year in most cases. Little clues, such as the gradual loss of comb marks in the hair and poor finishing are more helpful in age determination than such variables as poor decorating or improper firing, for instance. But it is getting to be a long time since the early 1900s and many of these little dolls are very satisfactorily old right now.

No. 154 In romper suits and boots, pre-World War I, this pair are good examples, but where the Germans got the idea that small American boys wore boots like these is difficult to fathom.

The 7-inch doll is tinted with orange and his belt, cuffs, and collar are deep orange. They can also be found in a wide array of tints with contrasting trim—pink, blue, yellow, and green. The 3¾-inch size has a natural white bisque suit with pastel blue trim. Both have brown boots and blond hair and the eyes are intaglio side molded with painted blue rims.

No. 155 Another, more modified version of this attire, this white romper suit has an all-over cloth pattern molded in the material. Unmarked, 4 inches, hip and shoulder jointed with wire, this one also has the large underarm pour holes.

He is complexion tinted, the cuffs and collar bands are pink, the belt is red, and the shoes are black. The bisque is sharp.

No. 156 Without marks, this 4-inch girl in a bathing suit has rubber strung arms. She is of good bisque and the modeling is good on the hair, on the circular ribbing of the hat, and on the high chest bow. The suit is white and her face and limbs are complexion tinted. Her shoes, leg bindings, and collar are blue, the bow is red, and there is a pale green rim on the hat.

No. 157 Incised on the head 576/1, this 3¾-inch Indian is good, old bisque and very well done, even to the molded flaps on the moccasins. It is wire shoulder jointed and deeply complexion tinted. The dress is pale yellow trimmed with red and blue, and the moccasins are deep yellow.

The head hole is covered with a small piece of dark material so it is not known whether there originally was a wig or not. The doll does not appear to have been played with at all, however, and the hair patch is a piled fabric, so the presumption is that it is original.

No. 158 In molded coat and bow, without marks, 3⅞ inches tall, wire shoulder jointed, this little girl has the gaping inside arm holes noted in the series, which may be from the manufacturer for Amberg. The finishing is not as good as some of the dolls but the coat is white bisque, the lapels are pink, the bow and shoes are blue, and the belt is pale green.

No. 159 Advertising symbols and characters from the comic strips were formerly, as now, in great demand. This boy in a bright red suit and red tam counts on both scores because he was the symbol for Buster Brown shoes and was the "Dennis the Menace" of the comics of his era.

The 3¾-inch specimen pictured is shown with a metal paperweight dog which is very similar to (and may well be) Buster's constant companion, Tige, an English bulldog who also invaded many phases of American life in both inanimate and animate form.

No. 160 Unmarked, 4½ inches tall, shoulder jointed with wire, this little Dutch girl is well molded and finished, and is of excellent bisque. The eyes are molded but only side painted. Her apron is pink, all the bands are taffy blond like the hair, and her Dutch sabots are brown. Her complexion tinting is even and nicely done.

Nos. 161 and 162 In the 1910 decade, long-waisted suits and dresses of this type were very popular for children in the United States, so, give or take a year or two, that should date this pair and the pairs which follow. Although all of them are unmarked, they are undoubtedly from the same factory.

Shoulder jointed with hard wire, these are each 7¼ inches tall; they have shallow intaglio eyes with blue rims around black pupils, black lid linings, and dark blond, one-stroke brows. The excellent complexions are pale.

The boy has dark blond hair. His white suit has a light green collar and belt, a dark tan tie, and yellow pants. His tan, tie shoes are flat soled and the socks are white.

The girl has light blond hair with a molded pink side bow. The white dress has light blue trimming and both the neckband and belt have a small design of molded depressions which imitate quite well the cutwork trim or the braid which often decorated these dresses. Above her pink,

158, 160 & 161 Author's collection; 159 Strong collection

162

163

164

165

162, 163, 164 & 165 Author's collection

heelless shoes, which have bright green ties, she has vertically ribbed, low white socks.

The bisque is sharp, both the finishing and decorating are good for the type and the modeling is accurate to a surprising degree.

Nos. 163 and 164 Unmarked, 7 inches tall, shoulder jointed with wire, this pair of Anglo-Saxon "Indians" have molded suits which closely resemble play outfits which have been available to American children since the early part of this century.

The feathers are tipped with yellow and orange; her headband is blue like the trimming down the front and around the edges of the blouse and skirt. His headband is tan, his collar is yellow, his fringe is brown, and the binding of the fringe forms an orange V down his chest. Her shoes are light brown and his exposed shoe tips are black.

They are of sharp old bisque which is well finished for the market they entered, but the decorating could have been much better. These are the same faces as those of the previous dolls but the quality is lower and this brings up the question: Are they later or were they made for a cheaper market?

He has a complexion coat but she does not, and her hands are tinted but his are not. There is an intaglio depression in the pupils but the eyes have no painted irises. Both have black eyelid lines and one-stroke brows.

These dolls have been seen with other color combinations, including green in the feathers and trim.

Nos. 165 and 166 The same pair, 6¾ inches tall, unmarked, shoulder jointed with wire and with flocked suits.

Flocking, which feels like rough suede, is made by a process wherein the parts to be covered are coated with glue or a substance resembling clear varnish and then subjected to a blowing treatment of flocking powder. This is done after the color decorating.

Greeting-card figures, pictures in books, and sometimes dollhouse furniture can be flocked. It is rather unpleasant to the touch, but some children enjoy handling such pieces, stroking them until the flocking eventually wears off.

In this pair the feathers are red and yellow at the tips; her headband is blue like the trim on the molded white front decoration, while his headband is tan and matches nothing else. Her collar is a reddish orange, his is yellow; the trim down his molded fringe is orange. She has white socks and brown shoes, his shoe tips are black.

On the boy the molded fringe around the bottom of the jacket and around the collar in back were flocked. He would be more attractive if it had been left white.

Although they have eyelid linings and red eye lines, as well as slightly intaglio pupils, the complexion tinting is not very good. It is adequate but nothing more.

Both have black hair but hers tends toward gray in the front curls; their arms are interchangeable because each has a closed right fist and an open left hand.

Nos. 167 and **168** The large doll in this pair and the doll which follows, each 6½ inches tall, are excellent illustrations of simple modeling variations in the same doll. They also point up the importance of the decorator in mass production of small articles.

Both have blue painted, molded headbands, but in the undressed doll the blond hair is pale and in the dressed doll it is much yellower. Both have blue painted eyes with high pupils, but in the dressed doll the eyes appear much larger because the decorator followed the outside molded line with the black lid lining and in the undressed doll the lid lining was run across above the center of the eye so that the outside, molded line appears to be the lid. In the dressed doll the mouth is much prettier because it is shaped and in the undressed doll it is a straight line.

The bisque is very good and it is by no means a thin shell. They are most attractive. The finishing on the little white dress is excellent and the floppy molded tie is painted blue.

These are quality products for their time and field. They were emptied of slip through the head but this time through a hole in the front mold which was carefully filled in at the greenware stage. They are rubber strung through good loops which fit into perfectly rounded and finished shoulder holes. An added point is that the arms are not alike. The bend in the left arm on the dressed doll is not as marked as it should be because she lost her lower arm and it had to be replaced.

The small doll is 3⅞ inches tall and she is a faithful reduction of her larger sister, even to the bent left arm. Precolored and unmarked, she may be a later issue or she may have been made for the price-conscious market because she is shoulder jointed with hard wire. The finishing is not as good

166

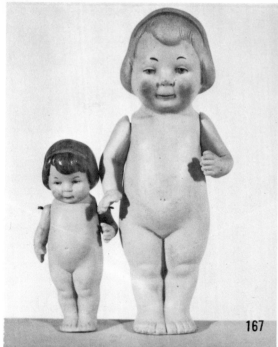

167

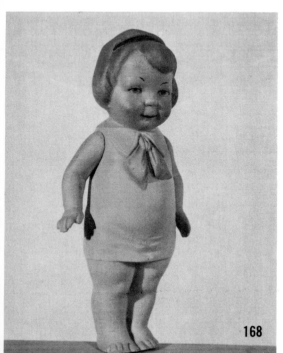

168

169

166 &167 Author's collection; 168 A Friend; 169 Strong collection

as that of the larger dolls because there is mold debris between her fingers, but this precolored bisque is far superior to the later type.

She has high pupils with blue rims and black lid linings; one-stroke brows match her hair which is "strawberry blond" and her molded head-band is glossy pink—both because of the precoloring. She has the same straight mouth as her sister.

No. 169 Not incised, but still wearing his good circular blue label with white lettering, this 5¾-inch lad in the knit sleeper is "Chubby" by L. W. & C., Germany. That is, of course, Louis Wolf & Co. who produced the "Our Fairy," **Nos. 262 and 263.**

Of excellent bisque which is well finished, he has molded hair painted a glossy, bright brown. His entire suit has a light blue wash and the trim is darker blue. There is a good, over-all herringbone pattern on his suit top and there is a molded closure with buttons in the back. His eyes are molded with side-painted pupils which have highlights and black lid linings. The brows are dabs of the hair color and his molded mouth is just a red line.

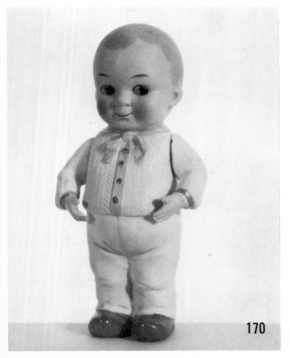

170

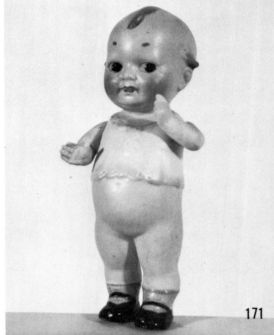

171

170 & 171 Author's collection

All the decorating is very good, the complexion is excellent and the rubber strung arms fit his rounded front to perfection. This is true of all the sizes examined.

In the November 1921, Butler Brothers Catalogue, under a caption: "A large variety of popular Japan imported dolls, including celluloid, bisque and china models" a doll closely resembling Wolf's "Chubby" was illustrated in bisque. He was without the molded suit, the size was given as 5½ inches and the price was 78 cents per dozen. The German "Baby Bud" was also shown in this listing and the price for these in the 5½-inch size was $1.25 per dozen.

In the December 1925 Catalogue, under "Imported Novelty Composition Dolls," the same illustration appears with shoes and socks added under the name of "Chubby Bud." In the 5¾-inch size these were 72 cents per dozen. Under "Imported Celluloid Dolls" the doll resembling "Chubby" appeared also and in the 5½-inch size the price was 84 cents a dozen and only $9.60 per gross. The German "Baby Bud" was still listed without any country of origin and in the 6¾-inch size the price had gone up to $1.95 per dozen.

No. 170 In knit sweater and pants, this 4¾-inch boy is not finished to satin smoothness, probably because the sanding would have removed the excellent herringbone design molded into his sweater. The bow, the band, the molded buttons, and the back detail are all equally good.

The suit is white, the tied neck scarf is light blue, the front band is pink with red buttons, and there are silver cuffs on the sweater. His boots are bright reddish brown and his hair is just a blond wash of color. He has a very good watermelon mouth and his side-painted eyes have white highlight dots.

No. 171 Another 5⅜-inch variation on this theme. Excellent bisque, well finished and decorated; the molded wisps of hair and the eyebrows are dark blond. The two-piece mouth is well done and the little shirt is molded to represent embroidery at the neck, down the front, and around the bottom. This edging is tinted blue and so are the socks, which are banded with dark blue. The one-strap slippers are black with yellow soles.

Like the previous doll, this one has very different hands. The bent right arm has a turned-back, wide open hand; the additionally bent left arm has a tight fist with the index finger raised in a "No! No!" gesture. The tiny index finger touches the cheek when the arm is pushed up.

172 & 173 Strong collection

No. 172 Unmarked, 5 inches tall, this little fattie in a knitted suit and cap is rather high in color and has poorly finished arms. He has side-painted eyes with highlights, black lid linings, and wavering blond brows. He is shoulder jointed and balanced to stand alone on very sturdy feet. The dark blond wisps of hair above each ear and at the top of the head are slightly molded.

The suit is tinted blue around the neck and at the bottoms of the sleeves and the pants legs. The slippers without heels are darker blue and have molded pompons. His cap, which covers the entire back of his head, has a peak and is also tinted blue. The back of the suit, although it has molded buttons, has been left undecorated and even the trim at the bottom of the pants does not extend around to the back.

He is made of very good bisque and, except for the arms and feet, is very well finished.

Nos. 173 and **174** Brother and sister pairs are always prized and these "action" twins are delightful. Unfortunately they are not marked, but that in no way decreases their desirability. Both the idea and the execution are excellent.

Each 5½ inches tall, shoulder jointed with loops which fit perfectly into flattened shoulder holes, they are well balanced and stand alone. They are made of good, sharp bisque and the finishing is very well done. Their blouses and socks are pale blue, the ties, the skirt and the pants are light brown, the one-strap, heelless slippers are dark brown. Both have well-molded, medium blond hair, bright pink cheeks and small, dark blond brows.

Her side-painted eyes have intaglio depressions, no colored irises, black lid linings, and white highlights. The left lower lip also has a molded swelling and her mouth is painted with droll, drooping corners. The backs of her tightly clenched fists are bright rose but otherwise there isn't a mark on her from this sibling fisticuffs.

The boy wasn't as lucky. He has one eye which matches hers but the other is closed and there is a tear molded on his cheek below it. His water-

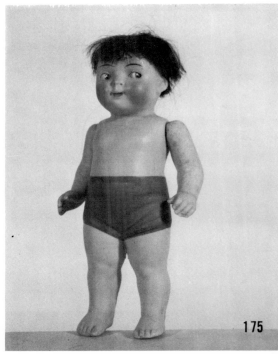

174 *Strong collection; 175 Hilsdorf collection*

melon mouth is deeply molded, his shirt has a triangular rip and his tie has obviously been yanked. What happened to the bottom half of his left sleeve is not quite clear because it seems to be neither rolled up nor ripped off, and his collar on the right side has been roughly treated.

His right hand is completely extended like a Kewpie's but his left hand is cupped and all his fingers are also tinted bright rose.

No. 175 This husky 5½-inch lad in molded orange trunks resembles the boy in the previous pair and is also unmarked. He is shoulder jointed with loops and there is a ball head under the brown mohair wig.

He has a watermelon mouth and goo-goo painted molded eyes. The irises are blue and there are highlights on the black pupils. The lid linings are black and the one-stroke brows are brown.

The bisque is good and he is heavy for his size but he could have been better finished. As so often happened, his arms mottled in the firing and do not perfectly match his good body in color. But he is very beguiling and stands alone quite well.

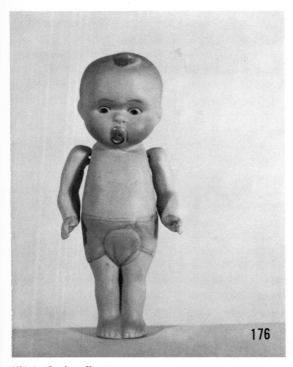

176 Author's collection

No. 176 At first glance this 5½-inch toddler with molded diaper and pacifier appears to be Japanese, probably because the coloring is not typically German. It tends to be buff rather than pink and ruddy—those German favorites. The modeling and molding and painting are acceptable as German and better than some.

The eyes have slightly intaglio pupils with blue rims and black lid linings, the one-stroke brows are blond and the hair is a reddish-blond wash with only the standing forelock molded. The pacifier is bright yellow, with a red ring; the diaper is yellow over the complexion color.

Infants

Modern parents, whose children have dolls which perform all kinds of human functions, are now faced with the problem of making up their minds about "Little Brother." Is he or isn't he an "obscene toy" because he has all the genitalia of a small infant? Will he or won't he "complicate existing problems of sex and perversion"? (*Time,* Nov. 10, 1967) They will have still another problem if/when "Little Sister" comes on the market with the same added female attractions.

It must be difficult for such parents to believe that many of their own mothers and even their grandmothers were permitted nothing but girl dolls, preferably in the medium to large sizes. Some dolls had "boy" haircuts, either molded or wigged, and such boy clothing as "Little Lord Fauntleroy," but many little girls did not have them and it was a matter of family policy that they did not. This same family attitude frequently extended to "baby" dolls.

If we remember—and some of us must because we were there—that mothers and grandmothers from the early 1900s were raised by mothers, often with a great deal of "help" from live-in grandmothers, who were soaked in the prudish Victorian tradition with lingering overtones of Puritanism, it will be more easily understood. The older the American roots of the family, the more likely the prohibition of boy and baby dolls.

Queen Elizabeth II causes such a small ripple in our modern American world that it is the more surprising to find that Queen Victoria influenced such intimate areas of life in this country. That she was held in great esteem is borne out by the fact that when she died in 1901 some American cities had elaborate reproductions of her wake. The details were relayed by the Atlantic Cable, which had been laid in 1866, and these "tributes" drew visitors by the thousands. One such, in an Eastern department store, complete with organ music, was the event of the decade.

There was a hush-hush attitude about babies and about the role of boys in the scheme of things. This hangover from the 1800s is undoubtedly the reason we sometimes find china shoulder heads with very adult faces dressed as infants. Some parents obviously did not have this baby phobia. It was among first-generation Americans that this attitude did not exist and that seems to indicate that Americans floundered in the Victorian morass more, or longer, than Europeans.

Butler Brothers Fall Catalogue in 1908 is a classic example of the avoidance of the word "baby" in its text. There are sketches of men standing around in heroic poses in "trapdoor" underwear and ladies in corsets, but baby bonnets are listed as "Children's Caps." There are only four items in the Index under "Baby"—baskets, cabs, cab robes, and walkers.

In the same issue there is only one baby doll per se—"Stuffed Baby with Celluloid Face." There is a "Crying Baby Doll" but it looks like a girl with long, straight legs. There are "Doll Carriages and Go Carts and English Cabs" but no baby carriages for live infants or for dolls.

Under "Doll Sundries" they list nursing bottles at 33 cents a dozen, doll baby sets with a bottle, small babies' rattle, and bone rubber teething ring at 42 cents per dozen sets, and hand-knit worsted fittings with sacques, hoods, tam o'shanters, and bootees, pink or blue with white, 84 cents assorted dozens and doll's bootees, "Popular dime items, 75 cents per dozen."

But the only infant dolls in that 490-page wholesale catalogue are small, frozen bisques in tubs and basins. These little sitting figures were 37 cents a dozen in 2⅜-inch basin and 78 cents per dozen in a 3-inch tub. They were listed as "removable," which was quite a concession.

It sounds truly ridiculous now but in 1917 or 1918 the author had over twenty German jointeds in various sizes but not an infant doll among them, although a young aunt, who was a trained nurse, had argued in their favor to no avail.

When Santa Claus brought the little girl next door a bent leg infant with about a 14-inch head circumference, she became the most popular child in the block. Hard feelings developed between some of the adults about the gift, however.

In spite of this, all-bisque infants enjoyed an immunity to this ban-all-babies attitude. The little pink hip and shoulder jointed infants caused no such furor and the unlifelike size was probably the reason. There were all kinds of small cradles and carriages available for them, but for some perverse reason we loved candybox beds which would hold half a dozen of them quite comfortably. This was considered "child's play" and very unrealistic before the advent of the Dionne Quints and we were indulged in these whimsies without protest.

There is one old family of infants, both immobile and jointed, which have molded yellow hair either with comb marks or excellent ringlets or both. The author has collected them for years without uncovering any information about them or anybody who remembers having them. They are especially interesting because of their body shaping. Unlike the later infants, all of these are potbellied, their spines are not straight, and the same face appears through several variations in body types.

No. 177 Unmarked, 3½ inches tall, with a very pale complexion, this is an excellent immobile specimen. The hair is very yellow and the mold must have been quite new because all the details are very sharp. The blue eyes have molded lids, black linings, and red lid lines and eye dots. The one-stroke brows are dark blond and there are red nose dots.

No. 178 Unmarked, 4 inches tall, hip and shoulder jointed with brass wire, this pair do not have the molded eyelids and only the one on the left has the red lid lines. Neither has red eye dots. They do not sit up well.

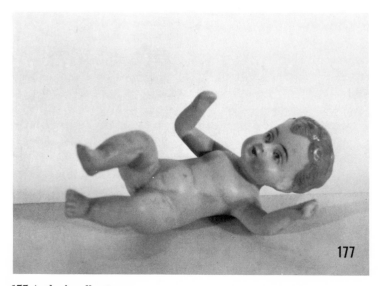

177 *Author's collection*

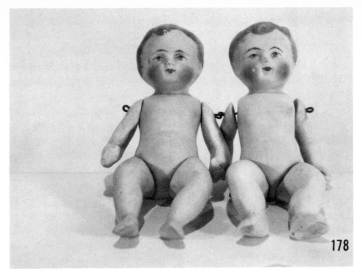

No. 179 Unmarked, 2¾ inches tall, another hip and shoulder jointed pair with brass wire. Both are shown because the one on the left has feature painting, including yellow brows, but no complexion tinting at all. Like the previous pair, neither has molded lids or eye dots but the legs have improved motion.

Because of the rounded back, all of these dolls keep their legs raised when lying flat, just as babies often do.

Nos. 180 and 181 A very odd little specimen with pegged arms and loop strung legs. Except that it is completely incised, it would seem to be a put-together affair by someone who was not too experienced with all-bisques.

Across the shoulders it is clearly incised 80.3/0, on the insides of the upper arms 80.3, and on the backs of the legs 3. It is 3 inches stretched out and sits up 2⅛ inches tall.

Like the previous dolls, it has the curved back and the leg holes were cut into the same potbellied torso, but it has a different, more oval face.

The blue eyes have pupils and black lid linings and the brows are one-stroke in blond. The dark blond hair has comb marks through the molded locks. The bisque is old and extremely good in all of these infants with rounded backs and in this one the complexion is very pale again.

A 3⅛-inch hip and shoulder pegged toddler in the collection has the same face and hairdo. The incised number on the back appears to be 505, and all the parts are incised 3/0.

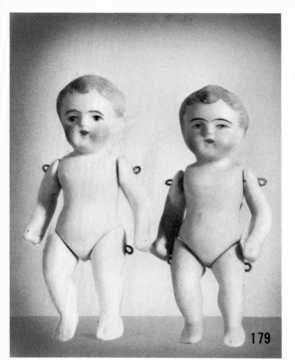

179

180

181

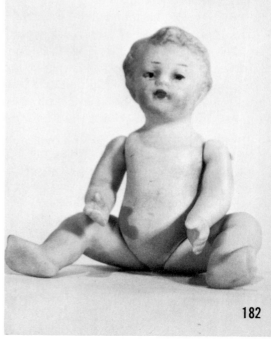

182

179, 180,181 & 182 Author's collection

The toddler has Kestner's white shirred socks with blue bands and black one-strap heeled slippers with pompons. The straps are molded but they were not painted, so the shoes appear to be pumps with the old, reddish-brown soles.

Could all of these be Mr. Kestner again?

No. 182 Another specimen with combination stringing. In this one the ball tops of the arms were flattened to fit the closed shoulder construction and then pegged. The hips are loop strung but the loops do not protrude from the leg. The leg flange is flat and the loop is a flat crossbar contained in the top of the leg. This must have caused assembly-line problems because the rubber had to be threaded through these difficult loops with a wire "needle," which could have been curved.

Across the back of the shoulders it is incised S299 or 8299, and below that, **Germany.**

Several things point to Heubach as the manufacturer. First, the leg loop. Heubach also made swivel heads (and in quite large sizes) with this type of loop built into the base of the neck, completely out of sight unless the head is turned over so the neck hole can be examined.

Heubach used large numbers, probably because of the quantity of their production in many fields, and the "G" in **Germany** is Heubach type.

Added to this, the molded hair is the type found on many piano babies and Heubach dolls, especially the shoulder heads.

The hair is well done but the face is not and the complexion coat extended into the edges of the yellow hair, turning it slightly orange. The eyes are well molded but only pupils and lid linings were painted and not too carefully. The brows are dark blond and the mouth is done in two sections, with a white line between. The complexion is mottled and more peach than pink. The bisque is quite good and would have made a very attractive and different infant if a few more seconds had been added to the decorating time.

No. 183 Unmarked, 4½ inches tall, hip and shoulder jointed with brass wire, this boyish-looking fellow is a later issue. He is still slightly pot-bellied, but much of the good modeling is gone, the bisque is not as fine grained, the complexion is somewhat mottled, and the decorating is inferior.

The hair has also been changed to a molded lock in front and comb marks out of a center crown. Instead of two closed fists, he has an open left hand and, for some reason, his brows are very dark brown.

After years of adult collecting, the large all-bisque infants came as a complete surprise to the author. As a child she played with youngsters whose parents were everything from millionaires to very ordinary working men. None of these large all-bisque infants ever made an appearance.

No. 184 The largest of these to join this collection is pictured with a ruler, but the complete measurements are: head circumference, $9\frac{1}{8}$ inches; sits erect, $9\frac{5}{8}$ inches; lies flat, 14 inches to the heels and 15 inches to the toes. It is hip and shoulder jointed with rubber.

The molded glossy yellow hair is beautifully comb marked out of a center crown and the ears are unusually fine. The painted eyes are bright blue with high-painted pupils and small highlight dots; the one-stroke brows are brown. There are black lid linings, red eyelid lines, and red eye dots and nostril dots.

The entire body is evenly complexioned in a pale tint. The pretty mouth is coral pink with a deeper color center line, and the mouth has the flat Kestner outer corners.

All of the modeling is good and quite detailed in the hands and feet, including fingernails and toenails and raised big toes. This particular doll was one of the first out of new molds because none of the elaborate detail was lost in the hair or the fingers and toes.

Surely this is one of the most thoroughly impractical toys ever created for a child—even those careful children of bygone days. Just washing it on a folded towel is a precarious job for an adult and it does have to be washed frequently if handled.

This is the doll sometimes identified by professionals as "the 13-mold infant." Careful inspection enables one to count the sections, even though it is beautifully finished. The arms and legs have two molds each, so that is eight. On the arms the mold lines extend down the inside to the heel of the palm and on the outside down to the wrist and the center of the thumb. This put part of the hand in each mold, the top in one and the underside in the other.

In the legs the mold lines go straight down the back, through the heel and across the sole of the foot, and down the center of the knee in front to the second toe, which put the raised great toe in one mold and the others in the second half.

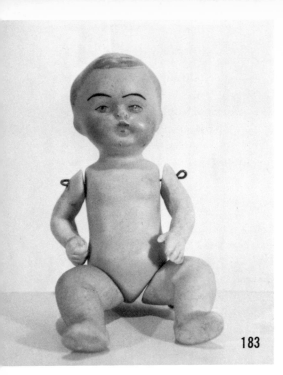

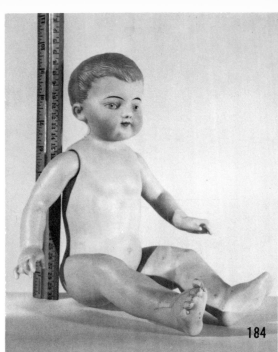

183

184

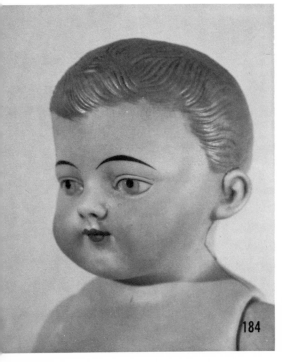

184

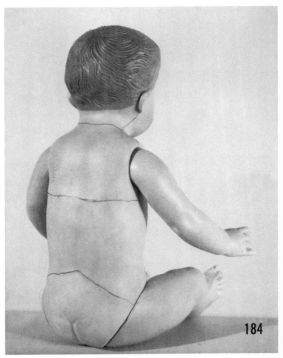

184

183 & 184 Author's collection

On the back of the body the mold lines have been penciled in for the third part of the illustration. There is a faint mold line across the head from ear to ear, which indicates that the entire front, including the torso, face, ears, and the front of the hair were in one mold, which makes nine.

Just below the hairline in the back there is another line, which means the mold was lifted off the head in one small piece, which makes ten. Just below the shoulders there is another line showing that another small section of the mold could be lifted out to preserve the deep arm sockets, and that makes eleven. The center-back mold ended at the waist line, which makes twelve. The buttocks mold came off in a pointed piece which touched the waist in the center, and that makes thirteen pieces.

All this elaborate engineering was necessary because of undercutting, which is a recurring problem in molding. Any protruding part, such as the ears, or any indentations, such as the arm sockets, would be broken off in unmolding the soft greenware under ordinary mold construction.

Oddly enough, too, the people capable of making these molds very often had no further contact with the manufacturing. The same thing is true today. Many of the people turning out quite acceptable reproductions cannot make their own molds. Except under unusual circumstances, however, artists producing original sculpings learn to make their own molds to protect their creations.

Kestner engineering is strongly suggested in the excellent, deep shoulder sockets and the ball tops on the arms of this doll. The sockets are every bit as good as those on the "French" and some of the "French-type." The stringing loops appear to have been cut from a completely molded ball top on the arm rather than just a molded loop.

This same construction is found on other suspected large Kestners, notably the large boy and the large girls, **Nos. 135** and **136.** Because the dolls are large and the parts are heavy, there is a tremendous pull on the loops when the dolls are strung.

No. 185 The next largest infant has an 8¾-inch head circumference; it sits up 8 inches; lying flat it is 10½ inches to the heels and 11½ to the toes. These are excellent proportions and were usually followed in German infants of all kinds. This one is unmarked.

The infants apparently were never subjected to the price cutting which resulted in the out-of-proportion legs on the girl dolls which are commonly identified as "stick legs" and known too well to all collectors. In the

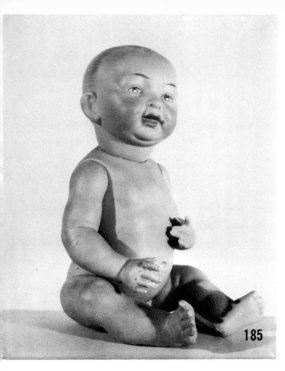 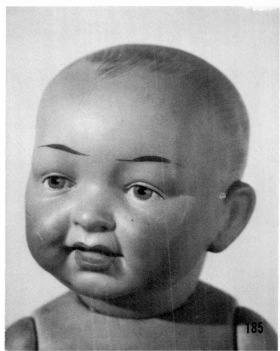

infants the head circumference should be more than the height of the doll when it is sitting and generally this is true.

Later than the 13-mold infant, this is a much more satisfactory plaything, although still highly breakable. The complexioning is quite ruddy; the open-closed mouth is toothless and deep; the head is a swivel with a kid lined neck hole, and the body is a much more babyish shape. The blond hair is only suggested with brush strokes and the only molding is the raised lock in front.

The gray-blue painted eyes have high-placed pupils with highlights of relief white. There are black eye linings and red eyelid lines; the one-stroke brows are blond and the cheeks are very rosy, like a baby's after being out in the winter air.

The tight-fitting, flat-topped arms have sturdy loops which fit into large shoulder holes. Even larger loops hold the legs firmly in place.

All the modeling is babyish and good; the finishing is excellent, especially in the dimpled hands and feet.

Without a doubt, Kestner made this doll also. The same head has been seen in many phases and sizes on infant composition bodies which have the same raised big toes and hands with free thumbs. There are twelve of these heads available for examination at the moment, ranging from a 7-inch to a 15½-inch circumference. A chart shows only two that are unmarked, this all-bisque and one on a composition body. And only these two unmarked ones have one-stroke brows.

The other ten have incised numbers and sizes and two have "made in Germany" also, which indicates that the face was used over a long period. All of them have multistroke eyebrows with painted, set and sleep eyes. Some have closed heads, others have cut heads for wigs. The incised numbers are familiar to all collectors: 142, 150, 151, 152.

This is another instance, as in the Amberg dolls, in which a certain face proved to be so satisfactory to the buying public that it was used over a long span of time with just "improvements" added, right up to sleep eyes and an open mouth with teeth.

It may also have been a very popular and standard Kestner item for distribution through wholesalers who sold in competition with J.D.K. marked infants.

No. 186 Like the Georgene Averill toddler (No. 280), this infant has an excellent flange almost all around the neck to hold it in place, but this one has the added feature of holes at the sides of the flange through which the rubber is inserted when the arms are strung. It keeps the head from turning, which is not a bad idea in a rather fragile child's toy because children do love to turn heads around.

It sits up 5¼ inches, has a head circumference of 5¾ inches, and measures 6½ inches to the heel and 7¼ to the toes when lying flat.

Incised on the back in three lines, 476 over 18 over Germany and 476-18 on the flange, it has a high complexion tint which is surprisingly uniform in such a deep color. Not as detailed in the modeling as the previous Kestners, it nevertheless is quite adequate and the hands and feet are very good. The hair is slightly modeled across the top and along the back in crushed curls, much in the order of the Bye-Lo Baby. The head is covered with a reddish blond wash. The sleep eyes are blue and there are both upper and lower painted lashes, but no eyebrows. The mouth is closed and painted with turned up corners which give it a happy expression. The cheeks are very bright.

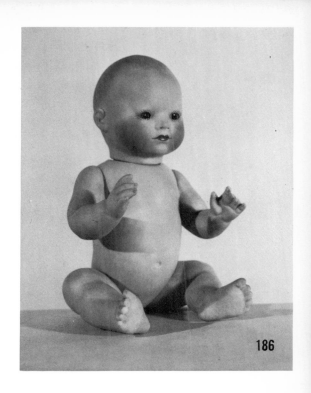

186

187

186 & 187 Author's collection

No. 187 This mint pair have been kept together because, while they look exactly alike, one is unmarked and the other is incised on the back in two lines 369. over **Germany.** Each has a head circumference of 6 inches, sits 5 inches, measures 6½ inches to the heel and 7¼ to the toe when lying flat.

The color is slightly high and not as meticulously uniform as some complexion coating, the modeling and finishing are very good, including minute fingernails and toenails. They have brown sleep eyes with painted upper and lower lashes, faint blond brows, and nose dots. The tiny mouths with molded, turned-down lip ends give them a pouty appearance. The cheeks are normally rosy. The original cap wigs are lustrous brown mohair pushed through cardboard caps and brushed flat from the center crown. A thin coat of glue holds them in place.

Why is one marked and one unmarked when obviously they were made from the same master mold? Close examination of the backs shows that the marking was not removed from the one doll in the finishing process.

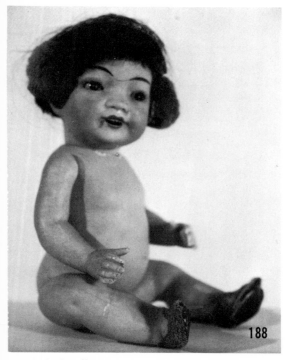

188

188 Author's collection

It was never there and it was purposely omitted, because the incised marks are made by raised figures in the molds. Since the marks were not removed from the doll, they had to be missing from the molds. This appears to be a case where the model for the doll belonged to the manufacturer, not to the distributor, as was the case with some patented dolls.

They could have been made to be sold in competition with each other. It is quite possible that the unmarked doll wore a paper label or a tag bearing some advertised name copyrighted by the distributor. The necessary "Made in Germany" could have been on that tag or label.

No. 188 The happy little Oriental miss sits up 5½ inches, has a 6¼-inch head circumference over her wig, is 6½ inches to the heels and 7 inches to the toes when lying flat. The swivel neck is held with a wooden plug and the arms and legs are strung with rubber through good loops.

German preoccupation with Oriental dolls fascinates many collectors and there is a great demand for them in any type. They certainly were not made for sale in the Orient, for there were no Chinese or Japanese colonies under German domination as there were French colonies for which many French dolls were made in black and in many shades of brown.

Then why? The principal reason was money. They sold well in the United States and that was sufficient incentive for the Germans to manufacture them. Their popularity undoubtedly was also truly American.

Anyone sixty years of age or over should have no difficulty remembering the stress in many homes and churches on Foreign Mission work. Collectors know that Mrs. Beecher introduced her "Beecher Baby" rag doll to the Mission Society ladies of her husband's church. There were "mission barrels" and "mission societies" all over the place among churchgoers and most Americans then were churchgoers. All of this activity had been going on long before 1900. The accent also spread into other fields and produced children's songs, books, and poems about the "heathen Chinee."

The wellsprings for this were the "Haystack Prayer-Meetings" in Williamstown, Mass., in 1806. A group of young college men at Williams College, led by Samuel J. Mills, held frequent meetings for religious conversations and prayers. Some of the meetings were in their rooms and when the weather became warm they moved outdoors.

Among other things they were studying geography and from these discussions was born a tremendous compassion for the heathens who lived in what were then just blank areas on the world maps. One summer after-noon, at such a meeting, they took refuge from a thunderstorm under a haystack and while the storm raged about them they pledged themselves to this cause. "We can do it if we will," Mills exhorted them and that became the watchword for the mission crusade which was to encircle the earth.

It is generally conceded that it was from these Haystack Meetings (a monument was erected to them in Williamstown, Mass.) that the world mission movement was started because other people were caught up in the blazing enthusiasm of these young men.

Many of the traditional American groups followed after these meetings and we know all of them. The Bible societies, the Sunday schools, the Society of Christian Endeavor, the Young Men's Christian Association and, finally, the Protestant foreign missions. It is because of all these things that so many prominent people in this country for many generations have been so proud of their birth to missionary parents in the Orient.

The late Janet P. Johl dates the so-called "enigma" or "taufling" doll back to 1856. A German manufacturer from Sonneberg had seen an Oriental doll which attracted a great deal of attention at the London Exhibition in 1850 (*The Antiques Journal*, April 1955). The bisque headed and all-bisque Oriental dolls were made many years later but they were probably Amer-ican-inspired and were a very natural addition to the manufacturers' lines in that eternal quest for "something different" in the doll field—especially if it sold well in America.

This doll has a good black mohair wig with bangs, commonly associated with the Japanese image. Chinese were usually designated in cartoons, dolls, and the like, by queues. The word "designated" is used deliberately. For an American to try to establish precisely the nationality of an Oriental doll made in a German factory almost a hundred years ago is ridiculous. Some of them do have what to us is an Asian cast to their features, but just as many more were ordinary dolls tinted yellow. We have little choice except to classify them vaguely as Oriental.

Unlike most open-mouthed dolls of every type, this one has molded teeth. In this method the teeth were molded under the upper lip, with the mouth opening cut below the teeth. In the ordinary open-mouth, the mouth was opened and the teeth were added from the back, held in place by a wash of slip that hardened during one of the firings. When a tooth is broken in this latter type, the group can sometimes be carefully chiseled out in one piece and replaced with reproductions. When molded teeth break, however, that is the end of them unless there is a skilled porcelain repair artist available.

The only German manufacturer known to this writer who made molded teeth in ordinary dolls was, of course, the pervasive Mr. Kestner and his offspring. The size did not seem to make any difference to Kestner either, and there are other quite small composition bodied dolls in this collection with these teeth, even though they were easier to do in the larger sizes. Molded teeth were a much more common practice among the French than the Germans.

This Oriental has a very thin outer lip line but at both ends it stops, rather than tapering off, and both ends are flat. Because of this extended lip line, she wears a perpetual and engaging smile. The one-stroke brows are pitch black; she has very fine upper and lower painted lashes and dark brown sleep eyes. There are red nostril dots but no red lid lines. The

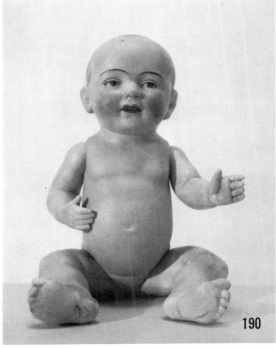

189

190

189 & 190 Author's collection

color is golden yellow, very evenly done, and the pretty hands have dimpled backs.

Her feet are most amusing. They are very well modeled but woven, colored braid, which is similar to the strip between her blue hair pompons, was glued to the bare feet and the soles were painted black, toes and all. This treatment has been noticed in other dolls.

No. 189 Incised 150 over 4/0 on the head and simply 0 on the arms and legs, this swivel head infant also has the stringing holes through the base of the neck. The head circumference is 5⅛ inches, it sits 4⅞ inches, and measures 7 inches lying flat.

Everything about it points to Kestner. The good, blue sleep eyes have been set but it has fine, thick upper and lower painted lashes and one-stroke, wavery, dark blond glossy brows. The very good hands have free thumbs, dimples, and molded fingernails. The big toes turn up on the well-modeled feet which have good heel detail.

Collectors are familiar with this open-closed type of mouth which seems to have a tongue molded inside the lower lip. In this doll that tongue section was carefully left white and looks like a tiny row of teeth.

The bisque is old and sharp and well finished but the complexion is higher than one would expect in this type. The white rim around the neck shows a very amateurish job of setting a kid lining in the neck hole. German infants seldom have kid linings.

No. 190 Stiff necked and husky, this is an unmarked German infant which looks more like a boy than a girl. He has a head circumference of 5¾ inches, sits up 5 inches, and is 6¾ inches lying flat.

Besides excellent arms and hands, this baby has well-molded upper and lower lids and molded puffiness under the eyes. The painted blue eyes have high pupils, black lid linings, and red lid lines; the one-stroke brows are brown. The hair is just brush strokes of medium blond, without any molded detail. The hands are beautifully done and finished on both the upper and under sides, with great detail. The complexion coat is inclined to be pink but it is in no way "high."

The arms have complete ball tops which were cut away to make the rugged stringing loops, the leg loops are balled and sturdy, and the large pour holes in the soles of the feet are filled but visible. The hip and shoulder holes are large and round so that the parts fit firmly.

His open-closed mouth is typically Kestner as are his baby feet with raised big toes and all the workmanship and detail.

No. 191 During and following the days of the Gibson Girls, everyone was addicted to "pretty" in children and this homely fellow would have made out poorly at our candystores. Hip and shoulder jointed with hard wire, 3¾ inches long and 2⅝ inches sitting up, he has an incised mark on his center back which may be **709**, or perhaps a larger number. The mold must have been old because the finishing is not good enough to have removed the mark.

For his age, the brush marks on the hair line around the face are good, the hair is dark blond like the eyebrows, and he has only pupils with brown lid linings. The complexion is mottled, the bisque is old but not at all sharp.

He is shown particularly because of the dark line like a brush stroke across the top of his nose. This is a kiln crack which developed in the firing and the complexion color worked into it. Kiln cracks are generally identifiable because of this color seepage.

In some very meticulous firms which made quality heads there are sometimes splashes of complexion color over kiln cracks on the insides of the heads. Many of us think that this practice by the decorators may have been for the guidance of those who did the final sorting for quality. This happens in Jumeau dolls, for instance. Many of these cracks are covered by the wigs, but they are not perfect heads and it is doubtful that they were sold as such.

No. 192 Unmarked, this seated, crying infant is one of a pair and his happier companion has a small animal, apparently a puppy, molded on his right side. He sits up 3¾ inches and is 2¼ inches from seat to toes.

All the workmanship is very good and a small chip on one shoulder proves that the good bisque was not precolored, although the tinting of the body is pale and very even. His loop strung arms do not match the main portion of the doll in quality on any count.

The hair is slightly molded over the temples and at the top of the forehead; there is a lock which looks almost like a bump on the left side and the hair is a reddish-blond wash.

His eyes, which appear to be closed, were molded like any others but simply not painted and they have only a very narrow lid lining and almost

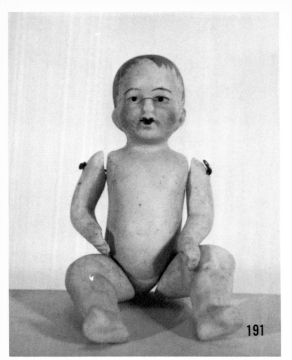

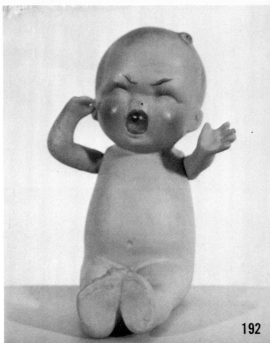

191

192

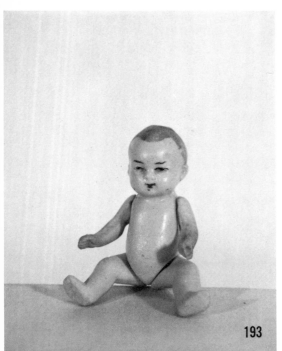

193

194

191, 192, 193 & 194 Author's collection

invisible lashes. His curving brows are also reddish blond and so well done with one stroke that they look as though made by two strokes. The open-closed mouth is an orange-red and two upper teeth were added in relief white.

No. 193 Only faintly precolored and incised **Germany** across the back, this is a much later doll. He is hip and shoulder jointed with good little loops. He has only pupils and lid linings in black, brown brows, and a wash of dull blond over the ball head. The modeling is not good but he would have pleased a child.

No. 194 This infant is precolored "candy" pink like the little girls with orange shoes who followed the Flappers. The incised **Germany** down this little one's spine is almost invisible. He has a small dot of blue for eyes, with an even smaller black dot in each for pupils, little blond dashes for eyebrows and a bright yellow wash over his ball head to hide the high color of the bisque. Children would have liked it, nevertheless.

ero **21**

Boots
Black and
Yellow

In a large collection of all-bisques, some method of classification has to be established so that new purchases can be compared to dolls already owned. If this is not done, duplicates can build up and while the collection will expand, it will not grow because growth means the addition of *new* material and duplication can amount to nothing more than a swelling in numbers.

The comparison of dolls also helps in the never-ending search for products from the same factory. Too often we do not have any definite idea which factory it was, of course, but the search goes on nevertheless because all-bisques are so poorly documented.

Black Boots

No. 195 This unmarked 4½-inch doll looks like some transitional experiment. The torso modeling and gloss of the bisque resemble Old Whites and the hairdo style, as well as the painting, is similar to some of the old dolls. It is hip and shoulder jointed with pegs and the arms have the old, flat shoulder surfaces.

The legs are almost shapeless. The tops of the socks are molded and the bands are purple; the black high button shoes have gold buttons only painted on, without any molded detail, and the tips and the heels are gilded. The painted bracelets are of the same gilt.

An unsuccessful attempt was made to flesh tint the legs but they are marred by countless flecks which are impurities in the slip similar to those in the Old White bear but finer grained. The legs are also very dull bisque which contrasts sharply with the body.

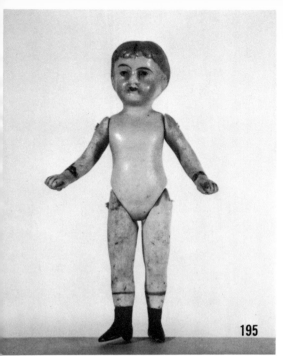 

The painted blue eyes have high-placed pupils, the brows are a single stroke in dark blond, the cheeks are tinted, and the glossy yellow hair has molded forehead locks and broken back curls.

No. 196 The 5-inch molded hair boy is incised across the shoulders **12-13**. He is hip and shoulder jointed with brass wire.

His arms are more shapely and closer to the body than the previous doll, the body is well molded but thick at the abdomen and his legs spraddle out. Except for the heels, the boots have no molded detail but they are painted with high-gloss black to resemble men's gaiters instead of high button shoes.

The painted blue eyes have high pupils, black lid linings, and single-stroke brows in brown. The side-parted glossy yellow hair is well done, once again with flat curls in back. The complexion tinting is excellent.

His black wool suit is machine made, hand finished, and the coat is fully lined and bound with old braid.

No. 197 The 2¾-inch girl and 3½-inch boy are smaller sizes of the same

197

198

199

197, 198 & 199 Author's collection

doll. Their glossy yellow hair is well modeled again. They are also blue eyed with brown one-stroke brows.

His shining black boots are painted higher than those on the previous doll but they have good heels; the little girl's legs were painted black for knee socks and her ankle-high boots are orange.

The interesting piqué clothes are quite soiled from years of children's fondling. The work is machine done and even the buttons on the girl's coat are machine set.

No. 198 This wire jointed 2⅝-inch boy and 2-inch girl are more of the same tribe, each with glossy, heeled, black boots, topped with vertical ribbed flesh-colored socks with red bands. These boots have tan soles.

The little girl may be professionally dressed. Her dress and cap are lace, the sewed-on sash and tied cap ribbon are matching yellow silk.

No. 199 These four, 1¼ and 1⅜ inches tall, are more of the family only in all of these the molded boot lines were not followed and only shallow slippers were painted, all with black soles except on the girl with a hat. The arms and torsos are complexioned but the legs were left entirely white.

They have yellow, glossy molded hair, pupils only, brows in the hair color, and tiny dabs of shapeless red for mouths.

Only the naked boy can be checked for an incised mark and it is on the center back: 6. Their clothing is professionally made and sewed on tight. The girl with the hat, third from the left, is very colorful. Her hat is dull green, the black jacket is laced with yellow over a white blouse, the tassel down the white apron is pink and green thread and the skirt is red.

No. 200 The author's favorite doll pin. This a memorial pin which originally contained a braided wreath of someone's hair. It is 2⅛ inches long, 1¾ inches across the glass and quite deep because it is not flat in back. The dolls are 1¾ inches tall, hip and shoulder jointed with wire.

The girl is the older of the two and she has the black boots with heels and black soles. Her lace dress and cap were copied from those of the girl in **No. 198**.

The boy is precolored bisque, his hair is golden yellow but not glossy like the girl's. He has the same crocheted clothes as the tinies in **No. 199** but he is much later than they are. The shirt is red, held together with two bars of thread which are tan like the pants, and the belt is just black buttonhole stitches.

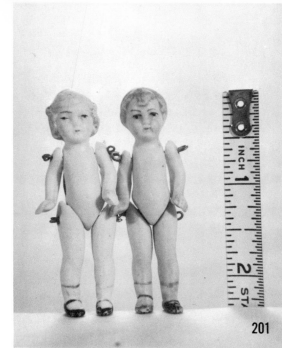

200

201

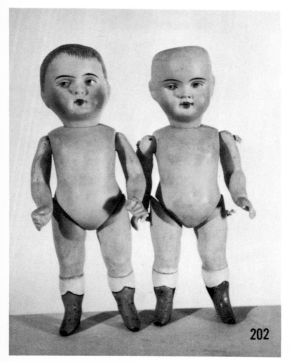

202

203

200, 201, 202 & 203 Author's collection

He has molded one-strap, flat slippers and low socks which were originally painted black but most of the color was worn off.

No. 201 This boy and girl are relatives of the boy in the pin. Hip and shoulder jointed with wire, precolored, unmarked, the girl is 2¼ inches and the boy is 2⅜ inches. The girl is paler than the boy; her flat, one-strap slippers are dark brown, and the socks have blue bands. The boy's shoes are the same but colored a reddish brown.

These final dolls with flat slippers are undoubtedly products of the same factory which made the dolls in the chapter called "Detective Story" and yet not one of these has the arm or hip holes which disfigure the others. As suggested in that chapter, they were capable of better work and they operated from the padded complexion period through precolored bisque.

Yellow Boots

Another distinctive group are these with yellow boots. The color is a deep golden yellow, the tops of all of them are molded to points in both the back and front, and the trim is all black. There are narrow black bands around the tops, the outside of the heels, and the sole rims, and the toe tips are also black. They are all topped with blue banded white socks with deep vertical ribbing. All these boots also have the molded gussets on both sides at the top, simulating the rubber which used to be in such footwear.

The first three dolls are certainly from the same factory. The modeling is so similar, the bisque is so old and so good and so well finished, the decorating is so alike, that it must have been done by the same people, under the same supervision, and possibly with the same paint.

No. 202 The 6⅛-inch pair of swivel necks are also very good examples of how the same bodies could be used with different heads or at different times.

The torso of the loop-strung boy with molded hair is incised **208** over **7** between the arms in back, and there is a matching **7** on the base of his swivel neck and on his limbs. The pegged doll intended to have a wig is incised in the same place **208** over **8**, and the entire mark appears on the back of her head, plus an **8** on each limb.

No. 203 The 5-inch wigged doll, with stiff legs and the same yellow boots is incised on the head **103** over **4** and each arm has a **4**.

Under these circumstances, which of the three with yellow boots is the oldest?

We generally presume that stiff legs and pegged arms came first in the tinted bisques, with pegged hip and shoulder joints next, followed by loop-strung arms and then hip and shoulder loops. Wire stringing came and went, only to return again.

The pegged doll is very likely the oldest. The two loop-strung dolls can be explained most logically by *price*. Because the doll with stiff neck and legs saved several molding and assembling operations, she probably is the cheaper model which competed with the boy with molded hair. This price approach puts the wigless one with pegged limbs first which is the proper order.

No. 204 Left, 4¼ inches tall, incised high on the head **154** over **2, 184.2** on the upper inside arms and no marking on the legs, this little blonde was just another glass eyed stiff neck until her companion came along.

Right: 4 inches, incised **184** over **2** in the same place on the head, **184.2** on the arms, with an air hole in the hip flange and incised **2** on the inside

204 Author's collection

of the thigh, this doll is all original and slightly cross-eyed.

Both have set brown eyes with upper and lower painted lashes and one-stroke dark blond brows. Both have excellent light blond mohair wigs on good cloth caps, with little silk bows sewed to the crowns, just like the wig on **No. 203.** Both torsos are excellent, clear old bisque, beautifully finished and decorated. The limbs are the same kind of bisque but not as well filtered and they show signs of impurities.

The yellow boots on the second doll are exactly like those on **No. 202** and she has the same white socks with the same very blue bands, but the ribbing is shallower.

The question is: How did the doll on the left get those different legs? Very likely some fortunate collector somewhere along the line added them to a legless torso because they make a presentable doll but they do not have a factory fit, especially in the back where they are ⅛ inch short in the flange to match the seat curvature. They are just like but one size larger than the legs on **No. 116,** so they are from a size 1 doll and are very likely Kestner.

In fact, this whole group of yellow booted dolls have more Kestner than any other characteristics and until something more definite can be ascertained, they are listed as: "Kestner?" in this collection. Because of their ability to create endless variations, these yellow boots are an eye-catching Kestner adaption of those on **No. 88,** in the author's opinion.

Candystore Dolls

Most of the German all-bisques in the small sizes are roughly classified as "Candystore Dolls" by many collectors. Commonest of all types, frequently incised and almost always with molded shoes and socks, they came to this country by the million. They also came in an amazingly wide variety. Price governed the type, the quality, the stringing, and the size.

They got the name because, prior to World War I, there were almost always boxes of these popular German imports in the same cases that held the licorice shoestrings, the chocolate-covered caramels, the sugar babies in pink, white, and brown (they resembled small Frozen Charlottes or penny dolls), and the lollypops in rainbow hues. These dolls were active, money-making items for small grocers, candy shops, and some novelty-goods stores because the average small town did not have any real selection of toys except during the Christmas season.

By the early part of this century the old "general store" had disappeared in much of the country, especially in the East where great ports dotted the coastline, and specialized stores were cropping up everywhere. There were drygoods stores in even the tiniest towns to supply material and findings for clothing made at home. There were hardware stores that carried the hand tools both workmen and homeowners needed and the garden tools and canning supplies of every description for American men who raised fruits and vegetables and for American women who canned, pickled, and dried them, or made them into jams and jellies for the winter.

At Christmas these stores added dolls and toys for the convenience of those parents who could not, or would not, travel to the nearest city where department stores simply added to the inventory of their year-round toy departments. Those were the days when children were supposed to be seen and not heard, and the words "trauma" and "frustration" had not found their way into family conversations. The shopkeepers loaded the windows with playthings all children wanted and the children took their lives in their hands by teasing for them whenever possible. Sometimes it worked; sometimes it did not. If it did, the shopkeeper gained without losing the everyday, year-round trade of the parents.

Although they were imported by the million, the sales of these little dolls during much of the year were such serious affairs to us that American parents wondered why the storekeepers, often of foreign birth, bothered with the things. Some of the American ladies who operated small shops permitted much less nonsense from small buyers and they were always the last ports of call. These shopowners were usually widows trying to support a family or spinsters ("old maids" in the lexicon of the day), who had no experience with or patience about trade with children.

Actually, these little Candystore dolls made up the first doll collections in this country because the purchases were financed by and dressed by the little girls themselves. In 1914 and 1915 some of the girls, this author included, had a sample of every doll sold within miles. The money came from windfalls from visiting relatives, from errands run for neighbors (your legs belonged to your family and you ran their errands quickly and for nothing), or through the proceeds from that budding new feminine profession, baby-sitting and baby-walking. Fresh air was a new vogue for infants and little girls pushed carriages for busy mothers who had no older child to saddle with the job. The pay wasn't good but it was steady work a good many months of the year.

Little American schoolgirls in the second decade of this century were the first children to have their own money to spend or save as they chose. They also had, or could borrow, bicycles and thereby broadened their buying area considerably, just as cars now take their children and grand-children to shopping centers miles from home. Even a boy's bike would do because most little girls wore that most modest piece of underwear, bloomers which matched the dress.

Before the precious coins left the owner's handkerchief corner where they were securely tied, the entire contents of the box or boxes had to be examined. It was never considered good purchasing strategy to let the storekeeper *know* how much money you could or would spend because your hands were then kept off the 19-cent or 29-cent dolls if you only had a dime.

Added to all this, the purchaser usually brought along a couple of her friends or a visiting child to make sure she did not get a doll with crossed eyes, a thin wig, or, heaven forbid, a smaller size than could be found in another store or in another town. In a last salute to those patient men and women of long ago, it should be said that not many of them stood over the children while the purchase was considered. Child thieves were anathema to parents in all classes of society, the storekeepers knew it and trusted most children. Known "pinchers" were watched, but other youngsters had a great deal of latitude and did not abuse it because one call *on* or *to* your parents, rich, poor, or middleclass, brought lightning from the clearest sky! No policeman then or now would dare to do what parents then naively considered their "parental responsibility."

There was, in fact, great competition for the children's trade because, in order to see the new dolls as well as those for which they were saving, girls would patronize one store over another when running errands. And little girls ran most of the errands because little boys just were not around when they were needed.

It is worth noting that little girls would go on strike against a store with no compunction whatever if a child from another town displayed a cheaper purchase than could be made locally or a larger doll for the same money. Some stores handled a full line of groceries and meats as well as a large case of candy with dolls, jacks, balls, marbles, cheap jackknives, and other money-grabbers from the children.

In prosperous communities girls could buy swivel as well as stiff necked dolls but the swivels were small sizes. Almost anywhere we could buy stiff necks with wigs or with molded hair and those with molded hair were generally less "expensive" than those with wigs. We cannot now tell whether it was our own preferences or the initial costs which governed the prices. Looking through old catalogues now we realize what little gold mines we were to storekeepers. We also realize that there must have been hundreds of thousands of these dolls in mid-Atlantic, in warehouses, in freight trains, and in back rooms of stores all over this country for years and years. It never occurred to us that another one would be waiting if we didn't buy each new love *now*.

Many of us can remember budgeting our funds to include the latest doll of our dreams, 10 cents for the Saturday afternoon movie, which included an episode of Pearl White in "The Perils of Pauline," and 5 cents for peanuts. We happily went from monied gentry to dead broke in a matter of a couple hours and, if the doll went along to the movies, we tucked the brown paper bag which contained our prize under the rubber of a bloomer leg so that our hands were free to crack peanuts or clap, whichever seemed most important at the moment.

The German manufacturers and the frequently German storekeepers knew far better than the children how the world conspired to break these hollow bisque dolls. When you find one now with a broken arm or leg, you can be sure it had its own baptism of tears long, long ago. The candy boxes full of clothes which frequently are found with all-bisques may not be very impressive to young or novice collectors but they are cherished by older women. They were so beautiful to the little girls who were training unwilling fingers to sewing and knitting skills which would serve them, their children, their grandchildren and often their communities and the Red Cross in that future about which they only dreamed then.

In countless conversations with women born in the 1900-1910 period, none of us remember buying dolls with pegged arms and legs. If we had them, they must have been given to us by older sisters or generous older neighbor girls who had outgrown them. It was common practice to inherit playthings of all kinds and accounted for some of the magnificent marbles in the author's chamois bag which she defended to the death because the boys generally played winners-keepers, losers-weepers.

We do remember that we much preferred rubber strung dolls to those with wire for two reasons. First, they had much better motion possibilities and, second, they did not rip their dress sleeves and pant legs. They had one big disadvantage, however. When the rubber broke we had to put them together with string and they were floppy afterward.

Those of us who are collectors now and able to take apart and reassemble even complicated mechanicals (with help from our husbands, to be honest about it), cannot really understand this. Rubber bands would have done the trick nicely and we were inventive enough to have thought of it but we cannot remember having rubber bands as a common household commodity or fine enough wire to use as a needle.

Several kinds of rubber bands are advertised in the 1908 Butler Brothers Catalogue, along with two slingshot rubbers which would have interested us no end, but they appear to be office and school supplies rather than household. The author can remember being paid as a child to put small rubber bands around carnations because they had a genetic fault and split in the calyx even in the budding stage. But in our particular group the chief source of rubber was from golf balls which we hulled and unwound. For our slingshots we mooched strips of automobile tire tubes.

Almost anybody's father could help restring a wire jointed, even though the excellent miniature tools we have now were not available then. Women's hairpins were often the source of wire because almost anything else rusted badly but, if your mother and aunts used bone or celluloid hairpins, it took a little searching in the neighborhood for the proper kind. Oddly enough, we never thought of combining pennies to buy a bundle of the things to keep for this repair work.

If the reader gets the impression that many little girls did not spend all their time with dolls, embroidery, and the allied arts, it is quite true. Millions of us lived in small towns where we knew everyone and had complete freedom of movement on foot, roller skates, bicycles, and even Irish Mails (you will have to look that up) and we know now that the bloomers we hated contributed much to our new liberty.

Besides being the first doll collectors, baby-sitters, and children with earned money, we were also very competitive with the boys of our generation in many fields. We jumped rope and played jacks together but we also walked fences, flew kites, belly bumpered down hills on our own sleds and raced the boys on ice skates.

Perhaps this is why we have lasted so well and so long!

No. 205 The 7¼-inch boy with molded curly blond hair and blue, strapless shoes is incised on the back, **Germany** over **8½,** and he is of quite good quality for this type. Because of the hair style, he appears to date in the early 1900s but they were popular for many years afterward.

His 4½-inch duplicate is incised simply **0 1/2** on the back and his hair is the deep taffy blond color. He shows marked signs of underfiring on his limbs because they are badly disfigured with mildew which appears in the form of heavy freckles over the entire surface.

These two are very good illustrations of one type of Candystore dolls —at least in the author's purchasing area. The small dolls found their way into the small towns outside Philadelphia in large quantities, but the large ones stayed in the city in department stores. Philadelphia was

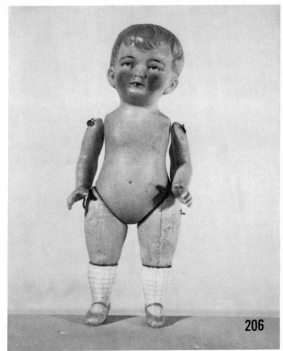

205 & 206 *Author's collection*

a great shipping port, of course, and we had access to many things which we cannot now find in the wholesale catalogues which served areas away from the Eastern seaboard.

No. 206 The 6½-inch boy with the much more "modern" haircut, typical of little boys in the 1910 period, is incised on the back **Germany** over **4½**, in the same print used on the 7½-inch curly-haired boy. Hip and shoulder jointed with hard wire, he is well molded and finished but the complexion tinting is very mottled. His white socks have a molded all-over screening design with green top bands; the one-strap heeled slippers are blue with blue soles.

The painted blue eyes have high pupils and the lower eyelid is nicely molded, which is unusual in these dolls

He is a very nice German all-bisque boy and there is a duplicate little brother in the collection, 3½ inches tall. He is incised in two lines: **Germany** over **1** across the shoulders. Hip and shoulder jointed with brass wire, the little one is a poor specimen when compared to the larger doll.

Candystore Dolls § 225

The bisque is old and good but the finishing and decorating are shoddy and he is quite dumpy in the smaller proportions.

Collectors continually ask, "Why aren't there more boy all-bisques?" The answer seems to be that they were not too popular with *us*, the children for whom they were made. It was a matter of dressmaking, very likely. Making pants for boy dolls, and shirts, was very difficult and, after we struggled with the tailoring problems, the dolls would not sit down. And if there was one thing we liked a doll to do it was to sit down in the small furniture we got for Christmas. Many of us made our own doll houses from several wooden orange crates, and even those orange crates are seldom seen today.

No. 207 Incised **145—11** across the shoulders, 4⅝ inches, hip and shoulder jointed originally with brass wire which broke in the legs, this is another nice all-bisque which probably was made by Kestner.

The well-done hair is bright, glossy yellow and has good comb marks. The painted eyes are blue with high pupils and black lid linings and glossy, one-stroke brows. The socks are a medium shade of blue done in the shirred pattern and the one-strap brown, heeled slippers have the old yellow soles.

The bisque is old and good and well finished and, while the complexion is not pale, it is by no means the late, high color.

No. 208 All of the previous dolls are superior in every way to the 3¾-inch twins which are incised **9770** over **2/0** on the backs. All the larger dolls have well-done blue painted eyes with upper lid linings in black; one of the twins has painted blue eyes with pupils but the other has pupils only.

The larger dolls have the old light blue slippers and the twins have brown. The complexion tinting in the twins appears to be properly fired but it is poor padding of the color before firing. They are also excellent examples of how a feature painter is responsible for a pleasant or an unpleasant face. This is one of the good reasons that little girl shoppers pawed endlessly through a box to get the best.

In a 1908 Butler Brothers Wholesale Catalogue a very similar doll in a 3¾-inch size is listed at 42 cents per dozen and in a 6-inch size at 78 cents per dozen to the stores. This explains any poor workmanship. They were ground out by the thousands for five- and ten-cent "penny-grabbers" and were so listed to the American stores.

With so few of these dolls incised with anything but a stock and/or size number, there is always the possibility that they wore pasted stickers which gave their country of origin, as Japanese items do today. It is even more likely, as we know from existing stock boxes, that "Made in Germany" appeared on boxes and box labels and this must have satisfied the U.S. Customs' requirements in small sizes or in items under a certain individual value. Small sizes were generally packed one dozen in a box, larger sizes by the half dozen, and the boxes were their collective passports.

To establish dates, therefore, rules of thumb and common sense have to be applied. And collectors should not lean backward in time—dolls should be brought forward to be closer to the true age.

No. 209 Unmarked, 5 inches tall, hip and shoulder jointed with hard wire, this is an excellent Snow Baby. It has a fine white grog finish which is not sharp or unpleasant to the touch. The suit is molded to the figure like a fuzzy snowsuit, the peaked cap is quite thick about the head, and the peak, the edge of the hood, and the tops of the shoes are lightly glazed.

The complexion tinting is bright and glossy like a child's while playing

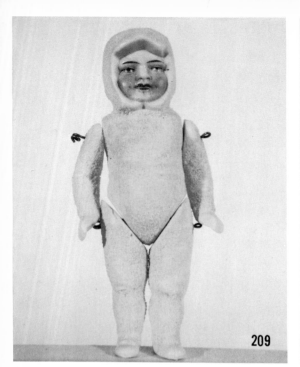
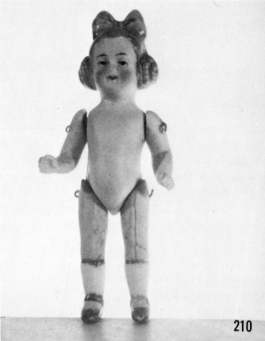

209 *Strong collection;* 210 *Author's collection*

outside in winter, the deeply molded mouth is painted in two sections, and there are dimples in the cheeks.

No. 210 Incised **3/0/½** and **a** on the back, this 3½-inch hip and shoulder wire jointed doll must have been very popular because little American girls by the thousands could "identify" with this girl, as we say nowadays. The braided bun hairdo was a very popular method of getting long, hot hair off necks. The cute top bow would have been a bit difficult to anchor on humans, however.

The hair is yellow (and there were so many blond children in this country in the early part of this century!), the bow is blue. She has pupils only, with black lid linings and dark blond brows. The torso and arms are of excellent bisque, the complexion coating is good for this type, but the legs are known to be replacements. She is so uncommon that anything approaching reasonable legs can be used and hidden partially by a dress.

As many collectors console themselves, "They surely aren't making them any more!"

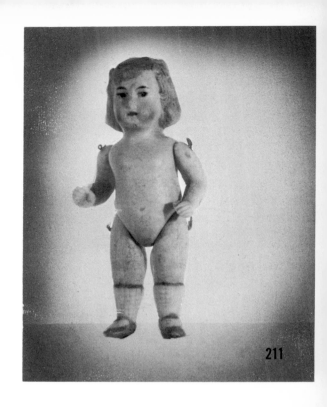

211

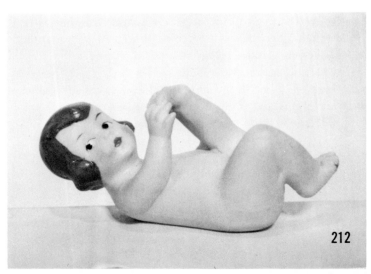

212

211 & 212 Author's collection

No. 211 Incised in two lines on the back **Germany** over **0 ½**, 3 inches tall, hip and shoulder jointed with hard wire, this is a good example of a common, cheap doll available just about anywhere before World War I.

She has a molded, side-parted blond bob with blue side bows, pupils only and black lid linings. The white socks with green top bands have Kestner horizontal molded ribbing, the one-strap slippers are blue and heeled. The complexion coloring is high and rather mottled.

No. 212 This immobile girl, 3½ inches long and 1¾ inches high, is incised on the flat of her back **1776-II** and there is a small air hole under the Roman numeral. She could be a product of the Kewpie era because the bisque feels the same and the complexion coating is pale like prewar Kewpies.

Her molded bob is a bright, glossy brown and so are her one-stroke brows. She has side-painted pupils only and the eyes have black lid linings. Her hands and feet are quite good.

She is not too common and it may be because she presented such an assembly problem. Her entire back, all of the head back of the ears and her seat up to the leg portions were in one mold. Her face, the head back to the crown and her body front were in the other half of the set. Both the arms were added and both legs appear to have been also because each has its own set of mold marks down the sides.

To the nonprofessional this looks like another case where there were incised marks on the lower abdomen to guide the greenware cutters. All the addition seams are clearly visible, especially those on the hips.

No. 213 Incised across the shoulders **Germany** over **241-8** (with a script G and not the print G on later dolls), this little boy is 3⅝ inches tall and hip and shoulder jointed with brass wire. He is apparently older than one would suspect at first glance.

He has blue eyes with high pupils, black lid linings, and dark blond one-stroke brows. The hair is brush stroked like many of the bisque headed infants and only the small lump in the center front is molded. The bisque is good and the tinting is above average.

The "girl" legs would have distressed us. There was a great division of male and female in our world and such a crossover as this would have been sissified to us. Girls longed for heels and played house in discarded shoes from mothers and aunts, but boys had no trucking with such non-

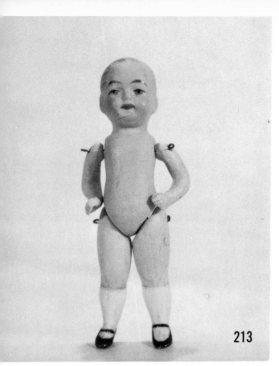
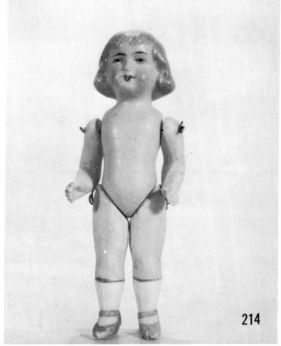

sense. These white socks have blue bands and some evidence of vertical ribbing; the one-strap slippers are black with tan soles.

No. 214 This 3¾-inch doll, on the other hand, would have pleased us. Not because she was high style or fine quality or even pretty, but because of her hair.

Like most crusaders, many of us were pestering our parents to cut the long heads of hair in which our families took such pride. We were tired of being braided, combed, brushed, curled with rags, hair bowed and barretted (usually pronounced bar-et then) to death. There was an overwhelming desire for neatness in our day which consumed quantities of time which we thought we could put to much better advantage. Many of us did not get to cut our hair until the 1920s so this little girl with her short hair completely unrestrained would have been good ammunition for our guns.

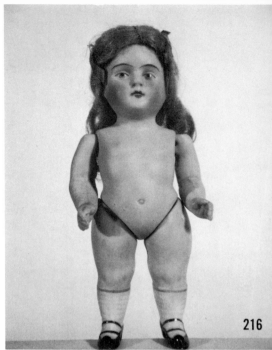

Faintly incised 6 across the shoulders and also on the leg flanges, she is hip and shoulder jointed with hard wire. Not too carefully painted, she has blue eyes with one centered and one high pupil, black lid linings, and brown brows. The molded hair is a soft taffy color of yellow; the socks have fine vertical ribbing and green bands; the one-strap heeled slippers are blue with blue soles.

Her complexion coating is pale but not the fine quality of the better dolls.

Candystore dolls with swivel heads and pretty blond wigs were high spots in our lives but none of us can remember paying any attention to the marks on them or the marks on our German jointeds. We gave our dolls names and ignored such small items as the marks which interest us so much as adult collectors.

No. 215 Left: 5 inches tall, incised 620 over 3 on the head, 620 3 on the back, and 1303 on the arms and legs, this closed mouth doll has her original blond mohair wig on a cloth cap. The swivel neck has the rubber holes at the sides of the neck. She has painted blue eyes with black lid linings and dark blond one-stroke brows. The bisque and all the work is excellent.

Right: With a poorly opened mouth and little teeth set too far back to show in a picture, this one is incised **620** over **5** on the head, **620 5** on the back, and **1305** over **5** on the arms and legs, so they must have been interchangeable with another torso.

She has the swivel head with the holes in the sides of the neck, very dark brown sleep eyes with pupils, and upper and lower painted lashes. The one-stroke brows are brown. The original light blond mohair wig is the woven type on a cloth base.

These two are good examples of how Kestner adapted the same legs to fit different dolls. Both of these have excellent centers of balance, although the legs on the small one spread a little and those on the larger doll touch. Both have two-strap brown shoes with molded buttons and bows and black trim around the soles and on the heels.

No. 216 Minus the swivel neck, here is the **620** over **3** doll (on the left in **No. 215**) but she is ¼ inch taller and has entirely different marks.

This may have been a doll for a private contractor-distributor. There

217

218

does not seem to be any other feasible reason for Kestner to change the incised marks to: 7203 over S and then to repeat the whole number in one line down the insides of the arms, to incise 720 on the inside of the leg flanges and 3S on the inside of the upper leg in plain sight.

The proportions of these two dolls are very different and the Kestner swivel head is by far the most attractive, with slender and attractive lines. This doll is pure German, with a fat torso, arms, and legs. The workmanship, however, is of equal quality but different. There is a machine sewn center part in this wig and two narrow pink bows are glued in place at the temple to hold the hair away from the face. The Kestner wig shows no part and the long bangs rise from a sewed center on the crown.

No. 217 Another stiff neck, 5⅝ inches tall, which appears to have been made by Kestner, perhaps for a quantity buyer such as Butler Brothers or an American house dealing only in dolls. She is incised 7713 on the back, 13 on the arms, and the full 7713 on the leg flanges. She is not a quality product but we would have liked her and she might have saved us a nickel or even nine cents.

Hip and shoulder jointed with loops, she has painted blue eyes with black lid linings and pupils, and one-stroke brown brows. The mouth is painted in two sections with a white center. The dark, reddish-brown wig, which has a machine sewn part done in black, may be original but it has been restyled with hand stitching.

Her blue-banded white socks have horizontal bands but not the shirred pattern of known Kestner dolls; while her one-strap heeled slippers are bright luggage tan, they do not have the black trim or the gloss of the better dolls' shoes. The soles are also the shoe color instead of yellow.

The face and torso are well finished and decorated but the arms are not and both the arms and legs have mottled complexioning.

Someone thought enough of her to dress her very appropriately and in old materials.

No. 218 Dearly beloved of the old candystore set, a doll with a look-alike doll, this 6¼-inch doll is incised 130 over 7 on the back of her stiff-necked head. She and her small duplicate are hip and shoulder jointed with excellent loops but both have long since lost their original wigs.

These are more Kestners. The large doll has blue sleep eyes with upper and lower painted lashes, shining multistroke brows, and the familiar wooden eye-bar plastered in place inside her head. The complexion coat is very pale and uniform; she has pretty hands with free thumbs, knuckle dimples, and very good finger delineation. Her white socks are high and horizontally striped and vertically ribbed, with blue top bands. Her good two-strap slippers are brown with molded side buttons and front bows. The bows, the shoe edges, and the heels are black, and the soles are brown like the shoes.

This brings up an old question: To rewig or not? It is actually a matter of personal choice and whether the dolls are collected for display or for study. Modern fiber substitutes and human hair wigs are *not* accurate. Old mohair wigs which are too far gone to use on large jointeds are about the only place now to obtain the proper material.

In a large collection, wigging can get to be a consuming passion which obscures collecting itself. There are never enough of them, of course, but old wigs from broken all-bisques are much more desirable.

Her little doll is incised **130** over **3/0** and the differences are due to the decreased size. The painted blue eyes have black lid linings and pupils;

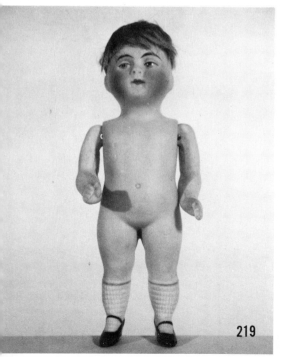

the one-stroke brows are dark blond. Her thumbs have been closed into the hand and the complexion coating is only slightly higher than that of the larger doll.

The old white dress bears description for the guidance of modern doll dressers. The material is an open basket weave and the sleeves are kimona cut. To eliminate bulky hems and seams, the neck, sleeve edges, the edge of the waist, and hem edge are all done in buttonhole stitch with very fine crochet thread. The back-seamed skirt is gathered with a raw edge, the edged blouse is superimposed and the front has an embroidered decoration. The little embroidered "purse" is a single thickness of cloth, also embroidered, and fastened into the waist with crocheted chain stitch.

No. 219 Incised **600** over **4** on the head and **6004** down the insides of the arms, this 5½-inch stiff leg is undoubtedly another Kestner product. The very good arms with excellent loops fit into narrow socket rims and even though it is not glass eyed, there is a circular open top to the head. The bisque is extremely good and so is all the finishing and painting. The complexion coating is very pale and uniform.

The side-painted blue eyes have pupils and black lid linings and the one-stroke brows are brown. The shirred white socks with blue bands are a familiar type for this firm and the one-strap heeled black shoes have bright brown soles. The old blond mohair wig is securely sewed to a good gauze cap.

No. 220 Not equal to the previous doll in quality, and rather pudgy, this 5½-doll would nevertheless have been very popular with us because skinny children and/or dolls were not the vogue in our day.

She is incised on the back of the head **150** over **3/0** and only **3/0** on the arms and legs. She has deep shoulder sockets and hip sockets with an almost completely closed additional depression to accommodate the large leg loops. She has good brown sleep eyes with upper and lower painted lashes, multistroke dark blond brows, and a long, light blond mohair wig on a good cloth cap. She also has a little plaster dome intact.

It is surprising that Kestner used the number **150** on her because there are several composition-bodied infants in this collection which are a Kestner 140 series and several others, including an appealing toddler, which are a 150 group of numbers. There is also the all-bisque infant, **No. 189**, which is 150.

Like many of these small dolls, the head and torso are much better

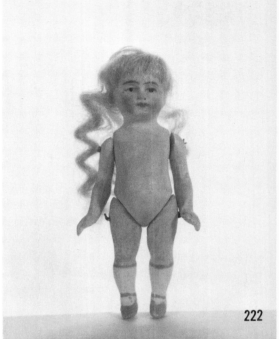

finished and decorated than the arms and legs. She has some mold debris in the fingers, her white socks have blue bands and a different type of vertical ribbing. The one-strap black slippers have tan soles but the heels are entirely black. The bisque is old and good but the complexion is not as pale and soft as that of the stiff leg before her.

No. 221 Nobody can say definitely at this late date, but perhaps this girl was an experiment by Kestner to make an all-bisque which would sit well. Perhaps they made it to order for someone else, but it undoubtedly was a failure because it is more than slightly ridiculous. Bent legs with shirred deep yellow socks and typical Kestner two-strap black slippers with pointed toes, front bows, heels, and tan soles simply do not go together.

Incised on the head peculiarly, it appears to be 30⅑ over 4, and only 4 on the arms, but 314 . 4 (and the dot turned out to be a small air hole) on the legs; nevertheless, she is NOT an assembled doll. The legs have been seen several times without torsos because collectors could not understand where they belonged. Other complete dolls have also been examined but the owners have always apologized for the mix-up in the legs.

The bisque is excellent, old, and well finished. She has blue eyes with high pupils and black lid linings; the brows are one-stroke in dark blond. The complexion is pale and very even and the little blond mohair wig is built on a very good pink cloth cap.

No. 222 Only 3¼ inches tall, this mint little girl has completely yellow one-strap slippers with heels. Shoes were mostly black, brown, and white in our day and this would have endeared her to us, poor quality or no.

She has an unfamiliar incised mark across her shoulders which appears to be 8106. Her decorating is poor and the complexion is high; she has pupils only, and brown lid linings like her brown brows. The waved yellow mohair wig with bangs is on a good pink cloth cap and there is a little Roman-striped ribbon across the top of her head.

No. 223 Unmarked and difficult to place in time, this 3½-inch stiff neck may be an old catalogue type because it could not have competed well with the Candystore dolls we could choose from.

Hip and shoulder jointed with hard wire, of very poor quality, there

223

223 Author's collection

are only painted pupils with black lid linings and brows. There is some vertical ribbing in the blue banded white socks and the high boots are orange.

Its chief point of interest is because it is "as found." The dress is old and the pleating quite heavy for such a small doll. The braid trim is also an old type and the style of dressmaking is before our time. The sewed-on sailor hat solves the problem of the wig which was lost from the center top push-in hole.

Precolored Bisque

Precoloring was an economy measure. The complexioning and padding operation could be entirely eliminated by adding pink color to the bisque. From the dolls in this collection, it would appear that many firms made both types at the same time. Reference examples will be given in the text.

The nicest precolored bisque has a dull finish which is so pale it is often difficult to distinguish at a glance because the rest of the decorating is fired.

Another dull type is much pinker and less appealing and much of it is postwar. It could have been simply a matter of adding too much color or, which is more likely, after the war some type of "ersatz" color had to be used because Germany had many substitution or, as they said, "ersatz," problems for quite a while. This must have been a great hardship because for many years Germany had produced some of the world's finest porcelain as well as some of the finest colors the world had ever known. In the blue shades, nothing could equal or surpass German colors.

Added to all this, they had Japanese competition with which to contend.

There is a third kind of precoloring which has a high, unattractive gloss and, since much of the decorating was not fired, the color washes and wears off because it could not get a purchase on the surface.

This unpleasant shine cannot be called "greasy" because that is a term applied to very good, old bisque which always retains a fine, low-grade gloss which gives the dolls and doll heads a desirable, freshly scrubbed appearance.

When there is any doubt about precoloring, there is nothing to do but remove the wig to examine the inside of the head. If it is closed construction, the arm and leg flanges will also be pink, whereas those with complexioning are white and the loops were left white. There is no mistaking the stark white of uncolored bisque. Even the slightest chipping helps also to identify precolored and uncolored bisque.

No. 224 A repeat of illustration No. 232. This pair is repeated here for quick reference because the large doll is precolored and the small duplicate is not.

No. 225 Precolored, with an almost closed head which is incised 516/3, this doll has the same numbers on her leg flanges. She is 5½ inches tall and quite a nice, dull specimen.

There are excellent tops to her rubber strung arms and legs, the body modeling is good and so is the finishing. In fact, there is little doubt that she is a Kestner because her legs are like those on both older and more expensive types. The socks are blue in a shade which hides the precoloring and the two-strap heeled slippers with pompons in front are the old type. There is an economy evident here, however, because the shoes are plain brown without the additional black trim which distinguishes the older types.

She has painted blue eyes with high pupils and black lid linings. The attractive closed mouth was painted in two sections, giving the impression of parted, smiling lips. The wig cannot be original because it seems unlikely that Kestner would glue a long hank of fiber across the head horizontally so that it could never be combed.

No. 226 Unmarked, very pale and dull precolored bisque, dolls with this molded bob were sometimes called "Buster Brown" during that particular craze. The same type was made with bent legs and appears incongruous because they are neither infants nor children.

This one is 4 inches tall and hip and shoulder jointed with hard wire; the hair is pale yellow. The side-molded, slightly intaglio eyes have black pupils and lid linings, with blue rims; the brows are brown.

The low molded boots are brown and very familiar looking with their brown soles; the low molded socks have vertical ribbing and were left uncolored. The workmanship is only fair.

No. 227 During the prewar period little dolls like this precolored with molded hair and bows were very popular—and cheap. We knew nothing about precoloring, of course, and were guided in our purchases strictly by our tastes.

This unmarked one is 4½ inches tall and hip and shoulder jointed with loops; the hair is yellow and the bows are blue. She has painted blue eyes with pupils and black lid linings and a fairly good body. The socks are blue with darker blue bands and the one-strap black slippers have yellow soles.

224

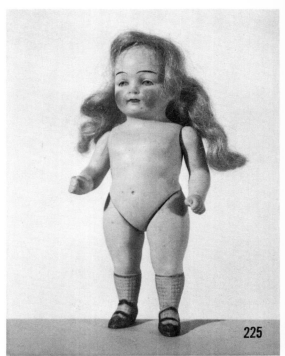

225

224 & 225 Author's collection

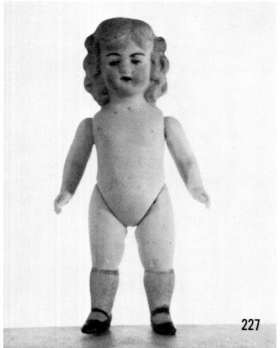

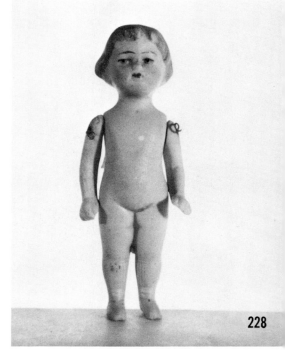

226, 227 & 228 *Author's collection*

No. 228 Even cheaper, this shoulder jointed precolored is 3¾ inches tall and incised in back in a fraction: **17** over a line and **9** below the line and below that, **Germany** in a crescent shape. It is doubtful that little girls paid more than 10 cents for these, and then only if financial difficulties had overwhelmed them—such as letting your roller skates be stolen and saving for a new pair out of your own pocket. Mass doses of sympathy seldom came our way.

The molded hair is dark taffy blond, the blue eyes have pupils and black lid linings, and the brows match the hair. The high socks and shoes are molded and if the shoes were originally painted, no vestige of it is left.

Other precolored dolls appear in the chapter called "Detective Story."

Detective
Story

No. 229 Because cobalt eyes in all-bisques are not too common, this 5½-inch doll has had more than her share of attention, even though her left arm is broken at the elbow and a replacement has never been found.

Hip and shoulder jointed with pegs, incised **3/0** high on the head, she is of excellent old, pale bisque. The light yellow bootines are trimmed with black and have dainty heels. Her body is slender and much less potbellied than usual dolls of her period. The head has a circular cut in the center top and the cap wig is woven blond mohair, like good wigs on larger dolls.

She also has red eye dots, there are no painted lashes, and her one-stroke brows are brown. The torso has shallow shoulder sockets but the arm tops are poorly engineered, as though they were an experiment. The tinting is the old peach color but the bisque is glossy and the coloring is not completely opaque.

No. 230 When the 6⅛-inch stiff leg came along, the facial resemblance to **No. 229** was immediately noted.

Incised high on the head 515 over 4, this doll is of fine quality bisque and compares well with the old tinted dolls (**Nos. 93 & 94**). However, this one has only a rim around the shoulder socket but the tops of the arms are well rounded and looped for rubber stringing. They are a vast improvement on the cobalt's arm tops.

The body modeling is very good and both the hands and feet were excellently finished before being decorated. The complexion tinting is slightly inferior but this very pale pink tone is more difficult to keep uniform than the peach color which is slightly opaque.

The head was flat cut to make the set eyes possible, and she has upper and lower painted lashes and one-stroke blond eyebrows. The old blond

229

230

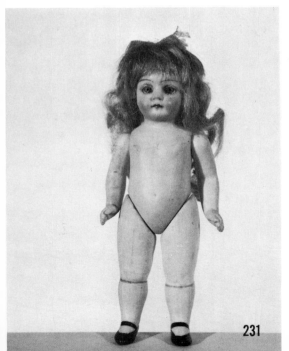

231

232

229, 230, 231 & 232 Author's collection

wig is of good mohair and like the cobalt's (**No. 229**). The socks are medium blue with deeper blue bands in a clear, sharp color. The shoes are glossy black and they are painted high in front with molded tassels; the soles are yellow.

No. 231 Incised high on the open top head **540/3**, this 5½-inch hip and shoulder jointed has the previous doll's face and the same light blue, set glass eyes, upper and lower painted lashes, and dark blond brows. She has the same narrow shoulder socket rims as the previous doll and the same arms. The knee socks are vertically ribbed and painted the same blue which appears to be white in the picture with only the dark bands showing.

Her one-strap slippers are shining black with slight heels and tan soles. The torso coloring is better than either the arms or the legs and all of it is a peachy pink. Her wig is reddish-blond mohair on a paper cap, held at the crown with a flat ribbon bow.

No. 232 These two dolls seem to prove that the same dolls were made of both uncolored and precolored bisque. Whether they were made for two different price fields at the same time or at two different times through the reuse of old molds cannot now be answered, but at least we can be sure it was done.

The smaller doll, 3½ inches tall, is a duplicate of **No. 231**. She is incised 540 0/2 and it is immediately evident that she is not precolored because her socks are white.

The larger doll, 5 inches tall, is incised **540/3** and she is precolored. This is quickly ascertained because her socks are a muddy blue to hide the precoloring and the bands are also darker. Both reddish-blond mohair wigs are built on paper caps—which was a late practice in the business—and this doll has a cerise velvet ribbon across the crown.

All the workmanship is satisfactory to good on this precolored doll, so, since there are upper and lower painted lashes and set glass eyes, collectors are entitled to wonder whether or not precoloring was not a much earlier economy than was previously realized, at least with some firms.

No. 233 Hip and shoulder jointed with wire, incised **320/4** on the head, this 6¼-inch doll has the same face as the others. She has a noticeable fault, however, which appears over and over again in the dolls in this group.

On the inner side of her arms, close to the stringing hole, there is *a gaping ⅜-inch hole in the arm surface*. This was where the excess slip was poured out after the arm had set and it should have been filled in at the greenware stage, just as the holes in the soles of the shoes were filled in after being unmolded. This was a company policy for economy sake.

The construction was changed to wire jointing and all the dolls have feet like hers, soft boots with a front tassel. With the exception of the doll with black shoes, **No. 230**, the modeling of which is very good, all these dolls have poor modeling and all the boot soles are painted with the shoe color instead of the customary yellow. It is not an unpleasant economy measure but it did save a great deal of time and effort and helps to identify the dolls.

All the socks have fine vertical ribbing which gets poorer and poorer as the sizes decrease. Except for the previous blue ones, all the socks are white with painted bands which are blue with the pink shoes and pink with the blue shoes.

Manufacturers fall into habits even today and this old porcelain house kept repeating the same face and shoes, with large pour holes left open in the arms, over many years of production.

The top of this doll's head is closed and flat, with a blond cap wig like

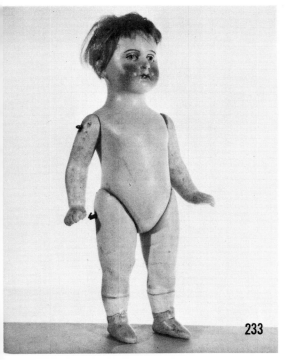

233 Author's collection; 234 Strong collection

those on the two previous dolls which have the same face. The painted blue eyes have no red dots but there are black lid linings and the old red lid lines. The one-stroke brows are identical.

The head and body finishing is far superior to that of the limbs but all the bisque is quite good. This may indicate that apprentice finishers did the limbs. Doll decorating is a trade which has to be learned and it would have been much more sensible to start finishers on limbs than on headed torsos. Limbs were cheaper to remake if ruined and easier to mold and unmold; they had to be fired only once, very likely; and since they were made in such large quantities, assembling would not have been delayed for a lack of them.

Accurately establishing the order of production at this late date is almost impossible. Observation, comparison with other lines, and available information can only help to form a pattern of progression.

Collectors must bear in mind that these dolls were not meant to be collected and that many factors controlled production quality, quantity, and changes. Every change cost money because new models had to be made and that also meant new casting molds. A long-term, lucrative contract with a wholesale distributor who catered to small stores, novelty houses, and peddlars, would have been more coveted by some manufacturers than a name in the trade for excellence. Contracts meant steady production and full employment for trained workers. All this also meant profits.

It is quite possible that this house continued to make both quality and economy lines but it would seem that in almost twenty years of collecting, with special emphasis on all-bisques, more of the superior type would have been found.

There is no question about this firm's ability to do good work because the following three bonnets attest to that.

No. 234 Shoulder jointed with wire, 5½ inches tall, this frozen-legged girl is marred only by the open pour holes in her arms. Her origin is evident in the white ribbed socks with pink bands and the telltale blue boots with tassels.

She has painted blue eyes with high pupils, black lid linings, and one-stroke dark blond brows. The bisque is very good, the complexion is quite pale, and the finishing and decorating are exceptional for such a competitive item.

The pale blond hair is expertly done and the detail of the bonnet is accentuated by the painting. The bonnet is pushed back on her head and the entire back is undecorated, but the front is certainly eye-catching. The outer rim of the brim is pale green, the inner rim is darker green, and the top bow and molded chin ribbon and bow are orange.

No. 235 Hip and shoulder jointed with wire, 6⅞ inches tall, this girl has a very large pour hole open on the inside of one arm, an even bigger hole in one hip flange and badly finished pour holes in the feet. She has the blue shoes and pink sock bands.

Her features are also the same; the bisque is good, but the complexion coating of the legs is somewhat mottled.

Her pale blond hair is even more detailed than that of the previous doll and the enormous hat has an entirely different shape, although it is also pale green with a dark green band through the turned-back brim. Instead of orange, bright pink was used for the bows and the back is again not decorated.

No. 236 Because her legs have been replaced, this girl is presented in a close-up which shows the detail of her head and hat to advantage. The

235 & 236 Strong collection

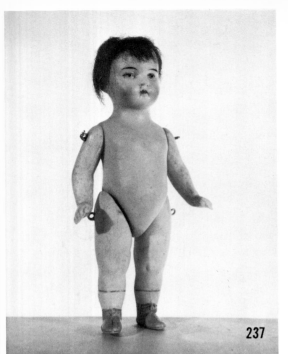

237

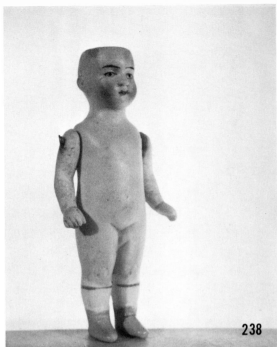

238

239

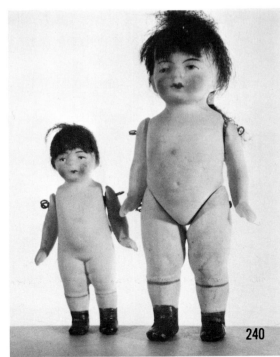

240

237, 238, 239 & 240 Author's collection

pour holes in her wire-jointed arms are positive identification. With the proper legs she apparently would have been about 7½ inches tall.

She is either older or was made for a quality buyer because she has red lid lines as well as the standard blue eyes done like the others. The long hair with bangs and only a suggestion of curl adds to her attractiveness by reducing the "busy" look of the other two. The bisque is very good, the finishing and decorating are excellent, and she has very good hands.

The bonnet, which is deeper than it appears to be in the picture, has a pale pink outer rim, a lovely rose inner rim and the bow ends at the top are a soft, dark green. As with most bonnets, the back is untouched.

These dolls are not marked in any way but it would have been very easy to identify them for factory purposes by the colors or differences in the bonnets.

No. 237 Hip and shoulder jointed with wire, incised **520** over **3** on the head, this little doll has all the faults of the others and, because she is hip jointed, the fill-ins on the soles of the blues shoes are visible.

The top of the head has a flat cut and she has a glued-on wig of inferior fiber. The painted blue eyes have black lid linings and poorly done red lid lines.

No. 238 Incised **510** over **2¼** on the head, this 4¼-inch wire shoulder jointed also has the pink boots which are not disfigured on the soles because the excess slip was poured from the head.

The bisque is sharper to the touch, the complexion color is higher, the eyes are painted blue with black lid linings but the red lid lines are gone. The head is open and flat cut but the wig was missing when the doll was found. The shoulder is still squared off at the torso and the open pour holes still mar the inner arms.

No. 239 Of a shiny bisque which did not take the fired color well, this wire strung shoulder jointed sample is incised in three lines on the center back of the torso **276** over **Germany** over **2½**. The arm construction is still the same, flat at the shoulder with flat inside arm tops, but the arm holes are filled in this time.

The original blond, glued-on wig is the same rough textured fiber noted in **No. 237** and there is a glued-on band of very narrow lavender tape.

The shoes are blue and unmarred, of course, because of the open top on the head. There is very little complexion tinting and, bcause of the nature of the bisque, this is not good. The eyes are blue and painted poorly.

No. 240 Of pale, precolored bisque with a dull finish, these two may be the last of the baby-booted line from this firm.

The 4½-inch hip and shoulder wire jointed doll is incised on the head **620/2** and the 3-inch wire shoulder jointed is incised **610** over **0.** The modeling is not complicated but it is adequate for the type and the decorating is typical of German work. The large doll has blue eyes with pupils and black lid linings; the small one has only pupils and black lid linings. The unpainted socks have ribbing and blue bands, and the little brown shoes have brown soles.

They have their original wigs, which are made of the previously noted brown fiber, and they also have the very narrow, glued-on headbands of the same type used on the blond doll. These two have rose-colored bands instead of lavender.

No. 241 Without any marks, of very pale, dull precolored bisque, the 4½-inch hip and shoulder wire jointed has the almost changeless face of the others. The molded, childish hairdo is tinted a very light yellow and the two molded bows are a medium blue. The boots have been changed to one-strap slippers which are painted brown, with brown soles, and the painting is either amateur or careless.

A limbless torso in the collection, also the deep pink color and with taffy hair, has the same two blue bows and is a size larger. Across the back it is incised in three lines, **Made, in,** and **Germany.**

No. 242 This 4½-inch doll is a later use of the same molds because the precolor is much pinker, the bisque has the later, unbecoming shine, and the hair is a dark taffy color to hide the pink scalp.

Instead of the two bows, this one has a molded band in back, which was painted the color of the hair for economy sake, and a molded band of leaves, painted green, across the forehead. Four small holes in the band held tiny artificial flowers secured by wires but only one flower is left.

Another sign of lateness is the incised **Germany** across the center of her shoulders. The shoes are the same brown.

No. 243 This 3½-inch precolored, hip and shoulder loop jointed little girl seems to belong to the same family. The featuring—black eye linings and pupils only—the glued-on wig of poor hair substitute, all point to this manufacturer, even though her shoes have small heels.

A dark spot can be seen in each arm top and in the right leg. These are

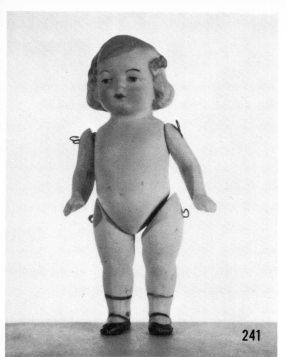

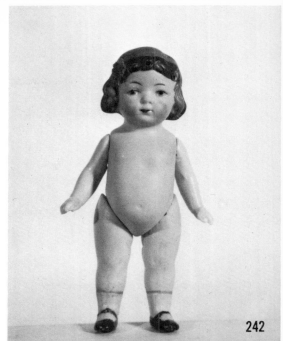

241

242

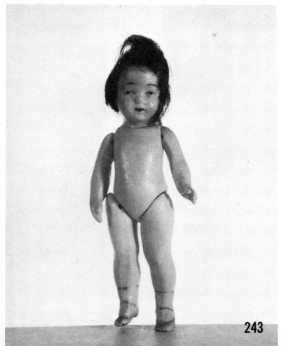

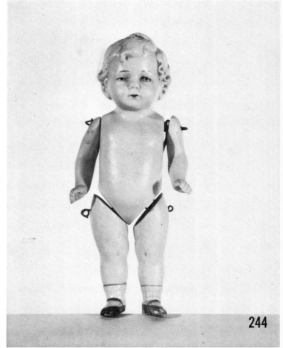

243

244

241, 242, 243 & 244 Author's collection

small channels in the bisque where a tool was run through in the green-ware stage to open up the stringing loops.

She is late, of course, and is incised **Germany** across the back like some of the others.

No. 244 This 5¼-inch doll with molded hair is also precolored and because of the type of bisque, most of the blond hair has worn off. It was painted but not fired and the paint did not get a good purchase on the surface.

Because it is wire strung, the small channels are not in the arms but the high hip on the torso has a gaping hole that was not filled in. There are also unfilled holes in the tops of the legs above the stringing holes—a new type of hurry-up defect. The unfilled holes on the insides of the arms are like those on the older dolls, only smaller.

The dimpled knees and shoes and socks are those of the molded-hair girls. Because he is larger, his back is incised in two lines, **Made,** and **in Germany.** It is the same print as that used on the other marked dolls.

These dolls were more and more puzzling as they accumulated through the years. Some of them we could remember from pre-World War I days but we were spoiled by the nice old German dolls and these did not have the same appeal to us. There must have been great quantities of old dolls in storage in this country, too, because at least in our area we did not have to buy these if we did not want to.

Dolls very similar to the doll on the right in **No. 240** appear in the Butler Brothers Catalogue for November 1921 but the illustration shows one-strap slippers instead of the boots. Under a caption "IMPORTED DOLLS," the subheading states, "A large variety of popular Japanese imported dolls. . . ." The individual listing is:

F9649—4¼ in., flesh colored china, mohair wig, painted features, shoes and stockings, jointed arms and legs. 1 doz. in box. . . . Doz. 42¢

In years of collecting, the author has never found one of these dolls of Japanese manufacture. Because they were only incised with numbers, this maneuver worked. Apparently it was just sensitivity about Germany which governed the listing.

In the December 1925 catalogue, a doll just like **No. 240** with the boots is listed in a 6-inch size at $1.95 per dozen. Not a word is said about their German origin but all-bisque Bye-Lo dolls with labels are in the group, as is the real "Baby Bud" and the little marked German dolls **Nos. 300 and 301.**

It was not until all the dolls and material and pictures were laid out for this book that the similarity to Amberg dolls was noticed.

Louis
Amberg
& Son

Nos. 245 and **246** These three precolored bisques, 5⅞, 4½, and 3 inches tall, are late, but they are identified as "Mibs" and were designed by Helen Drucker. They are fully incised and dated across each back:

ⓒ

L A & S 1921

Germany

The molded hair is much like that on the previous doll but the bisque is better, inasmuch as it is not so glossy and has retained most of the decorating. This may be because they were never played with, however, because the color is *not* fired on and washes off quite readily. They are rather well finished for that era except for the bungling closure of the pour hole in the largest doll's head.

All the hair and feature painting is slipshod and the largest doll has the whites of his/her eyes painted pale blue. They all have uncolored socks with blue bands and the telltale flat, one-strap slippers. In the two small dolls the slippers are brown and in the large one they are gray.

There are large, unfilled pour holes on the inside upper arms of the large doll which can be seen when the arms are raised but on the small ones these holes have been closed. The pour holes in the feet are visible but not objectionable.

As with doll **No. 243**, in all the arms and in the legs of the hip jointeds, the same channel is visible where the stringing loops were opened with a tool or a wire of some kind during the greenware processing.

It is quite possible that this whole series of dolls was made for Louis Amberg & Son, at least starting with the first dolls with blue and pink boots.

 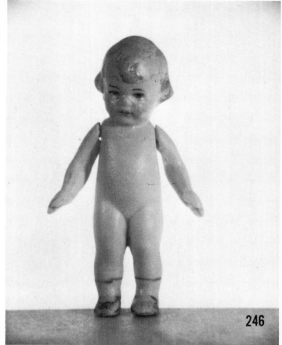

Like E. I. Horsman and other American importers, Amberg bought so
many German dolls that they eventually were incised with the buyers'
names, trademarks and/or copyrights, with or without those of the manufacturer.

This would account for the unchanging characteristics of these dolls.
The faults were all the result of pricing other porcelain competitors out
of the lucrative and continuous Amberg contracts.

In *Dolls, Makers and Marks*, Elizabeth Coleman gives 1872 in Cincin-
nati as a starting date for Amberg and places him in the doll and toy business in 1878. From 1899, when the firm moved to New York City, it was
a large doll distributor, best-known to modern collectors for their "New
Born Babe" which was copyrighted in 1914, nine years before the Bye-Lo.

In discussing these all-bisques, Dorothy Coleman says there is reason to
believe that Armand Marseille made a great many Amberg heads but she
agrees that so far there is no evidence that A.M. made all-bisques, and we
are all sure they were late-comers in the doll business.

The Colemans have also inspected marked "Herm Steiner" dolls in factory-made clothing which was labeled "Amberg." However, Hermann Steiner is listed as 1924, which is too late for "Mibs," let alone the earlier suspects from the same manufacturer.

German dollmakers kept their secrets well and so did American distributors, so there is a good chance we may never know the name of this manufacturer. When and if it is ever found, it will doubtless be quite by accident.

But American collectors must bear in mind always that their personal quest for perfection did not bother most doll manufacturers at all. These were toys for children and, because "der kinder" did not rule the German world by any manner of means, the same attitude invaded business concerning children.

This was even more true of dolls than of toys which would interest boys. German fathers, and this included those who had migrated to America, were less reluctant to spend money on work-oriented toys for boys—farm equipment, fire engines, and the like—than on doll babies for girls. Babies you got for nothing and buying make-believe duplicates for girls who had small brothers and sisters to care for was considered a pretty foolish expenditure. This was true right up to the World War I period in many German populated areas here.

If an object was salable, it was sold, and, just as today, it had to be quite poor quality not to find a buyer and a market somewhere. The object of the manufacturing was to garner American dollars and nothing else mattered.

Kewpies and Their Competitors

Kewpies, the impish brainchildren of Rose O'Neill's popular magazine illustrations, were apparently an instant success in bisque. Because Rowena Godding Ruggles' delightful book, *The One Rose,* is so packed with information and pictures of this beautiful American artist and her many accomplishments, it has become a standard reference work for collectors and students.

For the purposes of this book, a few Kewpies will be pictured to complete this record.

Patented in 1913, the dolls and Kewpie-decorated china, as well as all kinds of novelties, appeared in the 1914 wholesale catalogues. It has been said that within the next few years scarcely a home in this country was without a Kewpie in one form or another.

This is very believable because *Time Magazine,* reporting her death in the issue of April 17, 1944, said:

Died. Rose O'Neill, 69, cartoonist creator of the "Kewpie Doll"; in Springfield, Mo. Exquisitely beautiful daughter of an Irish ne'er-do-well who later retired to a Missouri chasm, the onetime Omaha convent girl became a newspaper cartoonist at 13, in later years attempted serious painting and sculpture, never really learned linear perspective. She copyrighted her epicene homunculus in 1909,* after first seeing its teardrop-headed form in a dream. Pirated the world over, the "Kewpie Doll" sold more than 5,000,000 copies, brought its twice-married parent more than $1,400,000."

* (This seeming disparity in copyright and patent dates arises from the fact that the first Kewpies were copyrighted drawings, paperdolls, etc. and the doll patents came under separate laws.)

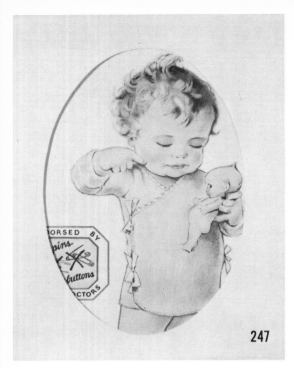

No. 247 Illustration from a VANTA BABY GARMENT full-page advertisement in *The Ladies Home Journal*, September, 1926. Printed in full color, the Kewpie in the child's hand actually measures 1½ inches.

No. 248 One of Rose's many signatures. This "O'Neill" is most frequently incised in the soles of Kewpie feet. In the Strong Collection, however, there is a standing Kewpie, approximately 5½ inches tall, which has the entire signature painted in black down the left side. A 4½-inch specimen still has the original price penciled in back and it cost 19 cents when it was new.

No. 249 The 4⅜-inch soldier is generally identified as "The Cadet," although Rose O'Neill constantly referred to him as "Army" in her writings. He has the usual bright red cap with a black visor, a brown gun, silver sword, and black belt, and his left arm is molded behind his back. The label is also bright red with a gold border and white print.

No. 250 The average standing Kewpie is barefooted and Rose called them "Plain." There is also this little girl with painted shoes with butterfly bows and white socks, nameless to the best of our knowledge. She is 5½ inches tall and incised **O'Neill** on the feet.

In the author's collection there is a much larger girl with black one-strap slippers without the bows and also without white socks.

No. 251 To collectors, "action" Kewpies are those doing anything at all besides just standing there smiling. This little banjo player in a pale blue, 3⅞-inch chair, is a good example. The only mark on him is a stamped ⓒ on the underside of the chair seat.

No. 252 Very much like the sprawling Kewpies in O'Neill drawings, this

249

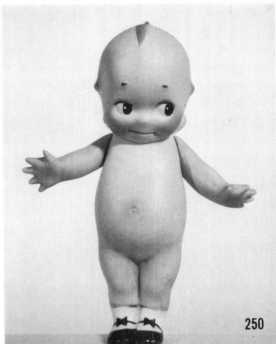

250

251

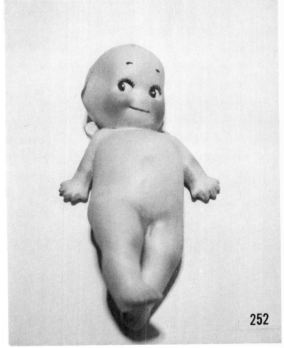

252

249, 250, 251 & 252 Strong collection

253

254

255

256

253, 255 & 256 Author's collection; 254 Strong collection

3⅞-inch creature flat on its back is often tied to a silk pillow, as is the companion which is flat on its stomach. On the oval depression in the middle of the back is incised **O'Neill** and **15 B,** and then the stamped ⓒ is superimposed over the lettering.

No. 253 "The Huggers" are very well known and this pair are 3⅜ inches, unmarked in any way, but O'Neill Kewpies nevertheless—perhaps missing their label.

No. 254 With a green book in hand and a brown book behind, this 3½-inch pair are more difficult to find and they are possibly another form of the "Instructive" Kewpies which appear in O'Neill's writings, always with at least one book. They are also unmarked.

No. 255 Only 2 inches or a shade less, this "buttonhole" Kewpie is eagerly sought, although they are generally unmarked. Some collectors have discovered that it is possible to have a jeweler wrap gold wire (the kind from which name pins are formed) around the button shank and then form a clasp and a pin in the two ends of wire. With such an arrangement, collectors can wear the doll more often and with greater safety than in the average buttonhole, especially those in a woman's suit or dress.

Another tiny one in this collection has the same outspread arms but has no buttonhole attachment. It is 1¾ inches tall, stamped **Germany** in blue down the spine and much higher in color than the one illustrated. There is also a minute air hole at the base of the head.

These appear to have been convention or party favors, the buttonhole type being for the men. The other doll can be dressed in a tiny ribbon or tulle skirt with a ribbon sash and then held with a safety pin fastened on the inside of the dress.

No. 256 Judging by the number of standing Kewpies and action Kewpies which have come to light in recent years, hip and shoulder jointed doll Kewpies were in the minority. This is surprising because here is an appealing little all-bisque about which speculations arise.

Production may have been interrupted by World War I and, no matter how tired modern collectors get of hearing about it, that event made their collecting much more difficult these fifty years later. We always have to bear it in mind when we run into problems.

This 5-inch specimen, with both the front label and the round, black and white back label still intact, has reddish brown instead of yellow hair.

Other original Kewpies in the collection have this same color, so it must have been a matter of the manufacturer's choice or error.

Not at all high in color, this one has more "blushing" than the average Kewpie with yellow hair. Long streaks of almost pure henna mark the knees, the toes are colored straight across the feet, the navel is marked, so are the insides of all the fingers, and even the seat is broadly splashed.

Standing Kewpies seem to outnumber the jointed variety by possibly as much as 50 or 100 to 1. On the other hand, so many standing Kewpies were made into pincushions and other decorative needlework items, and so many action Kewpies were kept in china closets, just ordinary destructive child play would, at first glance, seem to be responsible for the scarcity of the jointeds now.

This may not be true. Many women who vividly recall the Candystore dolls and the standing Kewpies they had, cannot remember seeing jointed Kewpies for sale or having had one. The author recently bought a doll trunk which had been unopened in an attic for fifty years. The owner's 8-inch, much-loved standing Kewpie was among the dolls. She remembered

257

258

257 & 258 Brewer collection

knitting sweaters and making ribbon skirts for it but she had never heard of sit-downs because she had not been interested in doll collecting in her adult life. There was no financial problem in her childhood and everyone in the family knew the Kewpie was her favorite doll, so she felt sure none of the adults ever had an opportunity to buy a sit-down or she would have had one or several.

Another point which argues against their production in the quantities necessary for survival is the dearth of large sizes. Many 12-inch standing Kewpies have found their way into collections, but this is not true of the hip jointeds.

German manufacturers were never reluctant to produce fast-selling items just because they were extremely breakable. Once loved and broken, the more likely the sale of a replacement. So many other types of large hip and shoulder jointed all-bisques have survived, there just could not have been enough of the Kewpie type made.

No. 257 Another unusual Kewpie is this 4⅜-inch boy with completely molded clothes and hat. Shoulder jointed, with typical Kewpie highlighted, side-turned eyes, he is a real charmer—and he was copied by the Japanese.

The flat topped hat was left white, along with the shirt, his necktie is pink, and his pants are teal blue. (There seems to have been something sacred about the blue of Kewpies' wings and green apparently was added to it whenever it was used as another color decoration.) Like little boys have always done, this fellow has a useless belt buckled around his middle; it is tan to represent leather. The molded suit with pants which buttoned onto the shirt was a popular dressmaking trick from the teens through the thirties to keep little boys together in public.

No. 258 Composition Scootles exist in fair quantities but the all-bisque type are much more difficult to find. Another of Rose O'Neill's brain-children, patented in 1935, Scootles never reached the Kewpie popularity, although modern collectors are fond of both.

Shoulder jointed, husky legs apart, this one is 5½ inches tall, and still wears his red and gold label. In four lines it reads, **Scootles, Reg. U.S., Pat. Off.,** and **Germany. Scootles** is incised, **Germany** is stamped on the sole of the left foot, and © **Rose O'Neill** is incised on the right.

The eyes are molded and the blue irises with pupils and highlights are painted to appear mischievous rather than goo-goo. The upper lids are painted light brown and the brown lashes rise from this band. The brows are blond.

The very pale yellow hair is molded in high locks on the head, into peaks above the ears and into a pointed cluster at the base of the head. The watermelon mouth has a dimple at each side and dimples, singly and in pairs, abound on the back.

The bisque and the decorating are good and the complexion coating is not high, surprisingly enough.

Nos. 259 and **260** This 5¼-inch hip and shoulder jointed doll with painted forelock was a competitive item for Kewpies and it is in good supply generally.

In old catalogues it is identified as "Cupid" and, to say the least, "Cupid" is a rather brash invasion of O'Neill's original word, "Kewpie." Without a doubt, too, this accounts for much of the misspelling of the O'Neill trade name because English does not lend itself to separating C and K in the spoken word.

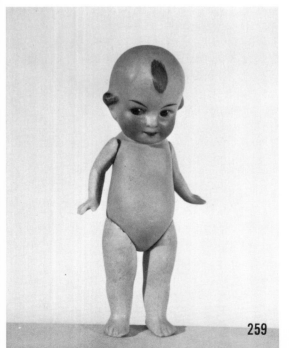

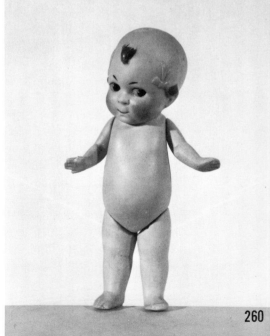

259

260

259 & 260 Author's collection

Above the listing of these Cupids in the 1916 Fall Catalogue of Butler Brothers, there is a note to storekeepers:

Novelty character baby with a winsome expression that will readily coax open the pocketbook. 1 doz. in box, Doz. 95¢

The bisque, the finishing, and decorating are on a par with the excellent but strictly copyrighted Kewpies and the eyes are side painted with highlights like Kewpie eyes. They are without the eyelashes Kewpies have and, of course, there is no evidence of or substitute for the tiny blue wings at the neckline.

Cupid is incised **GERMANY** over **10954** on the back. They must have been sold in great quantities because they are to be found in widely separated areas throughout the country.

Cupid's sister, with painted blue bows, is incised in back **10414** over **GERMANY,** and she is also 5¼ inches tall. For some reason best known to the designer, the ribbon ends point upward.

Even though they are both of good German quality, they would have been more attractive with heavier arms and, like some other late German dolls, the whites of their eyes are painted blue.

The girl of the pair is not as common as the boy although in the 1916 Butler Brothers Catalogue an attempt seems to have been made to correct that situation. The separate listing of the boy in dozen lots is marked "OUT" and yet on the same page, at the same price, 95 cents a dozen, they are listed together in assorted dozens.

No. 261 In 1914, about six months after the Happifats were copyrighted by Borgfeldt, Butler Brothers decided to get into the market with a doll of their own. Incised over the entire back in five lines, **THE / WIDE-AWAKE / DOLL / REGISTERED / GERMANY,** the doll appeared in the Fall 1914 Butler Catalogue, along with the Happifats, Kewpies and Kewpie novelties, and the little "Oh You Kid" doll.

The specimen pictured here is 5 inches but the advertising lists only two sizes: 6¼ inches at $2.25 a dozen and 8 inches at $4.50 a dozen. The 3½-inch Happifats are also $2.25 a dozen.

The bisque, the finishing, and the complexion coating on the Wide-Awake are all very good. The side-painted eyes have black lid linings and white highlight dots. The open-closed mouth is smiling and there are two small teeth of relief white under the upper lip. The molded tufts of hair in the center forehead and over each ear are colored dark blond like the

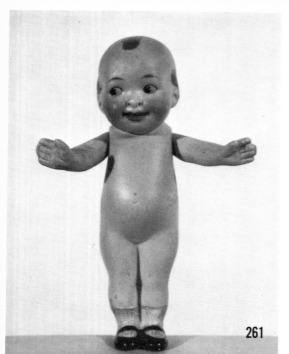

261

261

262

263

261 & 262 Author's collection; 263 Strong collection

one-stroke brows, but the tuft in back is untinted. The one-strap, heelless slippers are black, and the blue socks with blue bands have small dots which form vertical ribs.

The arms are the poorest part of the doll and the left hand is better than the right, which could mean that this right arm is a replacement. The incised arm marks are different but, with no numbers on the doll itself, they cannot be checked without assembling a number of dolls for comparison.

In the author's collection, however, there is also an unmarked 11¼-inch specimen of the Wide-Awake doll. This large one was probably made for and sold to toy specialty shops and metropolitan department stores. In the large size, the entire head is properly tinted and hair is indicated. Undoubtedly it originally had a front label which could have carried the same or another name, since it was intended for "the carriage trade."

The doll itself is a beautiful specimen in every respect. The bisque is very fine quality, it is of extremely good weight, and all the workmanship is in the best German all-bisque doll tradition.

No. 262 Complete with her original blond mohair wig on a pink paper cap, this 4½-inch, open-closed mouth little girl has blue sleep eyes and is incised in the head **222** over **11**. She has upper and lower painted lashes, one-stroke brown brows, and a medium complexion coat.

There is no doubt, although she has no label, that she is "Our Fairy" under a 1914 patent. Dorothy Coleman lists them as produced by Louis Wolf & Co. This is a small size of the following doll.

No. 263 Exactly twice the size, 9 inches, this labeled doll is incised on the head **222** over **22** and has the same good original light-brown mohair wig but on a very sturdy cloth cap. In this doll the brows are feathered in brown and the brown sleep eyes are set "goo-goo" fashion. The two upper teeth are under the upper lip but in the small doll they are dots of relief white on the lip.

The round label is dark green. Beneath the bottom bow of the label someone—undoubtedly in that World War I anti-German fervor which swept this country and changed sauerkraut to "libertykraut"—has scratched out the word "Germany" right through to the bisque.

The dark shadows at each side of her mouth are caused by the depth of the molded mouth. Unfortunately she has lost her original arms but she is valuable, nevertheless, because of her size and her label.

In the Strong Collection there is another doll, marked **222** over **28**, which is 11½ inches tall and has the same original blond wig and excellent original arms exactly like those on the first little specimen pictured. In these large sizes the bisque is very good, the finishing is well done, and the complexion coat is padded to perfection.

"Our Fairy" dolls were made as competition for Borgfeldt's Kewpies and they are sometimes erroneously listed as "My Fairy." The Colemans identify "My Fairy" as a 1922 trademark registered in Germany by Seyfarth & Reinhardt (usually shown as "S U R") and they have come to believe that it was for an entire line of dolls rather than for one specific item.

No. 264 Known to collectors as "The Medic," this 3⅞-inch immobile doll is unmarked but he must have been an early German product following World War I.

The side-painted eyes have blue rims, highlight dots and black lid linings, and the Kewpie influence is also seen in his tiny eyebrows and bare feet on molded-together legs.

The puckered mouth has an intaglio center like a whistler's. The mouth,

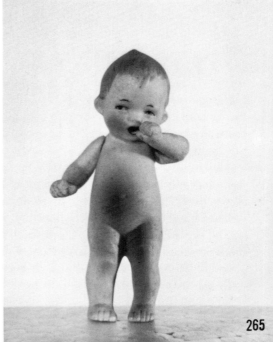

264

265

264 Brewer collection; 265 Author's collection

in combination with his spooky eyes, gives the amusing impression that he is awed by his responsibilities or scared to death about his mission.

There is a black peak on his green hat and the matching green coat with a molded collar and neck bow has molded black buttons, shoulder straps, and belt. Although it is not accurate, the shoulder straps give the impression that he is wearing the famous "Sam Browne" belt of that war.

And he is loaded with supplies! The molded pockets on his belt are bulging and a brown kit can be seen behind his left arm. The internationally known symbol of the Red Cross on his cap, sleeveband, and medical case hopefully mark him for special care on his errands of mercy.

All the finishing and decorating is quite good for such an inexpensive little item and the bisque is sharp.

He is an extremely good example of how the Germans captured the complete feeling of the popular Kewpies without infringing in any way on Rose O'Neill's patents.

No. 265 "The Thumb Sucker," a little German oddity, isn't common but he has been difficult to date. Incised only 0½ in the center of the back, he is 3 inches tall, and has a rounded open mouth which does not quite accept the thumb.

His modeling, finishing, and decorating are excellent, the bisque is very good, his slightly molded hair has a tiny, Kewpie-like peak on the top which is painted yellow. The eyes have a touch of blue around the side painted pupils and the small one-stroke brows are brown. He is in the best German tradition on every count and the chances are very good that he was more competition for O'Neill's money-making friends.

No. 266 A & B With **BABY BUD** incised across his back and **Germany** incised on the curve of the right shirt tail, this 5¼-inch toddler was patented in 1915. He appears in the Butler Brothers 1916 Santa Claus Edition Catalogue along with the Cupids, all kinds of Kewpies, Wide-Awake, Happifats, the Sailor Boy (**No. 152**) and the lad with the molded sweater and cap (**No. 153**). This size was $2.25 a dozen to the storekeeper and the 7-inch size was $4.25 a dozen.

Shoulder jointed, the bent arms fit close to the body. Both thumbs are free, the right forefinger is raised and the left index and middle fingers are held in a premature "V for Victory" sign which was not to become famous for more than twenty years, during another great war in which Germany was also terribly involved.

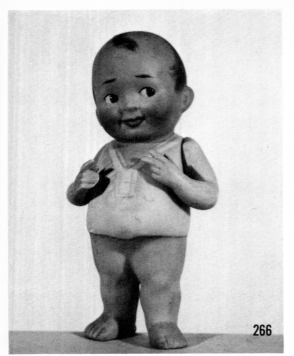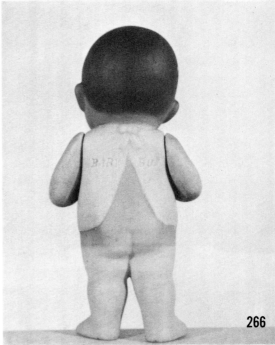

266 *Strong collection*

The Kewpie-influenced eyes are side-painted pupils only, with high-light dots, black lid linings and brown brows that waver. The open-closed mouth has the tongue molded sticking out and it is paler pink than the lips. Not too refined, of course, but different and it was "different" that sold dolls.

The short, molded, V-necked shirt is tinted blue around the bottom and down the molded neck trim. The molded back bow was left white. The left foot is extended slightly forward and gives him exceptionally good balance.

The forelock and ear wisps are molded and all the hair is a deep brown. The bisque is very good, the weight is satisfactory for the size and, while the complexion coat is slightly high, it is very evenly padded.

This doll was plagiarized by the Japanese, as shown in illustrations **Nos. 330** and **344** and either that firm turned out two kinds or it was stolen again by another Japanese producer. (See Chapter 32.)

Novelties abounded at one period in the popularity of all-bisques.

Whether the Kewpie rage had anything to do with some of these items is not known but they are delightful additions to any collection and cherished by collectors.

No. 267 This imp with huge ears, for instance, is a good example of the novelties. Shoulder jointed with rubber, 5 inches tall, he is of excellent bisque, the finishing is good, and the complexion tinting is uniform and a good color.

No. 268 The fanciful, 4½-inch creature with hoofs, pointed ears, abortive horns, and tail is also interesting. The sharp bisque is good but not as well finished as it could have been before the initial firing. His horns are gray and the hoofs are gray with blond hair fringe to match his back tuft and his tiny, molded tail. He is loop strung.

The two following dolls with movable hats are difficult to classify as to origin since neither is marked. The workmanship generally, however, as well as the bisque, is not Japanese quality, so until some marked ones come to light, most collectors consider them to be German.

267 Strong collection; 268 Author's collection

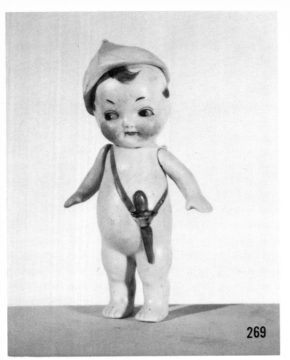
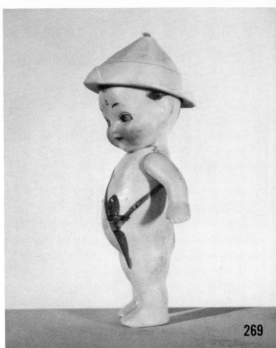

269

269

270

271

269 & 271 Author's collection; 270 Strong collection

No. 269 While this 5⅛-inch boy is sometimes called or sold as "an unusual Kewpie," he is not a Kewpie. But, if it were not for the fact that the known German Cupids (**Nos.** 259 and 260) have the whites of their eyes painted blue, that would be counted as a Japanese error in this doll.

The bisque, the modeling, and decorating are all of fair quality. He has brown wisps of hair painted on the forehead and nape of the neck, and molded and painted dabs over the ears. The molded shoulder strap is painted green and the dagger is orange-tan. His side-painted eyes have brown irises, black lid linings, and red lid lines—with the whites painted blue, as noted.

In both of these hatted dolls the tops of the heads are completely open and the white hats are attached by a rubber strand hooked over the arm rubber or arm wire inside the body and then secured by a knot on top.

No. 270 The 3½-inch little girl is shoulder jointed with very common wire instead of rubber and her legs are molded together, so possibly she and the boy above came from different makers or were made at different times. Her hat has flowers molded in the pink band and the molded ribbon on her chest is blue. She has blue eyes with high pupils and black lid linings; the molded hair is blond.

Although she is not as good quality as the boy, her vertically ribbed socks and one-strap slippers, plus the fairly good arms, argue further against a Japanese origin.

No. 271 Immobile, 3⅝ inches tall, unmarked but undoubtedly German, this youngster in a riding suit is quite good bisque, well done in every respect except the decorating and that appears to have been done by a beginner.

Drained through the feet, with the holes well filled in, it has a small air hole in the center of the neck in back. The cap, with a top button and molded ribbing, has a blue peak and all-around band. The shirt with a molded tie was left uncolored, the good little coat has blue lapels and a collar even in back, the crop is brown, the high boots are tan. The bobbed hair has a few comb marks in front and is a darker coat of the same color as the boots.

She has painted blue eyes with pupils, brown lid linings and brows— production speed-up again and not age—but the complexion is badly mottled and not extended to the hair line.

All of these molded dolls with stiff legs broke very easily and still do!

Without lumpy mohair wigs to save their heads and no bundling in little girls' attempts at dressmaking, one fall was all they needed. Added to this, they seemed to foster an irresistible desire in little brothers and visiting friends to make them stand alone. The mortality rate was phenomenal and unbroken ones at this late date are small prizes.

No. 272 In the early 1960s, in the midst of the Kewpie madness which overtook doll collectors, the Happifats suddenly boomed into renewed popularity. Patented in 1914, in the midst of World War I, they are hollow bisque of varying quality in two sizes and three types. They came in both 3½- and 4½-inch sizes and there are also 3½-inch Happifat Babies advertised "in painted chemise," according to the toy catalogues.

They are listed in Butler Brothers 1914 Fall Catalogue at $2.25 a dozen assorted. In the 1916 Catalogue the 3½-inch size is listed again at $2.25 a dozen and there is another listing of a 4-inch size, one pair to a box, 39 cents a pair, wholesale.

Only the arms move and, while they are sufficiently balanced by the ballooning clothes to stand alone, the breakage rate must have been

272

272

272 Author's collection

terrific because they topple with a breath. This must have endeared the little creatures to their manufacturers but parents apparently did not have the same ideas about them for they do not seem to exist in the quantities Kewpies still can muster.

Until she became an adult collector, the author had never seen Happifats, but the stores from which we bought our dolls in turn bought from wholesalers and their drummers, who were based in Philadelphia, rather than from catalogues. It could very well be that the storekeepers knew our tastes so well that they did not feel these would have been popular with us. They were undoubtedly right because these dolls have no appeal for many collectors.

The girl's dress is light blue shading into deep blue in the gathers. Her sash and shoes are pink. The boy's jacket and shoes are a pretty Hunter green and his pants are a lively brown, which deepens in the creases. The "Mohawk" hairdos are painted a reddish brown and, divided into two back locks on both dolls, are a sure sign of the breed.

These dolls have a copyright circle stamped on the under side of the clothes and some of them are found with an oval paper sticker intact bearing the name and also **Germany**. The quality and the painting compare poorly with the old German products but that is quite understandable.

The Japanese seem to have appropriated this idea also, as illustrated in **No. 329.**

Post-war Names
Bye-Lo, Averill,
Orsini, Kallus, Fulper

Bye-Lo Baby

Grace Storey Putnam copyrighted her Bye-Lo Baby in April 1923 and these 4-inch stiff necked all-bisques with painted eyes, hip and shoulder jointed, were being illustrated and advertised in Butler Brothers December 1925 Catalogue at $2.50 a dozen. This was through the efforts of our indefatigable Mr. Kestner, Jr., or his heirs and assigns.

We can get some idea of how quickly these dolls went into production by figuring backward from this piece of old American advertising literature.

The previous catalogue had to be completely checked and corrected. Then newly assembled information had to be added about merchandise which would be available for shipping. After that they had to be proofread, printed, bound, addressed, and mailed (probably third class because of the weight of over 600 9 x 13 pages with a cover) in time for last-minute Christmas ordering by shopkeepers all over the country. They were planned to be in the customers' hands about the middle of November because there is a notice which says: "The prices in this issue of 'Our Drummer take effect November 18 and supersede all others. We guarantee them against advances until our January 'Drummer' is out."

Under these circumstances, surely the material had to be in the printers' hands by October 1st. The Bye-Lo listing was not a late addition because it has ample space. Butler Brothers had to have the illustration in September and they had to know that they would have or probably *already had* the dolls in hand.

The dolls had to be manufactured, cleared through German ports, make the Atlantic crossing, clear the U.S. Customs, and then some of them had to make an additional trip by freight to other Butler Brothers warehouses in Chicago, St. Louis, Minneapolis, and Dallas because shipping from New

York in small lots would have added considerably to the cost in the mid-West, South, and West.

All of these points indicate that Mr. Kestner's establishment was still running a very tight ship in 1923 in spite of all the talk about the the destruction of the German doll industry during the war. They evidently went from copyrighting to shipping in twelve or fourteen months.

Eventually all-bisque Bye-Lo dolls were made in many types: with and without wigs, with painted and with sleep eyes in both blue and brown, with stiff and with flanged moving heads, barefooted or with pink or blue one-strap slippers and white ribbed socks. They have ranged in this collection from a sitting height of 6 inches to completely frozen miniatures only 2½ inches long.

Old illustrations show these dolls with a circular label on the body in front but in many instances this has been removed. The labels were generally dark green print on yellow (or yellowed) paper with **BYE-LO BABY** and **Germany** printed around the outside rim and a Ⓒ in the center. Most of them are completely incised in back, however, and the marking extends from the shoulders to the waist:

Copr. by
Grace S. Putnam
Germany

Ahead of the copyright line there is a stock and a size number, with the stock number on the left and the size on the right. This size number is also incised on the flange on the swivel necks.

No. 273 Brown-eyed, complete with the round green and yellow original paper label, this diapered and slippered swivel neck is a little gem and most unusual. The number is **886 12**, and is also incised on the leg flanges.

It sits up 3½ inches, has a 4½-inch head circumference, measures 4½ inches to the heels and 4¾ inches to the toes. The sleep eyes have upper and lower painted lashes and black eye linings and faint, light brown brows to match the wash on the head.

The diaper is not a matter of leaving half the body and the tops of the legs white. The top ridge, the center and side buttons, the leg scallops, the threaded ribbon, and the bows are all well molded, as are the tops of the socks, the vertical ribbing, and the one-strap slippers.

The finishing and decorating are excellent and the buttons, the ribbon, and the slippers are blue.

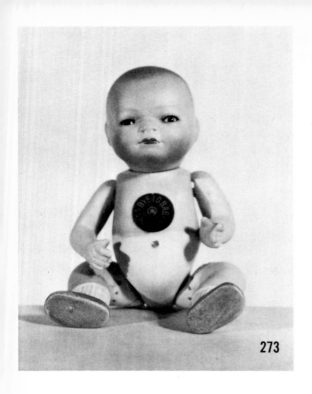

273

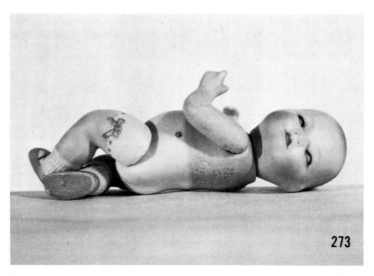

273

273 Brewer collection

No. 274 This slippered specimen has the same measurements as the diapered model above except that, because the legs are thinner and longer, it measures 5 inches to the toes.

The incised number on the back is 6-12, and on the legs 894-12. Perhaps the number 886 referred to the diaper because 86 and also 94 are found on slippered legs but not always with the first 8. In this doll the slippers are pink and the eyes are brown.

No. 275 Another version of the popular small size with a stiff neck, a brown mohair wig on a paper cap, and blue eyes.

No. 276 A little stiff neck which combines several Bye-Lo features. First of all, it is only 3 inches sitting up, 4 inches lying flat, and has a head circumference of 3¾ inches.

The incised number is high on the head, 16 over 10. The usual copyright information is incised on the back, and while those on the small arms and legs are difficult to decipher, they appear to be 20 over 10 on the arms and 94-10 on the leg flanges.

The silky brown mohair wig is on a paper cap, the tiny sleep eyes, with upper and lower lashes, are gray, the white socks have vertical ribbing and the one-strap slippers are blue. The bisque and the finishing are very good.

No. 277 Another stiff neck. The incised number is 20-10; the same mark is on the legs, which have bare feet. The measurements are the same as No. 276.

The small painted eyes are blue-gray with black linings; the brows are a very faint blond. The mouth was greatly extended by the decorator who added thin side lines to the lips, and there are red nose dots. The complexion tinting is pale and very good, as is the modeling, and the slightly indicated hair is washed a pretty brown.

The all-bisques are listed in the December 1925 Butler Brothers Catalogue:

2F 6717 "Bye Lo" baby. 4 in. flesh tinted body, painted features and hair, jointed arms and legs. 1 doz. in box. . . . . Doz. $2.50

No. 278 With the BYE- and © of the original label still intact, this 2½-inch frozen specimen is most appealing. The painted eyes are very gray-blue with pupils and lid linings in black. The eyebrows are little blurs of the dark blond wash used on the head. The complexion coating is quite even and pale and the feature painting is very definite.

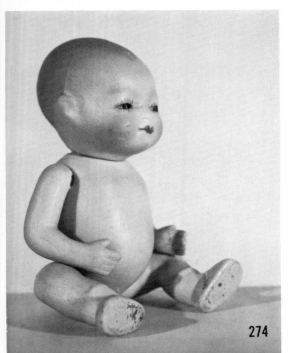

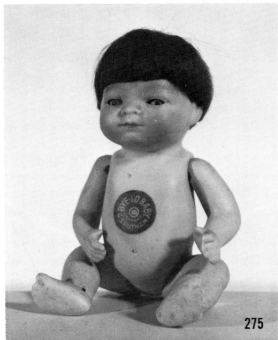

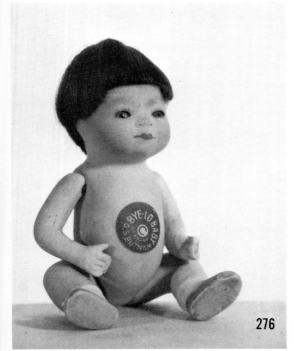

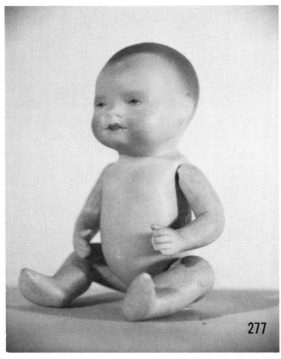

274, 275 & 277 Author's collection; 276 Campbell collection

There is an air hole in the inch-long flattened area on the back which keeps the doll in place as designed but there are no incised markings.

No. 279 Another 2½-inch frozen Bye-Lo, this one has an air hole in the depressed oblong area on the side which holds it in the proper position. There is an incised number in the depression but the air hole is cut in the center of the first figure so it is impossible to say whether it is **6000** or **0000**.

The complexion coating is pale and very well done but in this doll the feature painting is much less intense and lends a more dreamy, babyish air to the infant.

No. 280 Not common, and very desirable, this is the Georgene Averill "Bonnie Babe" infant miniaturized to become an all-bisque, flange necked toddler. The only mark, **11,** is found on the center front of the little neck cuff. The doll is, of course, from the mid-1920s and, like the Bye-Lo, proves that the German doll industry recovered to a great extent after the war, at least as far as quality production was concerned. The molding, the bisque, the finishing, and the decorating in these postwar dolls were all excellent.

Only 4½ inches tall, with one-strap flat slippers and white ribbed socks, this doll is correct; these slippers are pale blue but they also came in pink. The brown sleep eyes have black lid linings and painted upper and lower lashes. There are two lower teeth in the crooked, smiling, open mouth and the brown tinted hair is molded in small curls all over the back of the head, with curling wisps in front.

New collectors should note that these moving heads are properly classi- fied as "flange" type—that is, cut off flat at the shoulder line instead of having a rounded swivel base. In the all-bisque Averill head, however, an additional small cuff is molded under and back of the straight flange cut to fit into the neck hole in the body. This little unseen rim keeps the head from slipping forward when it is strung. It is an excellent idea and should not be mistaken for a break because it is cut off sharply just below the ears and extends only across the front half of the neck where it is needed.

No. 281 The legs on this "Bonnie Babe" are replacements of precolored bisque with white socks and brown one-strap slippers from a suspected Amberg doll. Even though they are not the proper legs, the hip fit is good enough to complete the doll until (and if) the proper legs can be found.

This doll also has the two tiny lower teeth but they are placed lower in the mouth and consequently do not show in the picture.

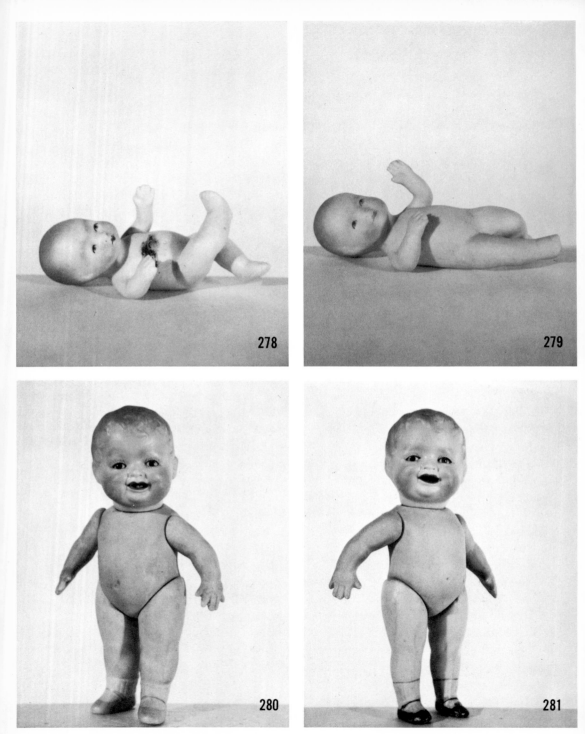

278 & 279 Strong collection; 280 & 281 Author's collection

Kallus

No. 282 Although he is not nearly as well finished or decorated as the Averill, this J. L. Kallus with part of the orignal brown and tan label is a small prize.

It does not take an expert to realize, with an Averill in one hand and the Kallus in the other, that the Kallus was rushed through the sanding processing before the bisque was silky smooth. The spread fingers were not properly cleaned and still contain mold debris. The complexion coat is mottled and looks like the mildew from underfiring.

His only slightly molded hair has an uneven brown wash, his sleep eyes are blue with upper and lower painted lashes but no black linings, and his brows are soft brown smudges. The one-strap, heelless slippers are pink; the molded white socks have vertical ribs. The flange neck is held in place with an inner rim like that on the Averill.

The Kallus is a miniaturization of the only bisque Kallus head familiar to the author—an open-mouthed boyish face with a protruding upper lip, sometimes identified as "Baby Bo-Kaye." This is the elongated head of a growing child, whereas the Averill is the round, curl-covered head of the picture-book infant. The head shape accounts for the ¼-inch difference in their over-all sizes.

With the dolls in hand it is immediately evident that their bodies were made from the same molds. This is verified by the fact that one of the incised numbers on the hip flanges is the same—897/11 appears on both Averill legs and on the left leg of the Kallus. The right leg of the Kallus is marked 897/37. There is also the fact that the hands are exactly alike, which was seldom the case when molds of a competitor's product were stolen. In these, the right thumb and pinkie stand free, with the other three fingers molded together. In the left hands, the middle and ring fingers are together and the thumb, index and pinkie stand free.

With only such small clues as these, is it possible for a collector to make a good guess as to the manufacturer of these dolls? Let's try.

George Borgfeldt & Co. bought the rights to the Bye-Lo from Grace Storey Putnam and Kestner made the tremendously popular all-bisque Bye-Los for them. That is a matter of record. It is also well known that Georgene Averill sold the rights to "Bonnie Babe" to the same firm and, completely satisfied with Kestner's work, there is no reason why Borgfeldt should have sought another manufacturer.

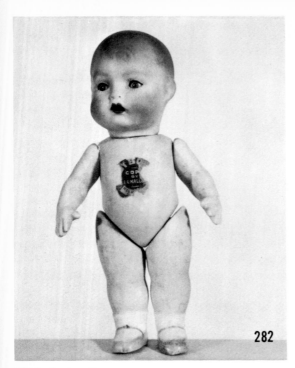

282 *Author's collection*

With these toddler body molds in Kestner's possession, and with the possibility that they were designed by the Kestner firm to fit the reduced Averill head, there is very little doubt that Kestner also made these small Kallus all-bisques.

This could have been through an arrangement with Borgfeldt, if they owned the rights to the mold, or through a marketing arrangement with the firm which had widespread retail distribution facilities, in which case Borgfeldt would have made the manufacturing contracts with Kestner.

Then, as now, doll advertising was based on constant change to make dolls year-round gifts to little girls on any and all occasions. The Averill all-bisque was patented in 1926 and undoubtedly had at least two years of popular sales leadership, after which it was time for another change. Borgfeldt would have been delighted with the opportunity to market this competition for the Averill because, given a choice, buyers purchase oftener than they do when no choice is available.

To the serious collector, the roughness of the body and the higher and poorer complexion coating of the Kallus are signs of the waning German bisque-doll industry.

286 § *All-Bisque and Half-Bisque Dolls*

Orsini

Working from a studio in New York City, Jeanne I. Orsini seems to have been a very busy lady for a few years. She obtained her first copyright in 1916 on a doll with a crying face which was called "Tummyache," from what Dorothy Coleman has been able to uncover, and there were many others after that. She had quite a penchant for short, repetitive names such as Mimi.

No. 283 On this 7-inch girl the original circular paper label is yellow printed in red and within the circle it reads:

DIDI
REG. U.S. PAT. OFF.
COPR. J. I. ORSINI
1920
PAT. APPL'D FOR

and outside the circle, in very fine print, **Germany.**

Clearly incised across the back between the shoulders, **JIO** © **1920.** The head and limbs are incised **41-17.**

The modeling is exceptional, the finishing is good but not silky, and the color is slightly high but beautifully even. She is hip and shoulder jointed with rubber, the brown sleep eyes with pupils have upper and lower painted lashes, and the brows are multistroke in brown. The open-closed mouth is fashioned into a wide smile and there is a set of even white teeth. She has a childish pug nose with red dots.

The above-knee white stockings have good vertical ribbing, the one-strap slippers have heels and tan soles. The nice brown mohair wig with end curls has a gauze base and a machine-sewn part, with tiny pink ribbon bows on either side.

The hands make Orsinis more than ordinarily interesting. The right hand has a raised forefinger out of a closed fist, both of which made the handling and the finishing more difficult. The left hand is cupped and the thumb is bent inward, which made it necessary to open up a hole between the thumb and fingers.

Like so many others, this doll has signs of Kestner manufacture—the workmanship is very good for the time period, the eyebrows are similar to Kestner's own, there is a wooden bar as an eye stop, and the shoes are like those on the better Kestner all-bisques. It gets monotonous, this business of crediting so many identifiable dolls to this firm as the manufacturer,

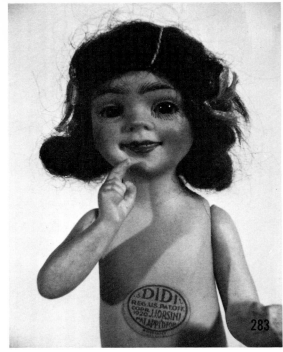

283

283

284

284

283 Brewer collection; 284 Author's collection

but they were in operation in the 1920s, they were turning out exceptionally fine dolls, and if the credit is due them, they should have it.

No. 284 Another Orsini, 5 inches tall, and incised across the back between the shoulders, **JIO** © 1919. She has no other marks but the leg flanges are incised with the number 14.

Hip and shoulder jointed with rubber, with factory set brown eyes with pupils and upper and lower painted lashes, her complexion is lighter than the previous doll's. This face has more character modeling, the open-closed mouth has upper teeth and a molded tongue, and the one-stroke brown brows have a smudged center to make them appear wider. Her hands are the same as those on the previous doll; so is the nose.

The ribbed detail of the stockings is largely lost and there is mold debris on one ankle. The one-strap slippers are brown with brown soles. The human-hair wig is a replacement.

Although she is just one year earlier than **No. 283** this doll has the smooth texture of the old dolls and there is more modeling to her torso and her legs. Her knees are smaller and better shaped in proportion, the calves touch and the ankles have more shape. There is no feeling of certainty about her manufacture, however.

Fulper

Many dolls designed by American artists—Rose O'Neill, Grace Storey Putnam, Joseph L. Kallus, Georgene Averill and, of course, Jeanne I. Orsini—were produced in Germany because all or parts of the dolls were bisque.

Fulper and Reinhardt are exceptions to this loose rule and both firms operated in New Jersey. Fulper was in Flemington and Ernst Reinhardt operated both in Irvington and Perth Amboy but, while Fulper made some all-bisques, there does not seem to be any evidence that Reinhardt ever did.

No. 285 This 9-inch, completely marked Fulper Kewpie is an excellent specimen and it is difficult to understand why a firm capable of this kind of work could not have continued in the all-bisque field.

The bisque, the finishing, and the weight are good, the color is slightly high but this is also true of many fine German Kewpies. It is quite a surprise to turn this doll around and find **Made in USA** on the back.

No. 286 Shoulder jointed, 10½ inches tall, this "Peterkin" was made by Fulper for Horsman and it has no incised marks. Originally he may have had a circular label at waist level in front because flakes of paper still cling

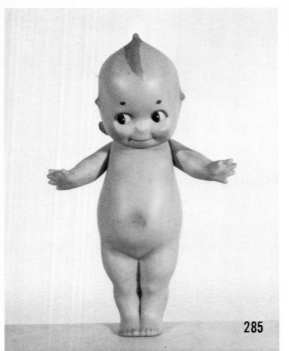

285

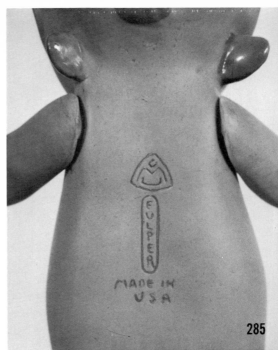

285

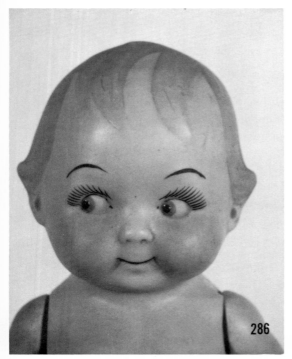

286

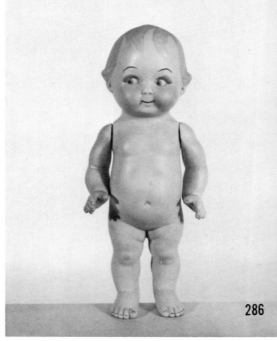

286

285 & 286 Strong collection

to the bisque and the body is lighter in a definite circle.

He is a sturdy lad! Short necked, long in the torso and quite heavy, he is balanced to stand alone extremely well. The bisque and the finishing are both good but the body is paler than the arms. Since the Germans also had this problem, in spite of their years of experience, it is easily overlooked.

The slightly molded hair has only a light reddish wash, all the nails are neatly outlined in rose, the painted eyes are blue with good pupils and highlight dots, the long eyelashes are black and the one-stroke brows are brown. The watermelon mouth is bright red, as are the small eye and nose dots.

It would be helpful to examine a number of these dolls because this specimen has a hidden but very interesting stringing method. Wire hooks, exactly like those in thousands of composition dolls, are implanted in his arm sockets. The inside arm tops are open mounds of bisque which fit the torso holes very well. After the first firing, wire hooks seem to have been secured in these open holes with dabs of doughy slip which then hardened during the color firing.

The only other method by which rubber could be used to string these open-topped mounds would be to use a wire or a wooden crossbar in the rubber and then to drop this wedge into the hollow arms. Celluloids were done this way but it does not seem too practical for bisque.

Because of this odd arrangement, one would hazard a guess that Peterkin was made before the Fulper Kewpie which has standard molded stringing loops.

Both these dolls fall in the 1918-1920 period but, unfortunately, neither one is easy to find. When they come to light they are generally offered to museums and this is only fair, really, because they can then be seen by countless visitors.

27

Flappers

When German production got into full swing after World War I, dolls typical of their own period came into the U.S. market. Those of us who were flappers in the 1920s and are doll collectors now are a little puzzled that it took so many years for the keen, competitive German manufacturers to become aware of the American image as opposed to the stolid, Teutonic type.

Because we were busy right here at home shortening our skirts, having our hair cut very close in what was called "a shingle," buying and driving our own "roadster" automobiles with "rumble seats," and learning the Charleston, we did little traveling abroad and, without TV to bring us world news almost instantly, we really didn't know whether or not Europe reacted to this "flaming youth generation," to quote our elders. Added to that, we didn't care.

Most of us had jobs, some of them very good jobs, too, and marriage was not our prime concern. So, unless we had younger sisters or nieces for whom to buy toys, we were unaware of these changes in dolls we had so loved ten years before. It seems unlikely that anyone of any age could have lived through the past ten or more years without being made aware of the Barbie and Ken dolls. To our generation the Bye-Lo Baby, Shirley Temple, and the Dionne Quintuplets were the only dolls to reach such a peak of advertising that everyone knew about them. The all-bisque Flappers never had this kind of promotion, so they are a surprise to many collectors.

Precisely because they are a surprise, collectors are sometimes misled about them. They are slightly breasted, slim waisted, and long legged and are sometimes sold as French but they are German dolls.

No. 287 Incised only **616.15**, this 5¾-inch hip and shoulder jointed girl

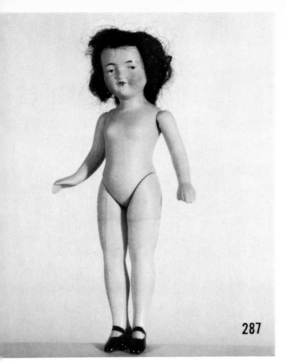

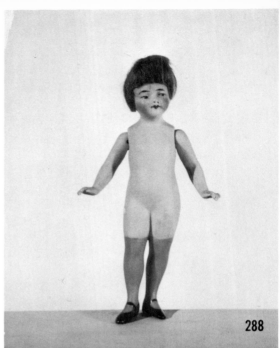

287

288

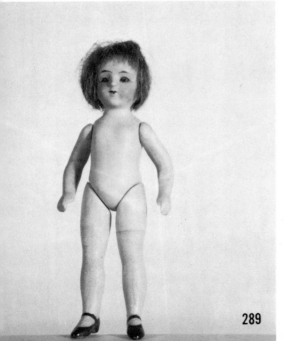

289

290

287, 288 & 290 Author's collection; 289 Strong collection

has a slightly turned head, side-painted blue eyes with large, high pupils, black eye linings, and one-stroke brown brows. The modeling, the finishing, and the complexion tinting are all excellent and in the good German tradition.

Unlike the old dolls, the high stockings on the Flappers have no molded texture; they are simply painted to represent the light-colored silk stockings which had replaced the old black, white, and brown in cotton and lisle. In this instance they are a soft shade of blue-gray. The one-strap black slippers have heels and yellow soles. The wig is a replacement.

No. 288 Incised **Germany**, this 5-inch Flapper is a stiff-legged version of the previous doll, with the same facial decorating. One stiff leg extends in front of the other, the high stockings are tan, and the one-strap, heeled slippers are glossy brown with yellow soles. She has her original brown mohair wig on a cap.

No. 289 A 4¼-inch doll of the same kind, hip and shoulder jointed with loops, this one has blue sleep eyes with upper and lower lashes but otherwise the same decorating. She has her original dark blond mohair wig on a cap, yellow stockings, and tan shoes like the others.

No. 290 A 3⅛-inch doll of the same kind, hip and shoulder jointed with wire. This doll has a molded aviator's helmet and glasses, and was factory dressed in two styles. One is a jump suit of stiff, suede-finished material and the other is a brown jacket of the same material with dark brown woolen knickers, which were considered very daring at the time. All the buttons are small beads and the legs are tinted yellow to represent silk stockings. The heeled pumps are black.

These are sometimes called "Amelia Earhart," but they are earlier than the famous woman flier, to the best of our knowledge. In the late 1920s some girls were learning to fly but more were just passengers with their flying beaux, but they nevertheless dressed the part to the hilt. All that is missing on the dolls is the white silk scarf which blew about with such a flourish in the open cockpit planes we thought so wonderful.

No. 291 These are 3-inch children, hip and shoulder jointed with wire, which are from the same period in time and perhaps the same factory, judging from the work habits. The little girls have hats molded like the felt hats in vogue at the time and the little boys have molded caps. All are incised **Germany** down the spine in a vertical arrangement.

From the variety in this collection, it seems evident that most, or perhaps all, of these little dolls were sold dressed.

The first child's velvet coat is machine made, the collar is some type of pile fabric representing fur and the buttons are painted dots. Under it she has machine-made cotton pants. Her hat was left white, but has a painted blue band and bow to match her full-length blue stockings and darker blue shoes. The undressed doll is wearing a pink hat with the band left white and her legs and shoes are pink.

Moths have taken their toll of the little boy's suit but it is dark blue felt of thin quality. His molded cap is darker blue than the girl's shoes and his feet have been painted above the ankles to represent shoes, although the visible molded slippers under the paint would have been dainty enough for a girl. The German decorators were in error, as sometimes happened. Little boys in the 1920s were wearing attractive oxfords which their grandparents persisted in calling "low cuts."

Both of these dolls were dressed for winter. The blue leggings painted on the girl and the fur collar on her coat, plus molded, buttoned-on ear

292

293

292 & 293 Author's collection

flaps on the boy's cap, and the striped muffler on the boy are ample evidence. This is interesting because it made necessary only one opaque garment and yet it must have encouraged the sale of them immensely. Dressing dolls this size is a difficult job for an experienced worker, let alone a busy young mother.

No. 292 The two little girls have blue felt coats with brass stapled buttons, although one has lost her white "fur" collar. Both have machine-hemmed and pleated blue and white checked skirts and sewed-on machine-made white cotton pants. Both hats are blue with pink bands but the darker one was also given a light wash of the brown hair color to make it slightly different. The same treatment was given the legs but the match is not good.

In all of these dolls the finishing is quite good and, considering the size, the featuring is more than passable. Some have pupilless blue eyes, some have pupils only, the mouths are bright red, and the hair and eyebrows are various shades of brown. They have surprisingly good hands which are cupped down.

No. 293 A smaller set consisting of a 3⅝-inch flapper mother and two 2⅛-inch children. This was considered to be an "ideal" family at the time and the American distributors must have ordered the combination. These were also predressed.

Mother's cloche hat (à la Greta Garbo) is blue with a brown band and her hair apppears to be a very short bob not visible under the hat except in front. This was the "shingle," with the backs of the girls' hair cut as close as the men's. Her legs are also painted yellow and her one-strap black slippers have heels. The long-waisted short dress is typical of the era also, but she has undoubtedly lost some of the decorations.

The bobbed hair with bangs on the children is true to the era and it was very convenient for doll manufacture because dressing distinguished the sexes. The little boy's pants are felt, this time in red, and the buttons are small white beads. His blouse is very cheap ribbon crossed at the chest, and the neck bow is held on with a red thread around the neck. He may have lost a small felt Peter Pan collar along the way.

294

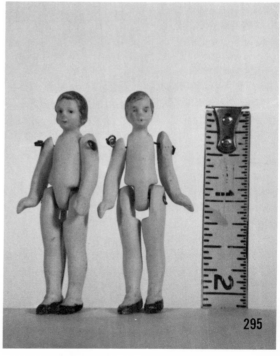

295

294 & 295 Authors' collection

The little girl has only her gauze underwear left but it is another indication of factory dressing, like the felt. Both children have slippers painted a more vivid blue than mother's hat.

No. 294 Incised 3/0 between the shoulders, this charming 2½-inch child attracts the attention of all the little girls who visit this collection. They sometimes carry her about all the time they are here and always beg their mothers to buy her, even though they know she is not for sale.

Made of dull, very fine, pale, precolored bisque, she is hip and shoulder jointed with wire and her decorating was fired. She has tiny painted blue eyes with pupils and one-stroke brows of the same golden yellow used for her hair. Her slightly tilted head has a nicely molded bob with a widow's peak and a molded loop to hold her ribbon bow.

She has the same molded socks and one-strap brown slippers as the Amberg "Mibs" (Nos. 245 and 246) and it would be easy to believe that she was also designed by Helen Drucker.

The little crocheted dress is a gem. It is vertically ribbed in blue and white, the skirt is a shell stitch in blue with a white border, and the sash is a chain-stitched string. The little basket is also blue and white, it is filled with multicolored bits of thread and is sewed to the dress.

No. 295 The hip construction on this 2½-inch brother and sister resembles that of some woodens. Incised **Germany** straight down the spine, they are wire jointed, and are made of of pale, dull, precolored bisque.

They are well finished and very simply decorated, having only brown hair, pupils, eyebrows, and mouth, plus the black flat-soled slippers on which the molded strap was not picked up in color.

No. 296 No mother has ever been found for the 3-inch, precolored, wire-strung little girls with bangs and bobs, nor for a similar doll in this series which has a much larger head but the same hairdo. Two have brown and one has yellow hair and they all have **Germany** incised on the inside area of the right leg. The molded shoes are painted a reddish orange and the socks are a paler shade of the same color to stand out against the precoloring.

Two are original, in mint condition. The white pleated skirt is processed voile, the underpants are thin cotton, and the blouse is teal blue felt with a red felt bow. The underarm seams and the back closing of the blouse are done by hand, very professionally.

296

297

298

296, 297 & 298 Author's collection

The other mint doll has a white felt blouse with amber bead buttons, a blue cotton gathered skirt, and a rose-colored sash of very cheap, thin rayon ribbon which is tied in a bow.

No. 297 Unmarked and precolored, 3⅛ inches tall, this little girl has a cheap brown mohair wig on a paper cap instead of the molded hats and hair. She is hip and shoulder jointed with wire, has blue eyes with black pupils, lid linings and brows, poorly done, and bright orange one-strap slippers with a light, unmatching, wash of orange for socks.

The jumper dress is made of gray rayon ribbon of very poor quality, machine stitched at the waist, and the shoulder straps are a narrower type of the same ribbon. She has a wrap around cotton petticoat, folded to eliminate raw edges. The hair bow is bright orange and the flower at her waist is a soft knot of orange ribbon with green folded ribbon leaves.

No. 298 Incised on the back, **39/96,** this 3⅜-inch girl is also of dull, good, precolored bisque. Shoulder jointed with wire, she has a lot of little relatives.

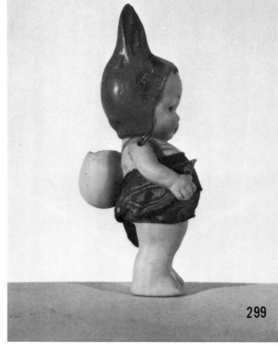

299   299

299 Strong collection

The whites of her eyes are painted blue; she has black pupils, lid linings, and hairline brows. Her center-parted molded bob is painted a bright yellow; the short socks are dark blue to cover the precoloring; and her one-strap slippers are black with black soles. The decorating is glossy.

No. 299 Undoubtedly an Easter novelty, this bunny-eared doll is 4½ inches tall and incised **Germany** across the little white egg. Shoulder jointed with wire, it has the same well-balanced stance as the dolls which follow, and is precolored.

The eyes are only black pupils with lid linings and the eyebrows are brown dots. The forelock, the cap, and the ears are a combination of brown and tan with a high gloss. The egg on her back is held in place by narrow molded shoulder bands, which are painted blue. Because it is white, the egg had to be separately molded and added.

In the author's collection there is a duplicate of this little doll, also precolored and similarly incised, but it appears to be a later issue. The precolored bisque is quite glossy and a darker pink, the cap shows no signs of the combination of tan and brown which are so attractive on the Strong doll. The dull brown paint is almost entirely gone and the shoulder straps are a very muddy blue because of the higher precoloring.

No. 300 One group of the little relatives, also precolored. From the left:

The 2-inch toddler is unmarked and the only one in the group which is shedding its coloring.

The 2-inch girl, 2⅛-inch boy and 3⅛-inch armless girl are incised in two lines on the back, **Made in Germany.** The little girl's molded hairbow is green.

The 3¾-inch girl with a very dark green bow and a coat is incised on the feet, **Germany.** This coat appears to be "original" and she is one of the dressed type mentioned below.

The largest girl, 4¾ inches, with the blue bow, is incised on the back, **Germany.**

These dolls are listed in the 4½-inch size at 84 cents a dozen in Butler Brothers December 1925 Catalogue. Boys and girls, 3¾ inches tall, are also listed at $1.80 dozen in "two color fancy costumes and hats." From the illustrations the costumes are made of cloth and braid or ribbon rather than being molded on the dolls.

Unfortunately, the loop strung types are not only difficult to string, but when an arm is missing there is very little chance of finding another arm,

300 & 301 Author's collection

and there is a good possibility that the remaining arm will get lost because all of them are so very small. The wire-strung types come apart less easily and, because they do not have to fit into a shoulder hole, satisfactory substitutes can generally be found.

These German dolls appear to have provided the bodies for the late and dreadful **MADE IN JAPAN** doll **No. 340.** There is no mistaking the stance.

These little girls have oddly molded and very distinctive hairdos. The hair comes from a side part, the section is braided and then tucked under the molded bow.

No. 301 Although their feet and hair appear to be different, these four were made by the same factory as the last group and there is a good chance that it was the firm that made the precolored Amberg dolls and perhaps even the "Cupid" and his sister, **Nos. 259** and **260.** They left many clues.

First, the apparent hairdo difference is the molded loop to hold a piece of ribbon and the girl without a bow has an altered hairdo which looks like a bob. Her companion, with a bow and bare feet, however, has the same loop and the barely visible remains of the tiny top braid of all the previous dolls with the molded bows.

Second, the shoes and socks on the two dolls at the left are exactly like those on the Amberg's and are as poorly painted. It is impossible to tell for sure that the color wore off from play and, since they are so much alike, the chances are that this painted strap and front rim were all they ever had.

Third, those with eyes big enough to have anything except a pupil have the whites painted blue. This is a very peculiar habit for a German firm, to say the least.

From the left the sizes are: the little girl with molded flowers across the forehead, $2\frac{1}{8}$ inches; the girl without a ribbon in her loop, $2\frac{1}{2}$ inches; the girl with a bow, $2\frac{5}{8}$ inches, and the little girl whose hair is worn off in front, 2 inches. All of them are incised straight down the spine: **Germany** in the same print and place as on the little pig, **No. 84.**

No. 302 Also precolored and incised **Germany** across the back, these twins are $1\frac{3}{8}$ inches long and $\frac{7}{8}$ inches wide at the shoulders—truly a precious "hand toy" a child could carry about unbeknown to her elders.

The author had many friends who were the young parents of the children for whom these toys were made and they were the first to be exhorted to "let the child express himself." Consequently some of these children annoyed everybody within sight and sound with the exercise of this new right. Instead of an adult hand on their posteriors, "the little monsters," as they were frequently called by the people not related to them, drove the shy child to use his own hands as a comfort and many of them went to first grade with a hand toy they would not relinquish, much as Linus in the "Peanuts" cartoon today holds onto his blanket through thick and thin.

Because they lack digital dexterity, children are not as prone to miniatures as adults frequently are, but many of the small toys made for the flappers' children answered a need some of the children had for a personal security which was lacking in the fast, erratic pace of those bootlegger days.

These dolls have pupils only and little dashes of eyebrows in dark blond. The hair is a wash of light blond and, right above the mark in back, they have loving little molded crossed arms.

They are a good example of dolls which must be strung with the spool rubber used on a sewing machine because the loops are very small. The arms are only ⅝ inches long over-all and the production problems they presented, even in precolored bisque, must have driven some of the handlers mad.

No. 303 This immobile pair evidently are the previous twins at a later age. They are precolored, **Germany** is stamped in dark ink on the narrow rim of the open bottom, and they are 1¼ inches high, 1½ inches across the hands.

Because they are a little larger, they have side painted pupils with black lid linings and dark blond dashes again for eyebrows. The hair is a darker blond wash and their arms are again molded across the back like the others. The plain head is a boy and the one with a molded topknot is a girl—the "ideal" family again.

These are sometimes mistaken for Kewpies but they are not.

No. 304 This 2½-inch precolored oddment has the same **Germany** incised across the back. The tiny gray-blue sleep eyes have waxed lids, the one-stroke brows are reddish brown, there are dabs of orange color on the cheeks, and the tiny mouth is bright red.

Like the others, this doll presents real problems if the arms or eyes are missing, and it is very difficult to find them with the small wigs intact.

No. 305 Where this girl belongs in the scheme of things is anybody's guess, unless someone knows.

Precolored bisque, she is a second girl with bent baby legs, although

302

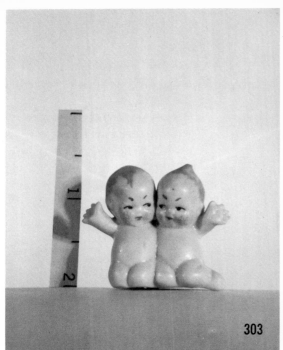

303

304

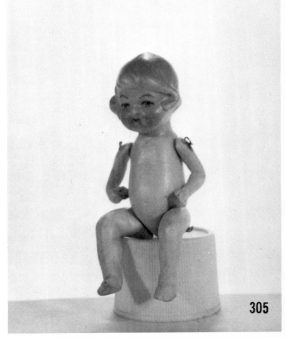

305

302, 304 & 305 Author's collection; 303 Strong collection

much, much later than **No. 221.** She not only has slightly curled bobbed hair but she also has a small apple molded in her right hand. Her back is incised **774** over a line with **3½** below the line, and **Germany** appears at the waistline.

The brown hair has been fired but the painting looks like work done with an air gun because the gradation of color is so even. The feature painting is poor. She has blue eyes with pupils, heavy black lid linings, and one-stroke brown brows. Again the mouth is bright red.

28

Moving Heads

A late, interesting group of dolls are those with moving heads and clothing molded on the bodies. They come in quite a variety, many times in boy and girl or man and woman pairs, and they stand unsupported. Sometimes they represent various nationalities and almost everyone is familiar with the Irish pair, for instance, the boy in a high hat, the girl in a shawl and sometimes decorated with or carrying shamrocks.

No. 306 This 3¾-inch Negro boy is larger and more unusual than others of this type. Unmarked, he is made of very good white bisque and well finished; his happy little face is a pretty milk chocolate brown. The glossy black hair is molded into little ringlets all over the head, his eyes are only molded slits which have black lid linings and he has tiny black brows to match. The lips of the open-closed mouth are bright red with the center left white and his cheeks have a rosy glow.

The shirt is white, his pants are pale blue with bright red suspenders, and there are green dots on the fronts of his white shoes.

Most of the dolls' heads are held by a rubber knotted at the top of the head, run through the body, and then knotted again, usually out of sight in the seat.

This lad is different. The stringing rubber is tied to the center of a small wooden crossbar which is dropped into the body vertically, maneuvered to the horizontal, and then pulled up until the shoulders hold it. The rubber is brought up through the head only and is tied on top where the tip of the knot can be seen above his forelock.

No. 307 "Our Gang Comedy" kids. In the 1920s Hal Roach gathered a group of children for a comedy series which proved so successful that, with various changes in the children as the original group grew too large or

306

307

306 Author's collection; 307 Strong collection

their voices changed, the popular comedies continued through the '30s and '40s.

These dolls are difficult to find as a group and even more difficult to assemble as individual purchases. The dog is the only immobile member of the group, all the others being strung from the top of the head through the body to the seat. The knots on the heads are all visible.

Because so many children eventually participated in this series, the kids are difficult to identify except through old movie stills but to the best of our knowledge these are, from the left in the front row:

"Wheezer," 2½ inches. He has a red cap with a peak, black hair, a white shirt with a big bow tie spotted with red dots, a yellow sleeveless sweater or vest, long blue pants, and black shoes.

"Pete," the 2-inch dog. He is dark brown and white with black eyes, a black penciled ring around the eye on the white side of his face, and a blue collar.

"Mary Ann Jackson," 3½ inches. Her hair is black, the dress is bright wagon yellow with black dots, and she has low white socks and red shoes.

Back row from the left:

"Farina," 3⅜ inches. His shirt is white with red stripes, the long pants are vivid blue with yellow suspenders, his socks are red and the shoes are brown.

"Chubby Chaney," 3½ inches, with reddish-blond hair. His head-hugging hat is red with a yellow border, the shirt is medium blue, the short pants are dark green with a red belt, and he has low white socks and brown shoes.

"Jackie Cooper," 3½ inches, with blond hair. His little round hat is brown, his white shirt has a pattern of little red slashes like quote marks, he has short black pants with blue suspenders, black shoes and low, flesh-colored socks.

In this group the boys in the back row do not have their legs molded together to provide balance. They needed additional support because they are taller than the others, so the legs were not separated. Instead, the bisque between the legs was left uncolored and a pointed column was added in the back up to their seats. This short pedestal gives them a triangular base and they stand beautifully—and safely.

All of them are complexioned very attractively and some of the light colors, like Chubby's blue shirt and Wheezer's yellow sweater, seem almost like old, fired colors. Inasmuch as they are borrowed, it isn't possible to scrape them to find out. Farina's complexion is peeling, however, as shown in the picture.

The pastel colors on the little Negro boy's clothing (**No. 306**) apparently were fired because they do not scrub off, but the intense colors, the hair and the red suspenders, may have been only oven dried because they flake with persistent scraping.

Nos. 308 and **309** The dolls in **No. 307** are glued to a mirror for display purposes but it was possible to isolate Wheezer and Mary Ann Jackson to show the detail and charm of these little movie-star portraits.

No. 310 Two more famous characters, Uncle Walt and Skeezix from the comic strips or, as they used to be known, "the funny papers."

These were the creations of Frank King and originally appeared as single cartoons on the back page of *The Chicago Tribune,* possibly as early as 1918. Conflicting information is given about the beginning of the "Gasoline Alley" strip which is now drawn by Bill Perry.

In an article, "Skeezix, King of the Comics," in *Coronet,* February 1949, H. N. Oliphant says that Mr. King also wrote all of the continuity which was so appealing in this feature and he always talked it over with his wife before anything was released.

Incised in two lines across the shoulders, **UNCLE WALT,** this doll with moving head is 3½ inches tall. He has a tiny white cap on top of his orange-yellow molded hair, the shirt is pale yellow with white cuffs, the bow tie is red, the pants are vivid blue, and the shoes are gray. He has a yellowish complexion, black pupils only, black brows, and a little red mouth. **Germany** is incised across his pants cuffs in back.

Incised **SKEEZIX** across the shoulders, the little fellow is 2⅝ inches tall. His hair is pale yellow, the shirt is white with a floppy red tie, the pants are green, and he has white socks and brown shoes. **Germany** is incised across his seat under the knot of rubber. He has the same complexion and feature painting as Walt.

No. 311 This doll with moving head is possibly made of "Bisqueloid," a compound which feels and sounds like a combination of bisque and plaster. Other dolls made of it are advertised by Butler Brothers in 1932.

This doll, which is 4 inches tall, is incised **Germany** across the back. The neck has a straight-cut base which fits into the neck hole in the body instead of the closed neck and swivel bases of most of these dolls. The head is held by a wire swirl which, when forced into the neck opening, spread when

308

309

310

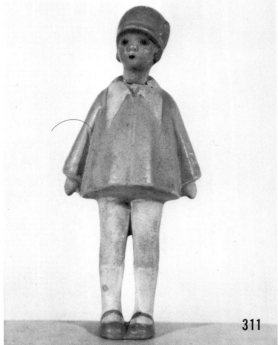

311

308, 309 & 310 Strong collection; 311 Author's collection

it got into the head. The rubber is attached to the loop at the end of the wire inside the body and tied under her molded coat edge in back.

The molded pink cloche hat has a front brim and a side ornament; the matching coat has long white collar points. The socks are white and the one-strap, flat slippers are blue.

Tiny wisps of very yellow hair show under the sides of the hat, the entire whites of the eyes are painted brown with centered pupils added, and her mouth is a dot of bright red. The complexion is very mottled and yellow.

Immobile Teenies

No. 312 A mint box of assorted Teenies—we just don't know what else to call them—including three children and three old folks. To this writer's knowledge there never were any young adults in this type.

All are incised **Germany** on the back. On the girl it is across the edge of her dress, on the boys it is across the waist at the belt line, on the old gent it is on the tail of his coat, and on the old ladies it is marked at the hems of the dresses.

The little girls without bows are 1⅝ inches; the girls with bows (**No. 313**) and the boys with pompons on their caps are 1⅞ inches; the ladies are 2⅛ inches; and the old gent is 2¼ inches.

Like the dolls with moving heads, they are made of white bisque, wildly decorated and not fired, so many of them are found without a vestige of color. In mint condition the children's complexions vary from slightly suntanned to very pale, the old folks' coloring is of a medium tone.

From the left across the box the descriptions are: A little girl all in white except for a hair bow, a skirt band, and a molded flower, all of which are teal blue. A boy with a bright red cap and pants. Another boy with a bright red suit with a white collar and a white cap with a blue top pompon. A grandmother with black glasses, white cap, yellow neck bow, and gray dress and shawl. A grandfather with a gray molded hat, bright purple suit, white vest and shirt, and a yellow tie. Another grandmother with a green molded hat and purse and a bright orange dress.

We often speak of boxes from Germany being marked but in this instance, because the dolls are marked, the cheap cardboard box which is stapled at the corners instead of glued and bound, is stamped only **1 1111** on the front end of the lid.

312

313

312 & 313 Author's collection

No. 313 Another little girl with yellow stripes down her dress and a yellow molded bow in her reddish-blond hair, holding a red flower. The first boy from the box is next. A different little girl with flowers and a band molded around her head, and with her hair in tiny curls in back; the entire head is painted brown. Her shoes, as well as the molded neck band and front tie, are painted blue and the molded ladle in her hand is green.

There may have been other animals in the group but the little lamb is most often found. This one has black eyes, red collar, and an orange bell. It is 1⅛ inches long and ¾ of an inch tall at the head.

The
Bonn Dolls

There is no way to determine the number of one particular type of all-bisques which are scattered through American collections. They are identifiable only by their incised numbers, which appear in the form of fractions on the heads, the upper number of which is 83.

In the December 1966 issue of *Spinning Wheel*, Lucy Cunningham wrote about and illustrated one of these dolls, giving Jack Fixit, "who operated a doll hospital supply house in Washington, D.C., for many years" as her source of information.

Mrs. Cunningham quotes Jack Fixit as having said, "The elderly lady who was making these dolls [author's note: in 1951 in East Germany, not far from Bonn] had to leave in the night when she learned she was going to be jailed for some reason. She has since died in Berlin."

The article goes on to say, "This short-lived factory also produced five sizes of all-bisque jointed dolls, from $5\frac{1}{2}$ to $7\frac{1}{2}$ inches in height. They had sleeping glass eyes and painted socks and slippers. The bisque was inferior but acceptable, and the hair was of bright synthetic material.

"These all-bisques were numbered in the catalog as:

> #25, $5\frac{1}{2}$" set eyes
> #50, $5\frac{1}{4}$" slp. eyes
> #100, $5\frac{3}{4}$"
> #125, 7"
> #150, $7\frac{1}{4}$""

Two dolls very similar to the illustration in Mrs. Cunningham's article have been in this collection for a number of years but neither of them fits the specifications laid down for the Bonn dolls. It is regrettable that we

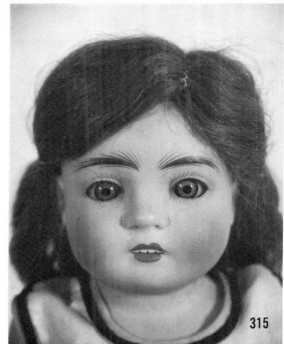

do not have more detailed descriptions with which to work but those we have must do.

Nos. 314 and 315 The largest, 9½ inches tall, is incised on the head, 83 over a line and 225 below the line, and below that, 24. The arms are marked 83 over 225 and the leg flanges 83/225.

She is hip and shoulder jointed with the enormous loops which characterized many Kestner dolls, and she also has very pretty hands which appear to be a Kestner type. Her very good wig is undoubtedly original and is made of pretty, light brown mohair on a good cloth cap, with a woven side part.

Her sleep eyes have been set and are threaded gray (a favorite Kestner color) with dark iris rims; she has upper and lower painted lashes and red eye dots. Her multistroke brows are brown with several strokes in each brow standing out away from the main group.

There are four excellent teeth cut into the center of her open-closed mouth, because the demarcation lines are too sharp to have been incised only. The white socks have good vertical ribbing and blue bands, the one-

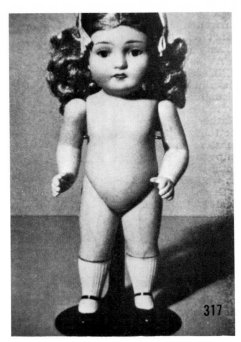

316 Author's collection; 317 Spinning Wheel

strap heeled slippers are black with tan soles. However, she does have big, thick, clumsy looking feet.

Nobody could ever classify her bisque as "inferior but acceptable" because it is good quality, well finished, and more than satisfactory in weight. The complexion coating is very even and only slightly high in color—pre-World War I if a guess has to be made.

No. 316 The second doll, 6⅝ inches tall, is incised on the head, **83** over a line and **125** below the line, and below that, **16 1/2**; her arms and legs are also properly incised. Even though she is larger than the listed #100 and smaller than the #125 in the Bonn list, her mark differs from the doll illustrated because the Bonn doll's lower mark is given as **16 0/2**.

She has the same Kestner stringing loops as the larger doll, bright golden-brown sleep eyes which have upper and lower painted lashes, but the red eye dot is missing. The open-closed mouth has no teeth indicated and the multistroke brows in brown are not quite as fringed onto the forehead.

Her wig must be discounted because it appears to have been made of reddish-gold human hair, and the maker was not an expert. It is hair pushed into a hole in the dome, then combed forward, and originally it was glued to the forehead to form a part of sorts. The author restyled it by cutting the bangs.

She also has the clumsy feet but in this instance they are not as objectionable as in the larger size. Her soles are also tan but one is light and the other is dark.

Her bisque is also good, not quite as smoothly finished as that of the big doll; the color is even and not high.

No. 317 Without a Bonn doll to compare point by point with these two, there is nothing to fall back on but the illustration in Mrs. Cunningham's article. Either because of the camera angle or the downward tilt of that doll's chin, she appears to have a prettier or more dollish face than the two described above.

The arms and the legs, however, seem to be exactly like those on the author's dolls.

The fit of the arms in the shoulder sockets and the free-thumbed hands are like those on thousands of known and suspected Kestner all-bisques. The same thing is true of the feet and yet we are not prepared at first glance to accept these thick, ungainly feet as products of the King of Doll Makers. We are so accustomed to the outlandishly unreal proportions of the hands and feet of all types of German dolls, the size of the feet on the Bonn dolls have almost been accepted as their identification factor.

It is not true, however, that they alone have oversized feet. Many dolls which have to be credited to Kestner on the basis of physical characteristics alone—until proof to the contrary is forthcoming—have the same heavy ankles, thick feet, and one-strap, heeled black slippers. Some of the older samples also have the small front bow which Kestner used for many years in several painted variations.

Without going into detailed descriptions, the following illustrations are included to prove this point and only the vital information is given.

No. 318 Incised only 150 on the head, 6¾ inches tall, with a slightly open mouth with four molded teeth.

No. 319 Incised on the head in two lines, 150 over 4½ 0., 5 inches tall, with an open-closed mouth without the teeth indicated.

No. 320 Incised on the head in three lines, 130, 6, and +, with an open-closed mouth without teeth indicated. This particular doll has blue socks in another Kestner pattern and her slippers have the old front bows.

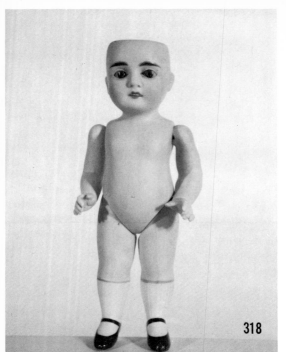

318

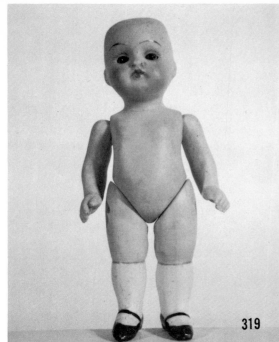

319

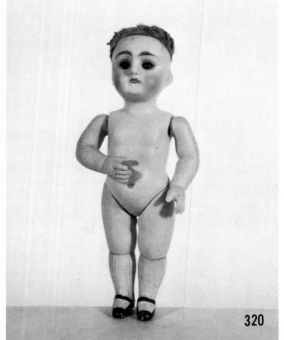

320

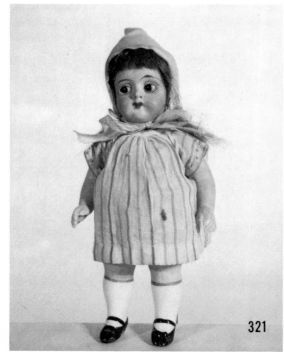

321

318, 319, 320 & 321 Author's collection

No. 321 Incised on the head in two lines **257** over **.16.** with **Made in Germany** in two lines on the back of the torso, this doll is 5 inches tall. The space between the lips in the open-closed mouth was colored and she has the vertically ribbed socks and the slippers with front bows.

No. 322 The only doll available with these feet and molded hair. She is 3⅝ inches tall, incised across the shoulder, **35. 8 1/2,** and is hip and shoulder jointed with wire. Her open-closed mouth has a white center, the hair shades from dark blond in back to brown on the front edges. In this doll the vertically ribbed sock pattern is different, inasmuch as it is a type of expanding rib which has wider panels at the top than at the bottom.

Some of these dolls have the warped heads which Kestner turned out, one has the Kestner wig base still firmly glued to the head without a hair of the original mohair, all of them have good shoulders, and the hands are all variations of established Kestner types.

Handling them, examining them, puzzling over them, it is impossible not to reach the conclusion that if the story about these Bonn dolls is true, and there is no reason to believe that it is not, then the molds for them were taken from a large Kestner, very possibly one of the 9½-inch samples like **No. 314.**

Without being a professional ceramist, but using the shrinkage factors explained in the second chapter, a doll of approximately that size would provide the size graduations listed in the catalogue from which Mr. Fixit quoted.

It would be interesting to examine a Bonn doll with the same thoroughness as the dolls in this collection have been scrutinized for years. Undoubtedly the bisque would tell the story because "inferior but acceptable" does not apply to any of the dolls pictured here. **No. 318** is very good bisque and the complexion is quite pale. The torso of **No. 320** is even paler and smooth as satin but her limbs are not well color-matched, a frequent problem in German decorating and assembly.

Unfortunately, this is a story without a proper ending. Possibly we can reach a definite conclusion by exchanging information and facts. If that becomes possible, the results could be published.

31

Modern Originals and Reproductions

Many collectors, both novice and advanced, fail to differentiate in their own minds between the *original* creations of modern ceramists and reproduction dolls by the same group. It sometimes takes the death of an artist to put the proper value on the work done in a lifetime which is too often prematurely ended. Just as frequently, the value of existing work by such artists is so exaggerated that serious collectors begin to wonder why any gifted artist bothers to stay in the doll field.

The late and beloved Martha Thompson is a shining example of this foolish phenomenon. To the author's knowledge, Mrs. Thompson did not make all-bisques, but her original creations in the portrait field are truly works of art. Yet no one would have thought of paying the artist herself the prices they fight to pay for her work now that she is gone.

An original is totally the work of the creator; a reproduction is a copy of a doll which has, through the passage of the years, become public domain. Most ceramists will not use the molds of an original for the full fifty castings. Consequently, if a doll has not been popular, the molds may be stored away after perhaps twenty pourings and that's that. For some reason they all feel reluctant to reinstate a doll into their production schedule once it has been ignored by collectors.

"Too few and too late" is the requiem tag on too many original creations, while reproductions roll merrily along.

The big mystery of the hobby is that the price of a good reproduction seems to bother no one. The buyers know that they are reproductions but, because the prices of the old, mostly German, originals have risen so drastically, there seems to be a point of comparison in their minds at which they rationalize the purchase. The same process does not carry over to the purchase of modern originals, even though they are entirely new and different, are made by the same people from the same materials, and the prices are the same.

We know that human nature has peculiarities all its own but some of them are difficult to fathom. It never seems to enter the buyers' minds, for instance, that the cost of one good reproduction is perhaps ten times the cost of the originals in their own day. Why a comparable original by the same artist who made the reproduction does not have the same value— and more—in the buyers' minds is beyond comprehension.

We show here a few samples of modern originals.

No. 323 A 4-inch all-bisque made and dressed by Eunice P. Tuttle of Scarsdale, N.Y., who specializes in "Original Modern Dollhouse Dolls." She has a wire strung swivel head, painted blue eyes with pupils and black lid linings, and is made of precolored bisque. The small hands are very well done, the heelless slippers are painted red, and she has a modern, glued-on, fiber wig.

323 Millar collection; 324 Author's collection

Mrs. Tuttle's 1966 catalogue lists her dolls in pairs. There are an 8-year-old, 4¾-inch boy and girl and, in both white and Negro, the following sets: 4-inch 5-year-olds, 3½-inch 3-year-olds, and two cunning 4-month-old infants which are 2¼ inches. Listed but noted then as "unfinished," is "The Infanta Marguerite" in two sizes, 3½ and 4 inches, representing the famous and very pretty little girl at both 3 and 5 years of age.

No. 324 "Lilli Ann," a 9½-inch swivel neck all-bisque by Goodie Bennett, Seattle, Wash., inspired by old paper dolls. She is hip and shoulder jointed and is sold with either blue or brown glass goo-goo set eyes.

No. 325 Another 9½-inch swivel from the hands of Goodie Bennett, this one inspired by a child portrait of her mother and named "Nathalie."

No. 326 A swivel neck dog and cat, each approximately 3½ inches, created by Mrs. Bennett, who signs all her work with her full name and the copyright year.

Reproduction samples.

327

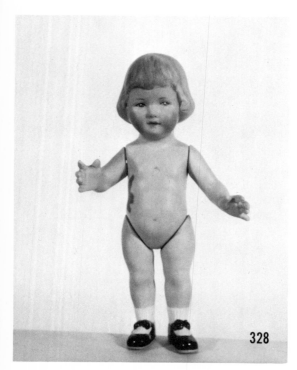

328

327 & 328 Strong collection

No. 327 A pair from Marianne DeNunez, Arleta, Calif. These are duplicates of the highly prized J. D. K. watermelon-mouthed goo-goos.

No. 328 Another all-bisque from Mrs. DeNunez who signs her dolls, "Marianne." Readers will recognize this one as a reproduction of the Heubach girl, No. 125.

Mrs. DeNunez is also known for her fine original doll creations, and all her work is deeply incised "Marianne" and the year of issue.

Japanese

Among dealers of all kinds, objects marked **NIPPON** are generally considered to be older, and sometimes much better, than objects marked **JAPAN**. Just when this changeover took place is difficult to pinpoint but it is interesting to check the Japanese entry into the doll field through old wholesale catalogues.

Butler Brothers Fall *1908* Catalogue, for instance, had a special listing in the Index for "Japanese Goods" and quite a few page references. There were six full pages of a wide variety of china items for the home and it appears they were not above copying their own fine china because there was a listing for a set of "imitation Amari ware" bowls.

There were no Japanese toy tea sets but there were thirty-eight German sets illustrated in the Toy Section, plus nine larger, "Juvenile" sets.

In a single column beside the first page of china there was a listing of Japanese dolls:

3½ in. clay body, painted features, felt topknot, gay paper dress. 1 gro. in box. Gro. 72¢

papier mache dolls, 3½ in., painted features, felt topknot, asstd. colors, crimped paper dress, with voices. ½ gro. in box. Gro. 98¢

4½ in., papier mache head with hair, imit. glass eyes, painted features, strong crepe paper asstd color kimonas with tinsel sash. 1 doz. in box. Doz. 25¢

7½ in., like above with cloth kimonas, 2 doz. in box. asstd. Doz. 27¢

Ht. 6 in., glazed clay head, feet and hands, painted features, good topknot, gaudy paper dress, 1 doz. in pkg. Doz. 35¢

8 in. like above with crepe cloth kimonas, Doz. 75¢

9½ in. glass eyes, painted features, natural hair, fancy cloth kimona, with voices. 1 doz. in box. Doz. 89¢

11 in. papier mache head, painted features, glass eyes, real hair, free arms and legs, fancy figured crepe paper kimona, moving head, each with voice. 1 doz. in box. Doz. 89¢

These are the dolls familiar to almost any collector and remembered by older collectors from all kinds of carnivals and parks in the early part of this century. It is quite obvious they were of little value then and they have little value now, although some are found in excellent condition.

In the regular doll section there was an ample selection of German all-bisques, but nothing from Japan. There does not appear to have been the national sensitivities which developed after the war, either, because Germany is proudly mentioned in many instances and, quite often, to conserve headline space, the Oriental goods are listed as "JAP."

In the *1916* Santa Claus Catalogue from the same firm, besides one page of Japanese toys, there were six pages of adult chinaware made in Japan, plus eleven toy tea sets and one chocolate set which look like and are priced exactly like the German ones. The Germans still had the edge on their great imitators, however, because they had twenty tea sets listed in the toy section and none of the bisque dolls appear to be Japanese.

In the November *1921* Catalogue Butler Brothers stated: "Here is as complete a line of European Imported Dolls as can be found anywhere today. Not since the pre-war days have the merchants of America been able to buy dolls of such beauty, originality and all-around attractiveness."

Be that as it may, there was no Japanese classification in the Index and no identified Japanese dolls, although where the German all-bisques were previously there is a headline: "A large variety of popular Japan imported dolls, including celluloid, bisque and china." Many of the dolls appear to be Japanese from the illustrations but "Baby Bud" was there without the bathing suit and that was the German version.

In the toy section the majority of tea sets were "litho metal, aluminum and decorated celluloid," and only three sets in china were advertised as: "Enamel coloring, varnished after being lithographed," which sounds very much like a Japanese operation to eliminate firing.

In the December *1925* Catalogue there were only four "imported china toy tea sets" with no country of origin indicated.

There were, however, "Fine Quality Imported Bisque Dolls" and among them, completely identifiable, were the dolls in **Nos. 300** and **301** which are incised **Germany**. The 4½-inch size, by the way, were 84 cents a dozen! There were also precolored bisque dolls which look like **No. 240** and they were German. The German "Baby Bud" **No. 266** was also included.

Several dolls which look very Japanese in the illustrations and much like **No. 339** in this book were shown but where the price should be the word "OUT" appeared.

By December *1932* the only special listing is "Japanese gardens" and there was no sign of an adult china section.

There were five small "Highly Lustered China" toy tea sets which are unidentifiable because of the packaging similarity, plus one large set with the material not mentioned, and another large set identified as "china."

The doll section carried no statement about quality and, compared to the 1908 catalogue, it was pitiful. There were some "5¢ and 10¢ Retail Values" listed under "Imported China Dolls" but from the illustrations they appear to be Japanese and one, "IF 9662," looks like a Morimura Brothers with a hairband and flowers. A small selection of "Imported Bisqueloid Finish Dolls" and a group of celluloids look German.

Japanese competition was vicious. They not only openly copied German dolls and toys but also undercut the prices to such an extent that no industry could have survived, let alone an industry recovering from a war. In order to do this they destroyed all semblance of quality and in the final analysis they wrecked the market for themselves as well as everybody else. There is a point of no return in lack of quality and the Japanese reached it very quickly.

American manufacturers also got a taste of this kind of ruthless competition. A city in Japan named Usa (pronounced Oosa) had long been a trading center in a rice-producing region. To circumvent our "country of origin" laws the city was developed as a toy-manufacturing area and objects made there were marked "Made in USA." At a passing glance this was mistaken by American shoppers for "Made in U.S.A."

It was necessary for our government to take stern measures to stop this infringement on a national identification. Japan suffered some serious boycotting of its other export items and during World War II the city was bombed.

In 1967 a world conference was held, without too much success, in an effort to establish patent protection. That it has long been needed is exemplified beyond the possibility of rebuttal in the sketchiest history of Japanese manufacture.

People sometimes ask, "With all your good dolls, why in the world do you collect such junk?" The answer is very simple—these dolls are part of an important industry which has provided a fascinating hobby for many people. It is true that they are part of the death scene but the beginning and the end of the story should be as important as the middle, the so-called "Golden Age of Dolls."

Nippon

No. 329 With **NIPPON** incised across the back, this 4⅝-inch stolen Kewpie is an excellent example of the flagrant plagiarism the Japanese practiced with complete disdain for the copyright and patent laws of other countries. With a little imagination and effort, the Germans competed for Kewpie trade with their own charmers but this Japanese doll was intended to divert Kewpie sales through price cutting alone.

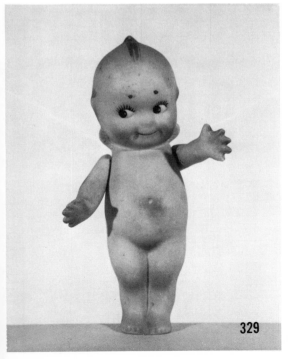 

329 Author's collection; 330 A Friend

The incised signature, O'Neill, in the distinctive lettering Rose used, was removed from the soles of the feet but it takes a practiced eye to spot this copy if it cannot be examined. The bisque is fairly good quality and the doll is a satisfactory weight for its size, the little blue wings are properly colored and so are the tufts of blond hair and the topknot. The white highlights in the eyes were done with paint instead of relief white and consequently barely show. The black lid linings are properly done but the eyelashes are longer and not as thick as those on German Kewpies.

No. 330 Incised **NIPPON** on the back, this 5¾-inch boy is a direct steal from the German "Baby Bud" **No. 266**, with the bottom of the German doll's shirt sanded off and a bathing suit illusion created by painted blue stripes around the base of the body and the legs. Even the oblong decoration from the front of Baby Bud's shirt and the gathers at his molded V neck were picked up in the copying molds.

In this particular doll the arms are known to be modern reproductions but it is an excellent illustration of how much Japanese dolls would have been improved by better arms.

331

331

331 Author's collection

The bisque and painting are fair; that is, passable for German but good for Japanese.

This doll appears again under Morimura Brothers as illustration **No. 344.**

No. 331 Incised **NIPPON** across the back in fancy type, this 3¾-inch girl certainly looks like a direct steal from the German Happifats, albeit with more finesse than the NIPPON Kewpie or Baby Bud.

Her clothes are colored in reverse, i.e., pink dress and blue sash. The different hairdo and up-painted eyes would have been ample protection if any protection were needed but other specimens prove it was not.

The bisque, the finishing, and decorating are all quite acceptable.

No. 332 With molded bobbed hair and bangs, this little **NIPPON** incised girl is 4¾ inches tall. There is a small doll molded on her right side, around which her bent arm seems to fit. The small doll's modeling is fair and the featuring is just dots for eyes and mouth; the dress is painted pink and the hair and boots are a blond tone.

The girl has feet which do not match and this has been true of all such specimens examined. The left one is pointed like the feet on the small Gebruder Heubach dolls and the right one is shorter, with a rounded toe. The original mold may have been made from a broken doll. The shoes are painted the bright henna which Heubach sometimes used.

The white molded shift has a ruffled neckline and hem, which are tinted blue only across the front surface. The features are not well molded but they are fairly well painted. The lid linings are black, the pupils are side painted with slight blue rims around them and the brows are dark blond. They appear to have been copying from something.

Like Japanese dolls almost without exception, the arms are very poor. They are too thin, they are not well molded or finished, and the complexioning is much poorer than that of the legs which, of course, were probably done by another worker. In this particular doll the arms do have a good fit to the body, however, which is unusual.

No. 333 Incised in two lines, **102** and **NIPPON** across the shoulders, this pair with rubber jointed arms have black lid linings, side-painted pupils with highlight dots which seem to be something like plaster because they flick off at the touch of a fingernail. The one-stroke brows are brown, and the mouths have intaglio depressions.

The molded caps are pale blue with narrow black bands and very glossy pink molded side bows. The hair is pale yellow but the edges are orange where it meets the complexion tinting and dirty brushes were used on the

332

333

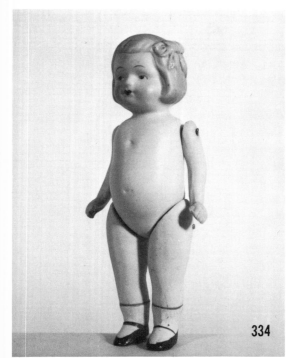

334

335

332, 333, 334 & 335 Author's collection

back areas. The short, molded socks are pale green and the shoes are glossy henna color.

All the finishing is very poor. There is mold debris in the hands and the doll on the left is made of lumpy bisque which did not shrink evenly in the firing. As a consequence, she has a swollen right side to her face, a bulging torso, and a rough, thick, left leg. A chunk of her hat brim stayed in the back mold but the area was colored in spite of this and it resulted in a triangular patch of a much darker color.

No. 334 Incised across the shoulders **NIPPON**, this 5⅝-inch hip and shoulder wire jointed girl has every sign of being cast from a German doll. She has pupils with little dabs of blue iris, black lid linings, and one-stroke brows in reddish brown. There is a bright pink, glossy, molded bow at the side of her yellow hair but the decorator did not follow the fairly good molded form of the hair and the yellow color mixed with the complexion coating across the forehead. The small mouth is bright red.

The torso is rather well finished and decorated, the complexion is pale and quite even, but the arms and legs are very poorly done from start to finish. They are rather shapeless, the color is bad, and the picture shows clearly the poor decorating on the feet—one strap is thick and the other is thin, one henna-colored shoe has no front, and the Prussian blue bands on the socks are especially bad in back.

No. 335 Incised **NIPPON** across the back, this Oriental infant is better than the usual Japanese doll. It has a 4⅝-inch head circumference, sits up 3½ inches and is 4¾ inches lying flat.

His body is barely tinted, one leg has almost no complexion coating at all and in places looks grayish rather than stark white. His feet and his entire head are very glossy black but this is not a true glaze. Drippings down the back look very much like yellow shellac and the doll has periods when either the temperature or the humidity can still make it feel a little tacky after all these years.

There is no question but that he is a "redesigned" German doll, maybe a Kestner. He has a stiff neck, is hip and shoulder jointed with loops, has the raised big toes and, like **No. 188**, his bare feet were just painted black, this time without even the glued braid to form the tops of the soft, typical embroidered shoes.

Anyone who can hold a paint brush steady could make this type of Oriental and he does look very Asian. The eyes are the answer. The entire molded socket was painted black, with extended lines out toward the temples and into the eye corners, then a highlight dot of white was placed in the center. It apparently was not relief white because one of them has rubbed off. Under the slanted eyebrows the mold marks of the rounded German eyebrows are still visible. The mouth, which is certainly no different in Asia, is the open-closed type with two tiny teeth painted under the upper lip.

The hair and feet were done with glossy paint because it scrapes off with a fingernail. The yellow shellac accentuated the pale complexion tint and left the face very glossy. Like **No. 188,** woven braid was glued all around the head with gathered circular pieces over the ears which have hanging drops of blue and red beads sewed to the center. The faded purple pants are probably original but the jacket could be a replacement because this fellow had a companion whose jacket was the only difference between the two.

No. 336 A more blatant theft than this MADE IN JAPAN copy of E. I. Horsman's 1925 "HEbeeSHEbee" is difficult to imagine because the design is unique in dolldom. The 4⅜-inch specimen almost lost its incised mark in the finishing, which must have been a fortuitous circumstance during its entire existence.

The round eyes are glossy royal blue with highlight dots of relief white, the bald head is barely washed with light brown color, the cheeks and mouth are a little on the orange side, and the clumsy bedroom slippers with a pierced hole for a front ribbon bow are enameled in a bright rose color. The little shift is white, the arms are very good for a Japanese doll, although the complexioning is poorer than the legs which are tinted like the face.

No. 337 A & B This 4-inch sit-down girl is not very well done but she is interesting and proves the point that the Japanese might have done better had they originated some doll ideas rather than just copied from other creators.

The straight legs are wire strung through holes in the base of the molded dress and they fit into rounded channels molded front-to-back on the under side.

The bisque in the dress is very white and of fair quality. The decorating seems to be very glossy enamel which does not wash off but does not appear to be fired. She has pink bows in yellow hair and blue bands on her dress. She is unmarked.

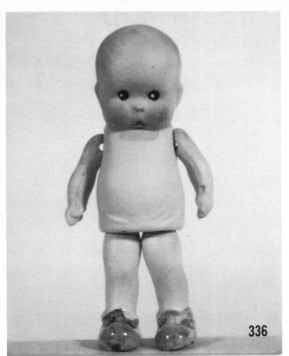

336

337

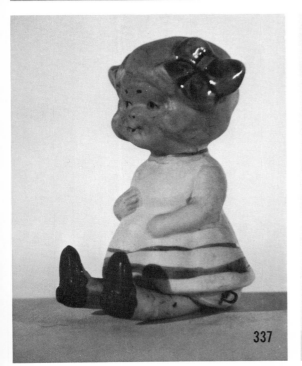

337

338

336, 337 & 338 Author's collection

No. 338 With a molded hat and dress, this 4½-inch doll is incised in back **Made in Japan.**

There is more than a possibility that this girl and the unmarked sit-down doll were made by the same firm. Although the previous doll's hands are molded to the body, they are the same shape, with an open, flat right hand and a pointed forefinger on the left hand. The arms are also heavier than the ordinary Japanese doll arms. The faces are also very much alike and there are two tiny molded marks under the hatted doll's painted eyebrows which match the funny black dashes on the sit-down but in this doll the decorators ignored them. Added to all this, the glossy band and bows on this doll's hat are almost exactly the same shade of rose as the bows in the sit-down's hair.

The hatted doll is made of a fair quality of bisque and the finishing is better than usual. Her side-painted eyes have black lid linings and the thin brows are brown. The complexion tint was used to decorate the molded jumper straps of the dress, the neckline, and the hemline but at the hem the color was not completed around the back. Her shoes are black

339

340

339 A Friend; 340 Author's collection

and the molded tufts of hair are light blond.

No. 339 Typical of millions of her kind in many sizes which came to the United States, this 5¾-inch shoulder jointed doll is incised in two lines in back, **MADE IN JAPAN.** The Kewpie influence is very obvious, with the body possibly molded from a German Kewpie.

Some modern artists use the odd word "tweekled" to express this type of stealing. In their parlance this means that the original doll has bits added or subtracted by means of modeling clay or sanding—à la Baby Bud. It takes very little stretch of the imagination to see the Kewpie under this doll.

The highlight dots are relief white, the one-stroke brows are dark blond, and the hair is a light blond wash of color. The bisque is fair, the finishing is poor, and the painting is slightly high in color.

According to Butler Brothers Catalogues these dolls were:

November 1921, not listed at all.
December 1925, illustrated, 5⅝-inch size is given and then where the price should be the word "OUT" appears.
December 1932, illustrated, 7½-inch size, at 72 cents per dozen.

No. 340 It is difficult to understand why anyone felt it necessary to mark this dreadful little specimen twice. She is incised in two lines across the back **MADE IN JAPAN,** and then, in smaller letters on her right foot, there is a black stamped circular mark, **Made in Japan,** which has a small fan insignia in the center.

Shoulder jointed with loops, she has poorly enameled pupils with irregular irises that appear to be some shade of Prussian blue, scant upper lashes, and a one-stroke brown brow on the right and only a brush drag on the left. The rather nicely molded hair is very pale yellow and the molded band is painted a dull Prussian blue with a bright pink oval decoration in the center front.

The bisque is very poor, the complexion coating is tinged with yellow, and the arms are poorly done without tinting.

This doll's body is like that of the German series, **Nos. 300** and **301.**

No. 341 Compared to the German swayers, **Nos. 78** and **79,** this 3½-inch Japanese specimen is rather worthless. Of typical Japanese bisque, it is held together by a wire attached to the large front button. The hat is black, the coat and the pants are green, and the inset in the front, representing a dress, is orange.

341 *Author's collection*

Morimura Brothers

This firm was the subject of a talk given by Elizabeth Ann Coleman before the Long Island Doll, Hobby & Craft Club in March 1967. A partial quote from the L.I.D.C. *News Bulletin* of June-July 1967 throws some interesting lights on the company, an important source of exports to the United States.

> . . . In recent years collectors have been made aware of the American dolls manufactured during the period of World War I. Also filling the vacuum left by the withdrawal of European products were the Japanese. Their period of influence ran the term when European imports were not available, roughly from 1915 to 1922. The largest concern was Morimura Brothers, an import house located in New York City, whose partners were subjects of the Emperor of Japan.
>
> Shortly after the outbreak of the war the firm began to produce as well as distribute dolls. They made no bones about copying popular European dolls; as a matter of fact, they noted in a trade journal of the period that their artists back in Japan, where the factory was

located, found it exceedingly difficult to produce faces imitating occidental features. However, these dolls were popular almost beyond belief. The dolls, some with socket heads, some with shoulder heads, some semi-rigid, some with character faces, some with "doll" faces, were all sold out for the year 1917 just at the point when the big rush for Christmas orders should have been beginning. The firm had to advertise that they could accept no orders after the 15th of February 1917.

The Morimura Brothers used as their mark the letters M B within a circle which has a central line with crossbars on either end. Usually under the circle the word, Japan, is found.

The first doll (1915) apparently manufactured by Morimura was "Queue San Baby." This semi-rigid doll was designed by Hikozo Arakia, a U.S. citizen residing in Brooklyn, N.Y. His design patent paper, which was assigned to Morimura Brothers, shows a figure with molded cap and queue. Morimura Brothers registered the trademark for this doll, "Queue San Baby" in 1916. Other dolls manufactured and distributed by this concern included "Dolly Doll", a doll designed by F. Langfelder, 1919; "Baby Ella", a doll with a bisque socket head on a jointed composition body, 1918-21; "My Darling", 1919-20; and "First Prize Baby", 1919-20. It should be noted that "My Sweetheart" frequently also appears on dolls made for B. Illfelder & Co. (B. I. & Co.) a German firm and that "My Darling" is the name given to a famous line of dolls made by Kammer & Reinhardt (K R).

No. 342 The 3¾-inch kneeling "Queue San Baby" still has his original diamond-shaped label but the red has faded to brown and the printing cannot now be read at all.

He is shoulder jointed with loops and his half-closed eyes have molded lids with black lid linings and only painted pupils. He has the starfish hands and a black queue down his back; he is a very smooth, golden yellow. The bisque and the finishing do not seem to account for the smoothness, how-

342

342

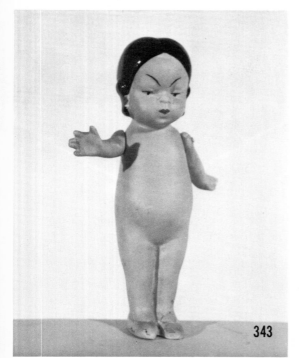

343

343

342, 343 & 344 Strong collection

ever. There is some quality about the bisque which probably will never be identified unless a broken doll comes to light.

Other standing Queue San Babies in the Strong Collection have the same cap, painted a variety of colors, all with the pointed shoes, the starfish hands and the queues of this doll.

No. 343 Although she has no label, this 4¾-inch girl is Queue San's sister. Her shining black hair is molded in double buns over each ear and tied through the centers with a molded band which has been painted a soft green. Her shoes are lavender.

Like the kneeling doll, her complexion is a golden yellow and she is also very smooth to the touch.

In the author's collection, with the faded diamond shaped label still intact, there is a 4⅝-inch Queue San girl which is also jointed at the hips. Like the sit-down Kewpie, she is more difficult to find than the one with the rigid legs.

Her painting is exactly like the shoulder jointed specimens but she does not have the starfish fingers. The arm are original and complexioned like the body but the fingers and thumbs are molded together in a slightly cupped form. The stringing loops on both the arms and legs are superior to those on typical Japanese dolls but she would be more attractive if the shoulder holes were large enough to accommodate the better loops.

No. 344 Another Baby Bud which is identified by the Colemans as the "Dolly" which was "designed" by Langfelder for Morimura Brothers and patented by that energetic firm because of "a change of design." Just how much talent it took to do this kind of designing is anybody's guess.

Since this one is not incised and the **NIPPON** doll has no label, it is not quite clear whether they are both from Morimura Brothers or whether the Japanese also stole from each other.

Except for the size, which is 3¾ inches (the **NIPPON** is 5¾), and the mouth, which does not have the white center, he is like the incised doll, even to the German Baby Bud's molded bow in the back of his neck. The Morimura gold, red and white diamond label bears only the word **DOLLY** on the center crossbar.

Both the bisque and the decorating are fair for such Japanese items but the skinny arms are typically poor.

The author has never had a penchant for Morimura Brothers' products but the record would not be complete without a few more samples.

No. 345 Not at all like the diamond-shaped label on the "Dolly," this

345

345

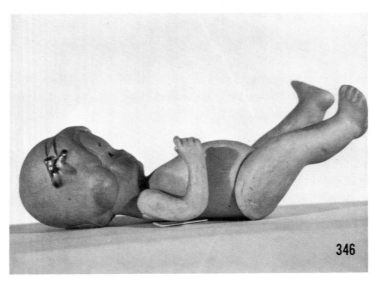

346

345 Strong collection; 346 Author's collection

yellow one is shield shaped. The outside edge and the bands on the red center bar are done in gold. The initials **M.B.** appear in red in the top section, "Baby Darling" is printed in white on the red center bar, and a red circle with a center line and semicircles at each end is printed in red in the base.

The doll is 4¾ inches tall, and has a tucked-in chin and yellow molded hair. There is a poorly molded, pink painted bow at either end of the blue headband with dark blue outer edges. There are dabs of blue beside the large centered pupils, black lid linings, and dark blond brows. The mouth is watermelon shape.

The body bisque is better than much of the Japanese ware and the finishing is quite smooth to the touch. The skinny arms are very bad and apparently were molded from the "Dolly" arms because the V form of the first two fingers can be plainly seen.

No. 346 Incised **NIPPON** across the shoulder, this is a 5½-inch specimen of the same doll with bent, baby-type legs. The Germans also did this in at least one instance, **No. 221,** so there is no point in blaming this on Japanese lack of know-how. The girl face and the full head of hair with blue band and pink bows, however, is a bit ridiculous on the babyish body.

It is interesting that the legs are infinitely better than any Japanese arms. They fit into hip holes with nice ledges to hold the legs close to the body. There is more than a suspicion that the legs were molded from a Kestner baby because the loops and the feet are so good. Unlike the arms, too, they are made of the same good Japanese bisque as the torso and as nicely finished and decorated.

No. 347 Incised **NIPPON** across the shoulders, this 4¾-inch pair are probably from the same firm. The previous doll is incised in the same manner and yet her head is definitely Morimura.

This doll has exactly the same body as the upright doll with blue band and pink bows. Besides the arms, the sameness is noted in the peculiarly flat seat and the thick molded-together feet so closely resembling those of Kewpies.

The yellow hair and the pink band and bow are well done, the whites of the eyes are painted blue and have large pupils, black lid linings, and tiny dark blond dash brows .The bodies are well painted and padded and the bisque is finished well but the thin, bent arms are shades lighter, of very poor bisque and barely colored.

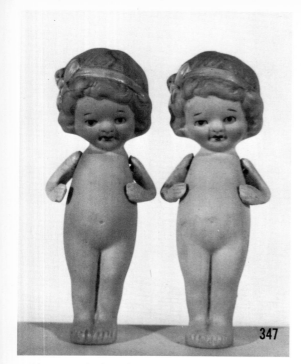

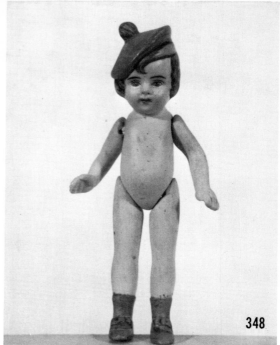

347 & 348 *Author's collection*

Occupied Japan

No. 348 One gets the feeling that someone with experience in Europe had a hand in this doll. If it were not for the incised mark in three lines across the back, that experienced person might have been an American. The mark is **MADA IN/OCCUPIED/JAPAN.**

The bisque is fair, she is 4¾ inches tall, the legs are long and straight, and she is infinitely better than many Japanese dolls. The size and fit of the arms, as well as the proportion and detail of the hands are very good. She is rather cute, except that we are not used to pure white all-bisques and this one has no complexion coat, not even blushed cheeks.

The dark blue eyes have high pupils, highlight dots, both upper and lower black lid linings, red lid lines, and red eye and nose dots. The one-stroke brows are black. The side-parted bob is fairly well modeled but the painting is poor and an odd, unbecoming brown color.

She has a blue tam with a yellow pompon, blue socks and completely yellow heelless slippers with molded instep bows which are highlighted in brown.

346 § *All-Bisque and Half-Bisque Dolls*

ひ *33*

*Instructions
for Care*

With the proper tools and supplies, almost anybody can work success-fully with all-bisques. Time and patience are the only other requirements.

To restring the pegged type, the proper size of rubber is drawn through the limbs and torso and then knots are tied in the ends of the rubber. Pegs are cut and fitted into the holes to be certain they hold the rubber without benefit of glue. The correct pegs for one arm and one leg are dipped in glue and set first. When these have had time to dry thoroughly, the rubber is pulled tight and the other pegs are glued and pushed firmly in place.

Mucilage or glue is available everywhere, so modern substitutes should not be used in pegging dolls. After another drying period, the protruding rubber and peg ends are cut off—some people like a penknife to do this and others use a small pair of cutting pliers. If you are very neat and want to sandpaper these butt ends, do be careful because the bisque complexion tinting will scar easily.

In loop stringing, the rubber is passed through the arm or the leg loops, pulled as tight as possible and a hard knot tied. These must be square knots and not "grannies" because they must not slip. The knots are then poked through into the hollow body to make a neat job, so all knots must be both small and strong.

Some collectors "infant string" hip and shoulder jointeds. That is, they thread rubber through all four loops and tie only one knot. The biggest problem is that infant legs are supposed to push up into a sitting position, but because their straight legs extend to an awkward width, all-bisques are displayed to better advantage standing. Sometimes, too, the legs take an annoying notion to flip backward when "strung on a circle," as other collectors identify this method.

Instructions for Care § 347

The commonest mistake beginners make in restringing dolls with arm and leg loops is that they tie knots in the rubber around the loops. This in no way makes the stringing job more secure, it can spoil the tightness of the fit and it inhibits the movement of the limbs.

The third type is wire strung and these are troublesome. Wire that is sufficiently rigid is difficult to form into the small loops on the outer surfaces.

All-bisque fanciers are constantly on the lookout for hard wire which can be bent with average small pliers. Although brass wire was used in some of the old dolls, copper wire was not and should not be used as a substitute. Some florists have a grade of wire in 18-inch lengths which is adequate and such odd items as hangers for Christmas-tree ornaments sometimes can be straightened out for this repair work.

A few words of advice and some suggestions about restringing and rewigging will help novices at least.

This work must be done on a table with a towel or other padding under a good light. These dolls and parts break and chip quite easily and, more easily, slip out of working fingers.

The first job should not be attempted without the proper tools and supplies and it is helpful to have inexpensive dolls with which to experiment.

Supplies must be gathered wherever they can be found.

The large sizes of round rubber have to be purchased from a doll-supply house and advertisements for these firms appear in almost all the specialty magazines. The two smaller sizes can be bought at variety stores or from notion counters. They are usually identified as "hat rubber" or "cord elastic" and are wound on cardboards in 3- and 6-yard lengths. The smallest size, used double for "teenies," is the fine rubber wound on spools and used on a sewing-machine bobbin to gather wrists and necklines.

If you have any Negro dolls, it is well to have black as well as white rubber in the proper sizes. Hat rubber, doubled, often has to be used in these dolls because large sizes in black are difficult to find.

Helpful tools include several sizes of crochet hooks; penknife or carving tool; sharp scissors in a small, pointed size; pointy-nosed as well as wire-cutting pliers in very small sizes; a hemostat or two, if you can manage to round them up, are unbelievably useful, and so are broken dental tools which can be sharpened to poke out softened old plugs, to force knots inside, and so on. You will also need a small spool of fine florists' wire to pull rubber through holes in bodies and limbs. Yellow mucilage or glue can be found with office or school supplies.

For plugs, gather a supply of both straight and round toothpicks, medical swab sticks, and both safety and kitchen matches. (Strike these matches and cut off the burned ends. Do not leave them around unburned or try to clip the sulphured ends with pliers!) Some wooden skewers from the butcher or small dowel sticks are also helpful for large dolls.

A few tips.

Pegs should stop at the bisque level of the hip or arm inner surface. Do not let them extend into the hole in the body. To eliminate this, properly fit and trim the fitted end of the plug before using the glue. An ample supply of plugs is necessary because they must be left in place while the glue dries and they must be long enough to provide a good finger purchase to set them properly in place.

It saves a lot of time if the holes are examined at the very beginning because they vary greatly in size in the same doll. In badly worn holes which are difficult to fit with pegs, the rubber can be doubled to ensure a tight fit if enough glue is brushed on the two pieces before the peg is inserted.

Large holes were meant to be pegged, no matter what method is used to hold the doll when it is purchased. It is good to bear in mind that someone else may have restrung either the arms or legs or both before it came your way.

Check any incised numbers on the arms and legs at the stringing points. If there are any, they should match some number on the head or the body.

Care should be exercised in building up an inventory of spare parts. Some collectors buy dolls without limbs for the torsos or odd limbs without any idea of the dolls to which they belong. If these oddments are not carried about continuously to be properly fitted when parts are available, a great deal of money can be tied up in these bits and pieces for a long time before they can be put to practical use.

Limbs should be kept with broken torsos in order to be sure that they are transferred to the proper type of body. Odd arms and legs should be kept in matched pairs on short lengths of florist wire. Unless they can be found when needed, they are useless and, if they can be found, they are sometimes useful articles of trade when someone else has a size or type you need and vice versa.

Small, open, swivel heads should be held with wooden plugs and not with wire up over the back of the head which is hidden under the wig. This is a much later German economy and good all-bisques in original condition seldom have this arrangement.

In larger sizes, however, the plug should be fitted with a wire loop. This is done by making a small T in the top of the wire so it cannot go through the plug hole and by making a loop in the other end to catch the leg rubber.

Plugs are nothing more than wooden buttons. Various sizes can sometimes be found in shops which make covered buttons and some husbands can make a supply on woodworking equipment. One source of tiny buttons for the smallest dolls (and the most difficult size to make) is old clothing with small, decorative, covered buttons. When the silk or satin is removed, the little center-holed button is ideal.

A peg or a piece of hard wire tied into the rubber and secured with a drop of glue is sufficient to hold the rubber firmly across the plug hole. When the plug or button is in place in the head, the two free ends of rubber pass through the hole in the plug, through the neck, into the torso and out the leg holes, or, if it is a small head, through the shoulder holes, with the aid of a florists' wire "needle," and pegged into the arms.

Swivel necks should never be X strung, that is, from one shoulder to the opposite leg, because it makes the legs slide up the body toward the waist when the head wire is attached in the center of the X. Instead, when the head plug and wire are in place, peg one leg, leaving the length of working rubber in place through the body and sticking out the other side. When this peg is dry, use a crochet hook to pull the rubber up into the neck opening, attach the wire and close the loop so that it will slide on the rubber but not slip off. The free hanging rubber is then pulled gently until it is taut and then pegged.

By using this method, it makes no difference how long the neck wire happens to be, although it must extend down into the body a sufficient distance to give the head stability. Doll shoulders frequently break because undue leverage is placed on them when the leg rubber is pulled up after the pegging in an attempt to attach the neck hook.

The arms are done last, although it saves time to peg one arm and set it aside to dry so that the last two gluing jobs can be done at the same time and the doll will be ready when the hip peg has dried properly.

Ball heads are held on with a strong wooden crossbar which is tied into the rubber, dropped into the head through the neck hole and shifted about until it gets a purchase in the neck. Or, they are held with a strong wire ⌄ or a ⌐⌄ of hard wire. This does not mean ordinary coathanger wire, however. It is possible to convert large stringing hooks for jointeds for this purpose and these can also be purchased from supply houses, or similar wire of that weight can be cut and shaped.

Like the wooden crossbar, these are dropped into the head and moved around until they fall into a horizontal position where they become wedged in the cheeks or the wide part of the neck. A single knot should also be tied in the rubber around the wire holders so that the rubber will not fall off during this manipulating. The free ends are pulled through the arms or the legs and then pegged.

Always use enough rubber! It is cheap and saves wear and tear on both the nerves and the temper.

The average woman enlists the help of her husband for this work, not only because he has most of the tools but also because men generally have more mechanical know-how and patience than women for this kind of fussy work. Lucky is the woman who loves all-bisques and whose husband ties trout flies!

Anyone who gets nervous and upset when things go wrong, or when something has to be done ten times before it is right, should farm this work out. It is time-consuming, nerve-wracking, painstaking, and downright tiresome unless you thoroughly enjoy solving problems. It delays things, for instance, to soak arms and legs before attempting to remove the plugs, but old-fashioned glue has tremendous holding power and a quick poking job often removes the top of a fragile arm or cracks the top of a perfect leg.

If you want to try wigs, you will need rolls of ½- and ¾-inch regular gauze bandage (1-inch if you have many large size dolls) and spray starch. If possible, examine the cap of the old wig and do the same thing—sew a piece of bandage to fit the head circumference, then crush and lightly baste the top down to fit the head. Spray with starch and allow to dry on the head to shape and shrink.

Human hair, hank mohair, or strands from an old wig can be used, but in the following instructions all types will be called "hair."

Backstitch a long piece of hair to the cap, laying the hair ear to ear and then stitching front to back. This makes good side fullness in one type. Next, wrap thread around another bundle of hair, secure it with a couple stitches, and sew this to the crown, placing it front to back over your previous stitching. Glue the under layer to the front section of the cap and cut off for bangs. Trim the back to make a straight line which can be thinned and curled, or taper the back line if end curls are not wanted. Brush with a straight toothbrush and glue into place. Enough glue from the doll's head generally will penetrate the gauze to hold the under layer of hair nicely in place.

For a part without bangs, use all the hair at once, backstitching a center or side part, and then apply a frugal coating of glue to the outside of the whole cap. Hold all the hair out of the way and allow only a few hairs all around to fall into the glue. Press this thin layer to the cap, tie the balance of the hair out of the way, and allow the glue to dry. Finish by brushing the dry hair over the whole cap. Some glue may penetrate the gauze when the wig is set in place on the head but it will not be enough to mar the brushed outer layer.

If the head is quite large and you are inexperienced, it may be necessary to build a wig on a cardboard dome. This was a common practice among German manufacturers and every collector has seen many samples.

Puncture a hole at the natural crown point in the dome. Take a length of hair long enough to reach from the back shoulder level to below the chin (you can barber or style it later) and, using nylon fishing cord, linen thread, or something else that will not break, tie the full strand in the center and secure it. Pull this bound spot through the hole in the dome and work a matchstick or pin a safety pin into the tied area on the under side.

Hold the hair out of the way, coat the entire crown lightly with glue and then spread the hair evenly, leaving a neat center spot. When the glue has dried, brush the hair, put the wig on the doll's head, cover with a plastic sheet held by a rubber band around the neck, and allow to shape overnight.

The following day, remove the plastic and style the hair. (Scotch tape pressed to the hair will help cut straight bangs or "Dutch" bobs.) After another good brushing, the hair can then be moistened and put on rollers if curls are desired.

If head holes are large enough to require a supporting dome for a cap wig, don't use flat cardboard with a build-up of cotton wadding. Look around you and pay attention to what you see.

Every house contains many sizes of bottles which have caps with slightly convex cardboard liners. Always check bottles being thrown out and re-trieve these caps. Remove the film of waxed paper or plastic and you have an ideal small dome which can be cut to the proper size. Then, too, molded papier-mâché egg cartons have good square bases in the individual egg cups. Cut the base off, round the corners and you have a dome with a slightly raised center.

If all else fails, cut a cardboard circle, soak it and then work it gently over the end of a knife handle or other rounded object to stretch the center. After it has dried it can be cut to the head size and will provide some rounded support for either a glued or cap wig.

Examine your dolls carefully while you are working with them. Learn to know exactly what you have and keep accurate records. Descriptions in this book will give you adequate samples of points worth noting in your own dolls.

34

Record
Keeping

Whether you consider it a nuisance or a fascination, as a collector you should keep accurate and adequate doll records. It is the only way to know what you have and to have a place to add information as new facts are uncovered or as your reading and club programs expand.

There is an added advantage, unhappy to contemplate but necessary to remember: Your family may be left with the job of disposing of a collection about which they know practically nothing and for which they may have only a sentimental attachment or a patronizing contempt. They will be prey to the unscrupulous as well as the scrupulous buyers who not infrequently put in an appearance while the family is still emotionally unable to transact business properly.

If there are certain dolls you wish to give as remembrances to friends or relatives, these should be specifically listed and easily and positively identifiable by your family through your records, the tags on the dolls, and the numbers or names you assign to them.

If your personal attachment to your collection urges you to keep the dolls intact by donating the collection to a museum or other institution, consult your lawyer and pay attention to what he tells you.

In many instances in the past, cherished "donations" have been sold by the recipient without ever being unpacked because the organization needed money for other purposes to which it had special devotion. This is not only unfair to your personal heirs but to yourself as well.

If you are led to believe that your dolls are desired for public display by an institution or organization, ask your lawyer to explain a "permanent loan" provision to you. This will prevent your treasures from being exploited by any group and will return them to your personal heirs if your wishes are not fulfilled.

The important thing is: DO IT NOW.

No matter what records are available about the dolls, some *other* safe place known to your family should contain an accurate account of the prices you paid for the dolls and when. If you think you paid too much, be honest and say so. If you are sure you got a bargain, give your family an idea of what the doll is really worth, if you know. If you don't, find out. This record should be added to systematically as your purchases increase and it should be reviewed and revised every few years, with current prices in mind. You have a great deal of money invested, no matter what the size of the collection, and you should leave sufficient information to guide those who must handle your estate.

There should be a record about the dolls at your own fingertips at all times and a 3 x 5 or 4 x 6 card file is ideal for this. A decorative file box will hold a world of useful information.

Abbreviations make these cards less cumbersome but be sure they are understandable. Learn the standard forms or make up your own because this will make the cards more easily read at a glance.

Use blk for black, bl for blue, br for brown, and wh for white. Pk does well for pink (but spell out rose), ppl for purple, grn for green, yel for yellow, orng for orange. Combine or qualify color information with further descriptive terms such as: pale, vivid, ye-orng, bl-grn, and so on.

In all-bisque recording, learn to differentiate between wigs and molded hair and between socks and stockings. Use "sox" for anything up to the knees and "stock." for anything painted above the knees. Also use the proper term for molded footwear: bootines, shoes, slippers, pumps, booties.

With all this in mind, here is a copy of the file card for the **S H No. 112.**

Name/ No.	all bisque
886	8½ in. swivel
S 5 H	hp & sh jtd w/pegs
(on head)	op. mo.—4 pretty upper teeth
	br. sl. eyes—ok (or set)
	orig. blde mohair wig & dome
	high color . . . very uniform
	vert. rib high blk stockings
	br. 2-strap w/heels & bows

And for the large infant, **No. 184.**

Name/ No.
Infant   molded blde gloss. hair w/comb marks
                hp & sh jtd w/rubber
no marks   red: eye-dots, lines & nostrils
                bl pt eyes w/hi pupils & highlights
circ. $9\frac{1}{8}$ 1-stroke brows in br
sits: $9\frac{5}{8}$ Kestner mouth w/flat corners
to heels: 14   pale color . . . uniform
” toes: 15

                13-mold type

Kestner ?

Any breaks, repairs, cracks, or chips should be noted; if the doll has a name, list that; if any parts are replaced, list them and tell whether they are duplicates of the originals, old parts that seem to fit, or modern reproductions.

If you want to keep your record of prices on the cards, figure out and use a code and use your maiden name, or your mother's first and maiden name for the source of the initials to number.

All-bisques are very amiable and you can pencil your numbers or price information in code right on their backs without worrying about getting it off.

And, if you are a camera buff, or have one available, be sure to take pictures of your dolls, both dressed and undressed, and file them either by number or name, or with the descriptions.

It is axiomatic that the more information available about them, the more valuable the dolls are or will be.

Bibliography

The Antiques Journal, April 1955.

Butler Brothers Catalogues, 1908, 1916, 1921, 1925, and 1932.

Coleman, Elizabeth A. *Dolls, Makers and Marks*, Privately printed, 1966.

Coronet Magazine, February 1949.

Eliot, Henry Rutherford, Article in *Century Magazine*, September 1906.

Johl, Janet Pagter, *Still More About Dolls*, H. L. Lindquist Publications, 1950.

Long Island Doll, Hobby & Craft Club, Inc., *News Bulletin*, June-July 1967.

Noble, John, *Dolls,* Walker and Company, N.Y., 1967.

Rada, Pravoslav, *Book of Ceramics*, Translated by A. Parfait, London, 1960.

Rhodes, Daniel, *Stoneware & Porcelain*, Philadelphia, 1959.

Time Magazine, April 17, 1944, and November 10, 1967.